Of Unknown Origin

OF UNKNOWN ORIGIN

A MEMOIR

Debra Levi Holtz

Council Oak Books
San Francisco / Tulsa

Some names and locations have been changed in this autobiographical
narrative in order to protect the privacy of individuals.

Council Oak Books, LLC
1290 Chestnut Street, Ste. 2, San Francisco, CA 94109
1350 E. 15th Street, Tulsa, OK 74120
OF UNKNOWN ORIGIN: A Memoir. Copyright © 2001
by Debra Levi Holtz.

Library of Congress Cataloging-in-Publication Data
Available on file

ISBN 1-57178-100-5
First edition / First printing.
Printed in Canada.
01 02 03 04 05 06 5 4 3 2 1

For my children, Jake and Sarah,
who teach me what it means to be a good mother.

chapter O N E

I stare at the postcard in my hand. On the front of the card is a painting of a naked woman lounging beside a vase of flowers and a tall bowl with three fish swimming in it. Behind her a window shade is partially drawn, revealing a tree. The colors are vivid and seductive, like a child's crayon drawing: reddish orange, goldenrod yellow, mint green and periwinkle blue.

The back of the card identifies the painting as *Goldfish and Sculpture* by Henri Matisse, from the Museum of Modern Art in New York City. A message, written in blue ink, reads, "Helen is very nice! Have a beautiful wedding." The word "very" is capitalized and underlined twice. There is no signature.

I study the anonymous card further, searching for clues. It is not addressed directly to me but to my last name, "Levi," at my parents' home in Chicago. The stamp pictures an aqua sailboat with the words "Iceboat 1880s, USA." The postmark is "Jamaica, N.Y.," mailed on October 7, 1986.

༄

The postcard arrived at a time when I had no desire to solve mysteries. My wedding was just a few days away and

1

my fiancé, Steve, and I had just arrived in Chicago from California to help my parents with last-minute preparations.

My mother was planning a formal ceremony and reception at her suburban country club and had invited more than a hundred of her friends and acquaintances. It was an event high profile enough to garner a mention in a newspaper gossip column. In my parents' social circle, invitations to such parties were a basic commodity and, as my mother put it, she had a lot of people to pay back. It was to be the kind of lavish affair that my mother reveled in and I had tried to escape from by moving two thousand miles away. Each time I returned to Chicago, I was reminded all over again of the world my parents lived in, where people impressed one another by the extravagance of their clothes, their homes, their cars, their parties.

My mother had reason to celebrate. I was marrying a Jewish doctor—one of the few decisions in my life that won her approval. Steve was nine years older than me, smart, confident of himself and had a sense of humor that no one appreciated as much as he did. He was light years apart from the men I had dated in the past whose lives were filled with problems and addictions that dwarfed my own. I was intent on being their savior even if they weren't looking for one, determined to untwist their psyches even if I couldn't straighten out my own.

The men in my past were rebels of one kind or another, and choosing them was an expression of revolt against my parents. It went hand in hand with the hippie clothing I preferred over the designer clothes my mother wished I would wear and my decision to become a journalist instead of the lawyer she had in mind. I worked hard at cultivating an image different from theirs because I knew that if I tried to fit in, I would fail. From the moment I introduced them to Steve, my parents began to accept me, to appear proud of me, as I knew they would. I was like the moon, visible only because of the sun's light reflecting off its surface. But perhaps the force that made me gravitate to Steve more than anything else was an underlying confidence that he would never leave me.

Steve and I knew very few of the people on our wedding's guest list because our friends lived so far away. I dissuaded them from coming; it didn't really feel like my own celebration. My mother had planned it herself, asking my opinions only rhetorically. I would have preferred a small wedding near our home in Oakland where we could celebrate with friends. But I acquiesced to my mother's wishes, both out of a desire to please her and a powerlessness to refuse.

At the same time, I felt like a hypocrite for going along with my parents' high life while scorning its excesses.

The postcard first surfaced one evening while we were gathered around a small marble table in the living room, having drinks before dinner. My mother was preoccupied with the final details of the wedding, alternating between phone calls to the caterer and the florist.

"I think this must be for you," my dad said, handing me the postcard from a pile of mail he was leafing through. I could tell by his serious scowl that he was tense, the way he got when he knew that my mother was spending too much money but felt helpless to challenge her.

I read the card several times, baffled but curious.

"Do you think this has anything to do with my adoption?" I asked my mother, placing it in front of her. She quickly read it and gave it back to me.

"I doubt it. It's probably from one of Steve's relatives," she answered, avoiding my gaze and picking up some other mail to look at.

"But didn't you tell me that my birth mother's name was Helen?" I persisted.

"Yes, I think it was . . . but I'm sure it has nothing to do with that. It probably refers to you and they got your name wrong."

"Steve, could this be from someone you know? It was sent from Jamaica, New York," I said, handing the card to him. He glanced at it briefly.

"I don't have any relatives in Jamaica. No, I don't think it's from anyone I know."

"But isn't it strange that no one signed it?" I asked, trying to recapture my mother's attention.

"I'm sure it was just an oversight," she said as she stood up and walked into the kitchen.

⌘

The wedding lived up to all of my mother's expectations. A hairdresser and makeup artist spent hours preparing the wedding party. Champagne flowed. Red roses in tall glass tubes towered above china plates and metallic-gold table-cloths. Guests marveled over the five-course meal. The rabbi, who chain-smoked Newports throughout most of the wedding, erroneously introduced every male in Steve's family as "doctor." A five-piece band played music perfectly suited to the over-fifty crowd. But when it came time for the Jewish wedding tradition of lifting the bride and groom on chairs and parading around the room, there was no one young enough to carry us.

While the whole scene was familiar to me, it was altogether foreign to Steve and his parents, whose middle-class values were firmly rooted in their own experiences as German immigrants and Depression-era survivors. They believed money should not be spent but zealously saved. Apart from his small family from New York, Steve knew nobody at our wedding. But he went along with the extravagance of it because he found it amusing and it wasn't costing him anything. Since this was his third marriage, he had plenty of experience with wedding etiquette. He smiled a lot, accepted checks in sealed envelopes slipped into his pockets and dashed into the men's locker room at carefully timed intervals to catch the first game of the World Series between the Mets and the Red Sox.

∽∞∾

I couldn't help feeling like a guest when I visited my parents. They lived in an apartment overlooking Lake Michigan that they had moved into shortly after I left for college. It was much larger than the one we had lived in before, just a block away. The apartment reminded me more of a museum than a home. With high ceilings and art-deco decor, the dining and living rooms flowed into one large space filled with delicate crystal objects, glass and metal tables, and furniture in varying shades of gray and white. The only colors in the room were on a single painted canvas—huge splotches of red, yellow and blue that reminded me of a brain on an acid trip. The apartment seemed even bigger than it was because there were mirrors on almost every available surface, making it virtually impossible to escape your own image.

I took great care in my movements because I always feared that I would break something. Unlike other people whose homes are their sanctuaries, their own private cocoons, my mother had designed her apartment to look more like an advertisement in *Architectural Digest*. It was immaculately kept; no newspapers lying around or beds unmade. After I ate, she would follow me around the kitchen with a sponge or a miniature vacuum to pick up crumbs that I couldn't even see.

That's also how it was with my mother when it came to the subject of my adoption. She had a way of sweeping it away like a bit of dust, insignificant but annoying just the same.

I was taught that the proper way to deal with unpleasant realities of the past was to pretend that they had never happened. My adoption was one of many embarrassing truths that were best ignored and certainly not discussed with people outside the family.

From my earliest memories I knew I was adopted, though I do not remember the exact moment I learned of it or who told me. It was a detail of my life that I accepted with little explanation, like an unsightly birthmark, and tried very hard to overlook for most of my childhood.

In private, my mother described me as a "chosen child," as if she had picked me from a window display of cute little babies wrapped in fuzzy blankets because I had some magical quality that lifted me above the rest. I was never sure what was so special about me, but just thinking of those other children who weren't chosen made me feel indebted to her.

"Where did I come from?" I remember asking my mother when I was younger.

"What's important is that no child could have been more wanted than you. We worked very hard to find you. Other people just have children, they have to take what they get. You should feel very lucky because you were chosen."

The first time I saw the postcard, I knew instinctively that it had something to do with my adoption. But it posed questions I wasn't yet ready to ask, so in the chaos of the wedding, I tossed it aside.

For five years I let the postcard remain "lost." While I suspected it was submersed in a pile of wedding cards and receipts for gifts of china and crystal crammed into my dining room cabinet, I repeatedly resisted the temptation to peek at it.

Yet it haunted me, just as the idea of searching for the woman who gave me up for adoption had ever since I became an adult. Both had to do with a choice between traveling down a straight, flat highway or veering off down a bumpy, unpaved road with blind curves.

Having my own children, the first blood ties in my life, was a secret wish I harbored but was too scared to voice. As familiar as I had grown to being a genetic anomaly, I couldn't imagine passing on traits like my ski-sloped nose, big ears or stubborn streak that felt like mine alone. How could I plant my own seeds if I had no roots?

I privately doubted that I would ever become pregnant. Perhaps it was because the woman who raised me had lost the ability to conceive. Or did it come from having no sense of having been born? While other children are told details of how they came into the world in funny anecdotes over dinner or softly spoken stories at bedtime, my mother had no such tales to tell me. She couldn't describe whether I kicked a lot in the womb, when her labor pains began, or how she got to the hospital. It was as if I had not been born, only adopted. My life began, not at the moment of birth, but when I arrived at my mother's house like some wayward spaceship landing from outer space.

Because I had not taken birth control very seriously, I got pregnant just before my eighteenth birthday.

The father was a sweet, insecure guy named Harry who hid behind the bravura of a gangster. He wore a black fedora and sped around Chicago in a black Cadillac. His father had some murky connection to organized crime and supplied his son with enough cash to eat at expensive Italian restaurants and avoid getting a job. Everything Harry did he did to the extreme; he ate too much, smoked too much marijuana, stayed up until the early hours of the morning and slept until noon, usually missing the classes he was taking at a local junior college.

Harry had given me a dog—a black long-haired Chihuahua that looked more like a cat—that my mother refused to allow in her apartment for fear it would soil her white carpets or chew on the velvet couches. This gave me the excuse I needed to move out. Harry and I got an apartment in a fancy residential hotel about a mile away.

Harry loved me in the possessive, suffocating way you love something you know you will ultimately lose but are desperate to hang onto nonetheless. He would become angry beyond reason if I said hello to a friendly stranger on the street. For kicks, he liked to drive around at night pitching pennies at people's heads.

He wanted me to have the baby, get married and cancel my plans to attend college in Los Angeles the following year. For my birthday, he gave me a book called *Mafia Wife*, both in jest and in a vain attempt to invite me to permanently join his fantasy.

For me, abortion was the only choice. Having the baby and giving it up for adoption was unthinkable. Never once did I let myself consider what my own birth mother would have done had abortion been legal in 1959.

In the beginning, an abortion seemed like a necessary inconvenience, a routine medical procedure that had to be performed like any other for health reasons. At a clinic in downtown Chicago, I filled out forms and met with a counselor who asked, "Are you sure this is what you want? Have you given it sufficient thought?"

"Yes," I answered, anxious to get it over with.

Once I put on the skimpy gown and sat with my legs up in stirrups, my outlook changed. The bright lights made everything seem grossly exaggerated. When the procedure began, I remember feeling like a giant vacuum was sweeping out my insides, making me as clean and sterile as the small operating room itself. In a haze of anesthesia, I wondered if this had been my only opportunity to have a child.

The days following the abortion were filled with unbearable pain. Each wave of stabbing cramps felt like punishment for giving up that chance. It may have been weeks or even months afterward that I began having the same nightmare: I had a baby, but the baby was miniature. While taking care of it, I would invariably misplace it and spend the rest of the dream searching frantically for the tiny infant—terrified I could crush it with every move I made—but never finding it. When I woke up, I felt a disorienting sense of despair that made me want to close my eyes and go on searching.

Two years later, while away at college in Los Angeles, I was overcome by crippling cramps worse than those following the abortion. A doctor performed exploratory surgery and found that I was suffering from endometriosis, an affliction of the reproductive system that causes tissue normally found inside the uterus to go astray and attach in lesions to other organs. Some researchers believe there is a genetic predisposition to developing the disease and when there is a hereditary link, the disease tends to be worse in the next generation.

The doctor told me the best treatment for endometriosis was pregnancy. Short of that, he said, I would have to take daily birth control pills to forestall menstruation and dupe my body into believing I was pregnant. I researched the condition and learned that endometriosis is a leading cause of infertility among women.

Yet I became pregnant only a month after Steve and I were married. A few weeks after I found out, just long enough for me to have told everyone I knew that I was going to have a baby, I began bleeding—not just a little, but in massive quantities. My sudden hormonal drop magnified my own doubts and reminded me of something Steve had said before we were married.

During a trip to Paris, as we watched children playing on the stairs of Notre Dame, he confided, "I've always had this fear that I'll never have children, and now that I'm getting older I'm worried that it may be true."

But a year after the miscarriage, our son, Jake, was born and for the first time in my life I had an anchor. I no longer felt as though I was drifting between storms. There was finally another human being in the world who shared with me an ancestry I had never known, a biological connection that most people take for granted.

Jake had the same blondish-brown hair I had as a child and even the same upturned nose that I did. His eyes were like blue marbles floating in a dish of white cream.

"He has the biggest eyes I've ever seen," people often said, stopping on the street to stare at Jake. After a moment, they would search my own face and say, "Oh, he got his eyes from you. He looks just like you." It meant so much more than the simple vanity of new motherhood. It reminded me of the kind of attention my own eyes attracted when I was a child, a kind of stunned delight from total strangers that made me feel charmed.

Often in the dark silence of the night, I would nurse my son and try to imagine what it would be like to give him away to people I did not know, never to see him again. As I held his warm body against my breast, feeling the vulnerability of his skin as milk flowed between us, the thought seemed inconceivable. He would never have to feel like a stranger in his own family, I promised him, as he slept quietly unaware in my arms.

Yet it was the birth our daughter, Sarah, two years later that preoccupied me with the thought of finding my own mother. Having a baby girl sparked a fire inside me that had been smoldering since the first time I gave birth. In her face I saw myself as a baby separated from the woman who had carried me inside of her for nine months. I had come to know how important that time of pregnancy was for the days that would follow, for when my children were born there was already a strong bond between us.

When you buy a flower at the nursery to plant in your garden, it is something that decorates the scenery and that you can admire. But planting seeds in the ground and watching them sprout and grow, leaf by leaf, gives you an extraordinary sense of wonder. It was a magic I could not have missed. While any bond I may have developed with my own mother was abruptly cut off thirty-two years earlier, I could no longer ignore that there was a stranger somewhere who bore such a primal connection to me.

One day as my children napped in their rooms, the idea of looking for the postcard struck me without warning, like an earthquake releasing an underground tension that had been building up for years. I walked into the dining room and tried to open the drawer of the oak-paneled breakfront. There were so many papers stuffed inside that the drawer jammed as I pulled it open. I slid my left hand in the crack to flatten the papers and pulled hard on the handle with my right hand. The drawer opened with a jarring thud, the crystal glasses on the shelves above shaking with a high-pitched rattle.

I took out the thick stack of wedding memorabilia, fell to my knees and began shuffling through it. That's how it had been with the different eras of my life: when they were over I just gathered up whatever papers or photographs I had collected into a chaotic jumble and hid them away. I had no reverence for the past, no sweet nostalgia that would inspire me to place mementos in photo albums or scrapbooks I could easily retrieve to reminisce about my experiences. Though I rarely threw anything away, I buried the souvenirs of my life the way other people try to forget bad memories.

For a few moments I feared that the postcard was really lost because of how carelessly I had tossed it aside five years earlier. My hands began to shake as I searched more frantically through the disorganized pile. Then the bright colors of the card glared out from under the white papers.

I read the words over again several times. A small, handwritten scribble at the very bottom of the card at first appeared indecipherable, but from a certain angle it looked like the number 27 had been written and then crossed out. I thought for a minute—I had been twenty-seven years old when I received the postcard.

The idea that someone out there knew about my private life yet refused to reveal his or her identity both alarmed and intrigued me. I felt my body falling out of rhythm as my stomach tensed and a rush of heat surged through my arms, making me tremble.

I realized at that moment why the simple words on that postcard preyed on my memory. My mother had once told me that my birth mother loved art. "All I know is that she went to the Art Institute every day while she was in Chicago," I remembered my mother saying. "She came here during her pregnancy and left shortly after you were born."

I sat on the floor with my back against the cabinet, my eyes fixed on the card, breathing in short bursts and searching my mind for any other information I might have been told about my adoption.

Once, when I was about sixteen, at a moment when my mother and I were alone in the car and I knew it would be impossible for her to ignore my inquiries, I asked, "How did you find that woman, Helen?" The question was so sudden that it might as well have just flown in the window.

My mother, turning just long enough to give me a suspicious glance, stared straight ahead and said, "It was a private adoption handled through a lawyer. I made sure that the woman was college educated, and I think she came from somewhere on the East Coast. She had some kind of an interest in art. But I didn't ask any other questions because I really didn't want to know anything else."

Knowing how secretive my mother could be, I had a lingering suspicion that she knew more than she was willing to tell me about the circumstances of my birth. But I had tried not to push it. I worried that my curiosity would hurt her, threatening the myth she had created that my life really began the moment she first held me when I was five days old.

But like other fairy tales of childhood, that story began to unravel as I grew older. No matter how hard I tried to fit in among my family, I couldn't help but feel different. "Debbie doesn't look like you. Who does she take after?" people would ask my mother. I, too, longed to know.

My own questions about my ethnic heritage irritated my mother. She would say, "You have the map of Ireland all over your face." It didn't sound like a compliment coming from a Jewish mother. I felt both enchanted and cursed, as though my life had another dimension over which I had no control.

Like any other teenage girl, I would spend hours staring at my face in the mirror. But my reflection was a riddle: Where did my blue eyes come from? Who else had those thin lips and big ears? I tried to envision myself as an older woman, hoping to catch a glimpse of my birth mother.

In my fantasies, I imagined her as a talented artist, probably a painter. She was an extraordinary woman, a combination of fairy princess and sorceress. I never thought about the details of her life, whether she was married or had any other children. She was a character frozen in time.

I glanced at the postcard again. Had she written it about herself? Had she been keeping track of the circumstances of my life? Was she inviting me to find her? I looked closely at the painting on the other side of the card. The sculpture of the woman had no face.

chapter **TW O**

"**G**iving birth is not the hard part," my mother would say. "It's what comes after that's difficult: raising the child. You'll understand when you have your own children."

While I did realize the truth of her words after Jake and Sarah were born, the message sounded like an embellishment coming from my mother. After all, she had not been a mother in any traditional sense. She did not change diapers, bandage knees or bake cookies. When I was a baby, my crib was placed in my nanny's room so that my mother would not be bothered by the nocturnal needs of a newborn. My brother, Howie, my mother's natural son who was twelve years older than me, was sent to boarding school in Massachusetts when I was two years old. As I grew older, there were no mother-daughter chats about adolescence, boys or the facts of life. My mother loved me, but what she enjoyed most took place away from me. Like other big city socialites, my mother's appointment book was filled with restaurant dinners, formal parties and trips. I stayed home with a procession of housekeepers whose names sounded like a committee of the United Nations.

I learned how to talk to myself. I had long conversations with my reflection in the bathroom mirror or with my imaginary sister who often sat on the spare bed in my room under a giant Paul McCartney poster.

I've spent years trying to be the mother I always wanted. I stopped working full-time as a newspaper reporter when Jake was born and quit almost entirely after Sarah's birth. Unlike my peers raising children in the 1990s, I've followed the lopsided philosophy that the quantity of time is more important than the quality of time that you spend with your kids.

Each morning when I see my children's first smiles of the day, I feel gratified for what they have and mourn what I did not.

I turn the brass doorknob. The door sticks, so I have to gently push it open. The jarring sensation causes the wooden unicorn sign on Sarah's door to jump toward me and then bang back against the door. As I slowly bend my head into the room, I see her little face rise up from the pillow in her crib. Perhaps the thud woke her or maybe she was just lying there quietly, daydreaming about the simple pleasures of being a one-year-old. Her wide eyes shine in the darkness. She is happy and begins to giggle, turning over on her back and hugging her pink, fuzzy blanket with her arms and legs. Her giggles turn into wild laughter, revealing her sheer joy in starting a new day. I put down the side of her crib and can't resist kissing her on the stomach. She has her own special smell, a warm and sweet aroma of comfort.

Sometimes when I feel particularly weary after a day of taking care of children, doing their laundry, cooking and washing dishes, I find myself picturing my mother who never did any of these things. A familiar resentment courses through me and I see it spilling out in unexpected, angry bursts. My children and husband look at me like I'm a fear-some stranger who just walked into the room. "Why do I always have to do everything myself?" I yell. My voice turns mean. I start banging the dishes together as I'm putting them away. I run into the bathroom, slam the door and look at my flushed face in the mirror. Am I angry at her or just jealous?

Since my children were born, my mother has often repeated: "Why don't you hire some help?" Each time she says it I feel the empty space in my chest expand.

Sarah was born by cesarean section. The surgery was fol-lowed by painful complications caused by the endometriosis and the scar tissue it left behind. After I left the hospital, my mother-in-law came to help for a week because I couldn't drive or lift Jake while recovering from the surgery.

The following week my mother came. She did not do any of the things my mother-in-law had done like wash the dishes or change Jake's diapers. Instead, she insisted on being treat-ed like a guest. She sat at the kitchen table and asked me to make her coffee or pour her a glass of wine. She never inquired about how I was feeling and showed little interest in my newborn daughter, choosing to lavish all of her verbal attention on Jake.

She seemed almost angry at me—as if I had done some-thing wrong. Sometimes she would ignore me altogether as though I were invisible. At other moments, I would catch her glaring at me with the same hostility in her eyes she used to get when I embarrassed her as a child. It could have been the painkillers or postpartum depression that made me over-react or even imagine that she was trying to hurt me. I couldn't help wondering, though, if my mother resented me for giving birth to a daughter, something she was not able to do herself.

My mother had a hysterectomy when she was thirty years old, seven years after giving birth to my brother. Adoption was her only alternative if she wanted another child, and she made it clear to the lawyer handling the case that she wanted a girl. She said the lawyer arranged the adoption with my birth mother before I was born, so I always wondered what would have happened if I had been a boy.

"I got a call shortly before you were born and I could have had twin boys from Florida," she once said. But it was what she didn't say that I heard the loudest—I was lucky and people in my circumstances should never question their good fortune.

❧

My mother was the oldest child of hard-working Russian Jewish immigrants. In order to gain a foothold in the culture in which they found themselves, my grandparents focused their lives on earning money and often relied on others to raise their children.

When she was very young, my mother spent her days in a small grocery store on the ground floor of an apartment building in Brooklyn, where her parents worked.

"I got so busy with customers, I forgot I had a baby," my grandmother recalled when she was ninety-seven. "People would be in the elevator of the building and see her creeping up the stairs. She could have been killed."

Once, my grandmother told me, she wanted to go out to visit some relatives and told my grandfather to watch my mother. He refused, but she went out anyway. She waited on the street for a little while only to witness my grandfather leaving the building alone. She returned to find her hysterically crying daughter stuffed into the apartment's dumbwaiter.

When the family moved to Painesdale, Minnesota, they bought their own grocery store and worked more than twelve hours a day. My mother was cared for by her grandmother and hired help.

"I was never at home," my own grandmother recalled. "But the store was close to the house and sometimes the children would come to visit. My husband would say to them, 'Go home, don't bother Mother.'"

My mother has told me that she cannot remember my grandmother ever saying "I love you" to her.

My grandparents taught their children that a person's worth was in direct correlation to how much money they had. It was a lesson my mother learned too well. Money was the language she came to understand best. As an adult, her sense of identity fluctuated with the balance in her checkbook. She showered me with material possessions as if the more she gave me, the more loved I would feel.

Unable to give me the physical affection or emotional warmth I craved, my mother forged a bond between us of appreciation and guilt. She was my benefactor. It was important to her that I felt grateful—grateful for the private school education, the expensive clothes and the braces on my teeth.

"Your head should be locked in a vault for all the money we've invested in you," my mother was fond of saying.

Most of all, she reminded me, I should be grateful for the fate she had saved me from. It was never clear what my lot in life would have been, but the message was that it would not have been as good as the one she had given me, and probably a great deal worse.

For my mother, the way one dressed was of vital importance. Clothes dictated how other people saw and judged us. I had more clothes than one child could possibly wear. When

I was very young, I had a private ritual of taking my clothes out of the drawers, folding them and carefully stacking them back in neat little piles.

I felt closest to my mother when she took me to a department store to buy clothes. She would sit in the dressing room as I tried on multiple blouses, skirts and pants. During those times, her attention was entirely focused on me and I felt special. But the moment we left the store, that would all change.

My mother spent hours every morning making up her face before a wall of mirrors in her bathroom. First came the thick brown foundation that she applied with firm, circular movements around her cheeks, over her lips, up her narrow nose, across her forehead and then up her neck in broad, sweeping movements. Then she went to work on her eyes; face to face with the image in the mirror she applied two or three different shades of shadow across her eyelids and framed them with thick black eyeliner, all with the precision of a painter. Most time consuming were her false eyelashes. She held the fragile black-haired fans in one hand while the other hand squirted them with a long line of glue. She stuck one after another over her own sparse lashes and then carefully poked them into place, her eyes nearly closed, her neck cocked upward and her mouth wide open in deliberate concentration.

"Putting on her face," as she called it, was followed by the anxiety-provoking task of choosing just the right outfit from her huge walk-in closet full of designer clothes. With her hair still stuck to her scalp in tight circles by pink curlers, she frantically searched the racks of neatly hung pants and dresses. She was nearly always in a hurry. By the time she was finished, she was usually an hour behind schedule but looked, nonetheless, like a well-manicured model in a glossy magazine advertisement: glamorous, attractive and appearing younger than her years.

It did not occur to me then how much self-doubt she was burying beneath all of those layers of decoration. It was easy to miss because once her mask and costume were in place, she seemed to have superhuman confidence. She could persuade a maître d' at a packed restaurant to find her a table and, once inside, chances were good she would know many of the diners. People seemed to gravitate to my mother. I marveled at how she could create conversation with everyone she met. No matter how upset she was at home, she never let her problems show once she walked out the door.

As for the way I looked, my mother was seldom satisfied and often disappointed that my appearance was not as important to me as she thought it should be.

"Let's see how you look," she would yell from her bathroom before I left the house during my teenage years. I would hesitantly walk in for my inspection, bracing myself for an inevitable criticism about my choice of clothes ("Your shoes don't look right with that skirt") or about my hair (she insisted that I blow-dry the natural waves out of my hair).

"Stand up straight," she'd say and pull my skirt around my hips to make sure the seams were perfectly lined up or tuck my shirt into my pants, her hands sliding down my backside to remove any unsightly wrinkles.

Instead of appreciating her notice as I should have in those moments, I resented her for making me feel like a fashion failure, or worse, as though I fell short of whom she expected me to be. I longed for her to care about the real me, to want to know who I was inside.

I grew more defiant. I dressed in baggy sweaters and shredded jeans, choosing friends who lived fast and fearlessly.

In the city it was easy for me to hang out on the street, drink in bars with forged ID cards and cruise along the lake in older kids' cars. But instead of taking my rebelliousness in stride as my friends' mothers did, she took it as a personal affront.

She often reminded me of how difficult I had been as a young child, recounting in mocking detail moments when I had embarrassed her.

"Once we were walking in Saks Fifth Avenue when you were four years old," she would say. "You were dressed magnificently—in a mink jacket and hat with white lace stockings. My friend Sophie Cohen met us and said, 'My how beautiful you look, Debbie.' Instead of saying thank you, you kicked her so hard in the leg that she dropped her packages and doubled over."

Her disapproval magnified my own sense of being different and not fitting into the world in which I found myself.

"You were like this from the day you were born," my mother would often say to absolve herself when she was angry at me. We both knew she meant I had inherited some flawed behavioral gene, and though I tried to deny it, I came to believe it too. After all, there must have been something wrong with me for my real mother to have given me away.

Knowing I had been rejected before, I repeatedly tried to tempt fate with my mother. How bad do I have to be for you to abandon me too? During our frequent verbal jousts, she sometimes accused me of taking out the anger I felt toward my birth mother on her. While it may have been true, I denied it. Instead I felt oddly tied to the woman who had given birth to me despite our years of separation. I convinced myself that there must have been a good reason why she had put me up for adoption.

⚭

After I retrieved the postcard, I placed it on the fireplace mantel like a family memento. It made an odd scene: a miniaturized painting of a naked woman propped up between a row of framed photographs of my children. The whole room was a study in contrasts: an awkward attempt at Southwestern decor in the living room of an old, English Tudor–style house.

One chilly morning in early January, I took Jake to preschool and put Sarah in my bed to watch an episode of *Barney*. I took the postcard off the mantel and maneuvered my way to the kitchen through a clutter of toys in the otherwise empty space meant to be a dining room. I placed the card on the breakfast table, careful to avoid the small puddles of spilled milk and cereal. Gulping a sip of cold, hours-old coffee, I knew what I had to do.

If I wanted to search for my birth mother, I had to start with unlocking the memory of my adoptive mother. A steady series of drafts blew through the panes of the large window in the breakfast room, and I shivered at the idea of calling her. Admitting what I intended to do would violate our unspoken agreement not to dredge up the past. She had tried so hard to stake her claim to motherhood, to make me believe that what mattered most was who you grew up with, not what came before.

It was with that thought that I dialed the telephone. We talked for about five minutes before I mustered the courage to bring up the subject. I began to speak in a voice that sounded like that of a sinful parishioner in a confession booth:

"Mom, I know this may come as a surprise to you, but I've decided to search for my birth mother."

There was a long moment of silence before she responded. "I expected this to happen. I just didn't know when it would."

"I need you to tell me everything you remember about my adoption."

"I've already told you," she said, her voice striving for control. "I wanted a little girl very much. I had your brother and couldn't have any more children. So we contacted an attorney. Eventually we got a call that a little girl had been born and we only had a few days to prepare for you. After we brought you home, I was so happy. No child could have been more wanted than you were. I spent the next few months on pins and needles, afraid they might come and take you away."

"Who would have taken me away?" I interrupted.

"A social worker made several visits to the house to make sure you were being well taken care of. I never knew when she would show up. But no child was ever taken care of better than you were. You were the best-dressed child I knew. I only dressed you in the very finest clothes. Florence Eiseman knit dresses with lace stockings. I even sterilized your bottles for two years! Your nurse, Ruth, wouldn't even let people near you. She was afraid of the germs."

Again I felt like a doll she had purchased, or a porcelain figurine that could have broken at any moment.

"What about my mother? Where did the lawyer find her?"

"I've told you, I don't know. I didn't ask any questions. She was college educated, from somewhere out East. She loved art. That's all I knew."

I was getting impatient listening to the same old story. I imagined her standing in front of her bathroom mirror, putting on mascara, the telephone receiver tucked between her ear and bent neck. She was always in a hurry, trying to do more than one thing at a time, and talking on the phone was usually one of them. It amazed me how she could tease her short, bleached-blonde hair with a metal comb, spray endless clouds of hair spray on it and still have electronic discourse.

Trying to talk to her when I was a child always made me feel like a secretary interrupting a busy executive with a trivial question. She would lift her hand up in front of her face with her index finger lifted, gesturing for me to be quiet and wait because the conversation she was having always seemed more important than anything I had to say. I would usually give up either because the other telephone line would ring or she would hurry into the bathroom to continue dressing, forgetting about me altogether.

"What about the lawyer?" I asked. "Is he still living? Maybe he could tell me who she was."

"He must be dead by now. Debbie, we did everything we could to make sure she didn't know who we were so she could never find us again. On the day we were to get you, the lawyer arranged a meeting on a street a few blocks away from the hospital. The lawyer came with us and so did our friends, Bill and Marlene Erlich, who had adopted children of their own. We rented a car and a few hours later we switched to another car. We covered the windows. We even wore veils so she couldn't see our faces. The woman pulled up in another car and walked over to us. She handed you to me through the car window. I'll never forget the big smile she had on her face, as though she was happy to be getting rid of you. Can you imagine? She was smiling."

I suddenly felt the need to protect this stranger, my mother.

"Maybe she was smiling because she appreciated that you were going to take care of me," I offered.

"No, that wasn't it. She was happy. I can't imagine giving away a child and smiling." Her voice was now indignant.

"Why didn't you ever tell me this before? What did she look like?" I asked.

"I've tried to put it all out of my mind. But now I remember. She was taller than you. She had brown hair and her eyes were smaller than yours . . .

"You'll never know how much I went through to get you," she continued. "I had to wait for six months until she signed the papers." Her voice trailed off.

"What papers?"

"The final adoption papers. The courts gave the mother six months to change her mind."

"Where are those papers now?"

She hesitated. "I have them in a safety deposit box, along with your original birth certificate. I pulled some political strings to have that removed from the court file so the woman could never come and take you back. I had read about a Catholic mother who found out that her baby was adopted by a Jewish family and reclaimed the baby. I wasn't about to let that happen to us."

"Why didn't you ever show them to me?" I was angry and impatient. "Do they have her name on them?"

"I suppose they do. I already told you her name was Helen. I didn't think it was necessary to give them to you. I thought you were happy with us. We've always given you the best of everything, the best education. Your father and I have always treated you as if you were our own. There was never any difference to us . . . "

"I know that and I appreciate everything," I said, my voice softening, apologetic. "But I need to know where I come from. I don't need another mother, I just want to know who I look like, what my history is. This has nothing to do with you."

"Even when your dad adopted you when you were nine years old, after your father, Manny, died, you were always treated the same as his own daughter. People even said you looked like him. That you both had the same blue eyes," she said with a touch of melancholy.

She had repeated that story many times over the years, as if the more times it was said the truer it became. I felt a sudden pang of guilt for attempting to open a door that was meant to be kept shut and sealed.

"Listen, you will always be my parents," I said with halting reassurance. "Trust me. I need to see those papers. I have to do this for myself and for the kids. Will you please send them to me?"

"I'll send them to you. I just hope you don't get hurt by all of this." I believed her, but couldn't imagine how knowing the truth could be any more painful than not knowing anything.

As I hung up the telephone, I took a deep breath. The heel of my foot was tapping the carpet in nervous beats. In a few days I would see my mother's name. I wondered how old she was. How tall she was. Where did she come from?

I had waited my entire life to ask these questions and suddenly I felt a desperate urge to know the answers.

chapter THREE

My first true childhood
memory is of the night my father was murdered.

It was late at night when I was awakened by a commotion. I was six years old. I can see myself in the housekeeper's
small bedroom, located off of the kitchen, but I don't know
how I got there. The window overlooked an octagonal courtyard and garage encircled by the tiers of the building we
lived in. I remember looking out of that window from fifteen
stories high, through the black bars of the fire escape, and
seeing red and yellow lights racing in fast circles across the
walls, illuminating the darkness. Police cars and ambulances
were parked haphazardly in the courtyard, blocking the
entrance to the garage.

The heavy footsteps of people rushing around the apartment and the deep, urgent sounds of men's voices spread
goosebumps up my arms. I huddled in the sympathetic arms
of our housekeeper, Alice, a big woman with a calm, loving
voice and a reassuring touch. But the look on her face was
barely concealed fear and I knew that something was very
wrong.

I do not remember seeing my mother that night. Nor do I recall who told me my father had been shot and killed. My memories are vivid but disjointed, like the images that remain long after watching a violent action movie.

c∞ɔ

Up until the time I mustered the courage to look for my birth mother, I let the past remain a collage of my own vague recollections, my imagination and the little my mother had told me.

We lived in a high-rise building on North Lake Shore Drive overlooking Lake Michigan for most of my first six years. The building, an imposing fortress of red brick and gray stone, curved around the block. Its tall windows and doors were covered by heavy black wrought iron bars with intricate spirals and spikes on top like the ornaments on a Gothic cathedral.

Our apartment was large, impeccably neat and formal. A white, gold and black color scheme could be found in nearly every room, from the gold silk chairs in the living room to the black bathtub and gold-plated faucets in my mother's bathroom. A giant mirror with gray hazy swirls covering the dining room wall had a funny way of making you appear to be wrapped in a puff of smoke. I imagine myself as a toddler slipping and falling on the marble floor of the foyer while learning to walk.

When my parents gave parties, my mother would put me in a fancy dress with white lace anklets and black patent leather shoes and briefly parade me before the guests like a trophy. Their parties were loud, smoke-filled affairs that went on late into the night.

I have been told that during a New Year's Eve party when I was three years old, my brother and his girlfriend begged me to come out as the "New Year's Baby" for the guests, naked except for a sash draped across my torso. But I refused to be treated like a toy.

"No, I want to be dwessed up," I said. Then I marched into my bedroom to put on a fancy dress before joining the party.

My mother always seemed very busy. It seemed to me that she worked with my father, but I was never sure what his job was. I remember my mother telling me he was in the women's clothing business, but I do not recall ever visiting him at a store or an office. At other times, she said he was in real estate. I sensed that my father did not earn a living like those of my friends.

I remember some dinners late at night at dimly lit restaurants where there were no other children. The waiters and waitresses brought me Shirley Temples with extra maraschino cherries on a toothpick. My father would not stay with my mother and me for very long, migrating instead to a more private corner table with men who were huddled together in hushed conversations, their faces barely seen through a thick cloud of cigarette smoke. They drank scotch and sodas and ate large quantities of steak and spaghetti.

"What is Daddy doing?" I would ask my mother. "Why isn't he eating with us?"

"Your father is doing his business, dear, and we don't want to interrupt him." His job always seemed clandestine.

His murder and the attention it attracted dispelled any myth that he was a legitimate businessman. My mother tried to shield me from the media frenzy and police investigations that followed his death. I was not allowed to attend his funeral and, shortly after, was sent to live with my grandparents for two years while my mother pulled her life back together. Manny quickly became a taboo subject, particularly after she married a straight-arrow insurance salesman three years later and created a new identity for herself. Yet the secrecy surrounding Manny's life and death served to cut off the first six years of my life as though they were no longer mine.

When I did raise the issue, my mother's explanations for why he was killed often changed. Sometimes she said he was murdered by the Mafia on account of "guilt by association." He wasn't *really* involved in organized crime, she told me, but had fallen victim to some bad people he had gotten involved with. Occasionally she would speak of a hotel they once owned called The Sahara. To me, it evoked images of a Las Vegas gambling casino that seemed out of place in Chicago. I imagined a small desert oasis just outside of the city where it was hot, even in the winter. In the middle of that oasis, I pictured a glitzy hotel with blinking lights rising incongruously from the sand.

When I was a teenager, though, my mother reinvented the story. She told me a cautionary tale of how my father was probably killed by my brother's drug dealer.

"I've never believed that Manny was murdered by the Mafia," she said. "He had once confronted your brother's pill supplier and I think that's who killed him."

The sketchy and conflicting accounts had the lure of a good mystery, and as I grew older I became more curious about the true cause of his death. When I first began to question who my birth parents might have been, Steve speculated that Manny might have been my real father, perhaps even arranging my adoption to cover up an affair with a pregnant mistress. The idea seemed farfetched to me, but I asked my mother about it.

"That was a theory my friend Millie used to believe, but I don't think it's true," she said. Even though she denied it, the fact that it had occurred to someone else lent the story some plausibility.

⌒∞⌒

The answers to my questions came one night on a trip I'd made to Chicago to help my mother pack up and move out of her apartment. After she'd gone to bed, I started snooping through boxes that had been brought up to the apartment from the storage locker in the basement. Buried underneath crates of old plates and table linens were two large boxes of newspapers and gossip column clippings. The papers inside felt dusty to the touch and were faded to a light peach hue. Among them was an issue of *Time* magazine, dated June 15, 1962. I leafed through the pages until I reached an article with a Chicago dateline. I sank to the floor and started reading.

Out of the Desert

The place was a little bit of Las Vegas, but without any gambling tables yet, and just two minutes from Chicago's O'Hare Airport. A salmagundi of Italian marble, Japanese carpet, matched rosewood, Hawaiian monkeypod wood, gold foil and tropical fish, the Sahara Inn is like a movie set for a dream sequence in a musical starring George Jessel and Zsa Zsa Gabor. Complete with boot-shaped swimming pool, fully grown palm trees and a still uncompleted 1,400-seat auditorium, it cost $10.8 million, and is staffed with waitresses appropriately undressed.

The room called the Sultan's Table has a mosque-like dome, a 25-foot "grape tree" (from which wafts the artificial fragrance of grapes) and ten strolling violinists. "I wanted them to play Stradivaris," said Sahara's Host Manny Skar, who was once convicted of burglary, "but my insurance wouldn't cover it." Manny is aggrieved that local newspapers have been digging up his past. "It is callous and unkind to repeatedly allude to my mistakes of long ago. Some of the people whom I know may not be entirely antiseptic. But most are banking, labor, civic, industrial, philanthropic leaders and members of the press."

The grand opening last week was graced by Bobby Darin and George Kirby—with such headliners as Jack Leonard, Vic Damone, Keely Smith, the Kingston Trio, Joe E. Lewis and Ella Fitzgerald booked for future stands.

On opening night, guests wandered around the huge pool (where during daylight hours bikini-clad "starlets" would bring the indolent customer a drink or a cold cut) under the flickering light of a huge gold torch, which belched flames. But most excitement was caused by the waitresses. Their flowing harem pantaloons caught on chairs and customers; the snaps gave way, entangling legs, chairs and customers in a delicious fricassee. Cried George Jessel: "It's the most beautiful place of its kind."

As I read, the Sahara was becoming less of a mirage. It felt strangely reassuring to know that my memories, no matter how vague they had been up until then, weren't entirely fantasy. The ornate hotel sounded like a little bit of Hollywood and a whole lot of Miami Beach and Las Vegas.

Each article brought the past into sharper focus. Memories, long buried, were rising up and finally making sense, obliterating a huge gray area in my mind where truth mingled uncomfortably with doubt. The people in my life were being transformed into characters on a much larger stage than I could ever have imagined. In giddy fascination, I read a story dated May 21, 1962, on the front page of the *Chicago American* newspaper. Beside a photograph of Manny was a headline that read "Hoodlum Tie to Sahara Inn Probed."

. . . Skar says the lot, building, and furnishings will have cost $10,800,000 by the time the project is completed. It is in the heart of what soon will be Chicago's new glitter gulch, a fast-developing suburban version of Rush Street.

In recent months there have been disquieting reports that some of the newly built motels and clubs are a new-found haven for investment of crime syndicate profits earned in gambling and prostitution. Government tax agents are reported to be trying to establish the true ownerships of several of the new motels whose owners of record appear to be mere fronts for other yet unknown interests.

Until a few weeks ago, the free spending Manny Skar was virtually unknown except to the headwaiters from Chicago to Las Vegas and New York, and to the bookmakers of Chicago and Miami Beach.

"You go anywhere with Manny from the lowest dives to the finest places and everyone knows him," one long-time business acquaintance said. "There can be 30 people waiting in line for a table, but when the maître d' sees Manny, Manny goes right up in front."

In recent weeks, Skar has been the subject of an intensive publicity buildup in the gossip columns—offering to promote the Liston-Patterson fight one day, winning a bundle at the races the next.

"We want to create an air of mystery about him," says the Sahara's press agent. "We want people to ask. 'Who is Manny Skar?'"

One thing I knew for sure about Manny was that he was a well-known womanizer. Once my mother was driving down Rush Street in Chicago and was stopped at a light when she saw Manny's limousine across the street. As the two cars passed each other in the intersection, my mother looked into the backseat and was stunned to see Manny lounging with a leggy blonde next to him.

"I looked at him and he looked at me. The driver turned white," my mother recalled.

She drove home slowly in a state of shock. Manny must have barreled home, because once my mother got there she found him lying calmly on the bed in his boxer shorts, reading the newspaper. She just stared at him.

"Who are you going to believe, me or your eyes?" he asked her. Having grown accustomed to his rampant infidelity, my mother couldn't help but laugh.

She didn't always find it so funny though. Sometimes late at night, I was awakened by angry shouting from the next room. I lay in bed, shaken by the belligerence in my parents' voices.

"C'mon Manny, do you think I'm the only person in the city of Chicago who doesn't know about all these women? Do you think people don't tell me? You take them to all of the same places we go to. I'm humiliated when I walk into Alfredo's or the Pump Room. People are always turning their heads to see who you're with that night."

"It's none of your damn business. Don't be a goddamn bitch."

Sometimes I would hear a thud against the wall between my bedroom and theirs and the sound of breaking glass. I'd run down the hall, clutching my pillow, to the bedroom of my nanny, Ruth, a grandmotherly British woman.

I called her Boovie. With her big breasts and large, round stomach, she was my protective cocoon. With her I felt safe. She was the only person in the house whose lap I could just crawl into for no reason in particular and lay my head against her white, nurse's uniform. She always smelled of lilac bathing powder and her graying hair fell softly around her face. Everything about her was proper, from her British accent to the way she always dressed in white and blue, switching off between a blue straw hat in the summers and a navy blue wool coat in the winters.

My mother told me that when I was three years old, Ruth suddenly tried to quit.

"I think it is time for you to find a replacement for me, Mrs. Skar. I believe I am becoming far too attached to Debbie and it would be better for all concerned if I left now."

"Ruth, please, you can't go," my mother begged. "I'll pay you whatever it takes to make you stay. We couldn't function without you. I could never replace you."

Ruth stayed. Even on her days off, she would leave only reluctantly. Worried that my mother could not handle the burden of caring for a young child, she would linger at the front door in her wool overcoat and hat, giving my mother a rundown of the daily schedule of my needs.

I can only imagine what Ruth must have thought about my parents' lifestyle and the people they associated with.

I learned from the newspaper clippings that before I was born, Manny was in business building houses with a man named Rocco DeStefano, who had been named before a Senate crime investigating committee as a racketeer in Chicago and Miami. Just three weeks after I was born, the two men formed the Sahara Motel Corporation and built a small hotel before building the larger one a few years later.

I didn't know any of that when I was seventeen and my boyfriend, Harry, introduced me to Anthony DeStefano. Anthony seemed unusually nervous around me. Anytime I looked at him, his eyes would quickly dart away. His behavior made me uncomfortable so I asked Harry about it. He said:

"Don't you know? Anthony's father Rocco was in business with your dad, Manny." It was obvious the relationship had ended badly and Anthony's family harbored bitter feelings. Anthony's awkwardness toward me became more understandable as I read the old news stories.

When asked by reporters in 1962 who really owned the Sahara, Manny said:

> "I own all of the stock, every share of it," he replied. "I'll take a lie detector test that there is no syndicate money in here."
>
> Asked about Rocco DeStefano's interest, Skar declared:
>
> "He's not in it at all. I bought him out about the first of the year. I put up every dime of my own and borrowed from every source I can think of. There's a lot of borrowed money in there."
>
> Asked where he had borrowed the money, Skar said he would rather not say.
>
> Told that there were reports the Sahara Inn was being financed by Sam [Mooney] Giancana, boss of the crime syndicate, Skar replied:
>
> "I never even met the man. I'm willing to take a lie detector test on that, too."
>
> Asked if he had any idea why anyone would be questioning his apparent sudden affluence, Skar replied simply: "There are a lot of envious people."

I was riveted by the stories, with their aura of scandal. While flipping through the pile of papers, I came across a faded yellow newspaper called the *Miami Beach Reporter*, dated March 1963. The front page of the newspaper is dominated by a pink-hued photograph of a flashy revue dancer who is modeling a skimpy, beaded bikini with strips of cellophane flowing from her hips and balancing a chandelier-shaped hat on her head. Underneath the picture, a black and white close-up shot of my face leaps off the page at me. My smile seems forced, reluctant. Underneath, in small print, it says, "Darling Debra Skar, 3-year-old daughter of Manny Skar, of Chicago, is visiting at the Eden Roc Hotel with her parents. Debra divides her time between the hotel and her daddy's yacht, *Sahara,* anchored on Indian Creek opposite the Eden Roc." Next to my picture is one of a fat woman dressed in a bunny costume trying to kiss Milton Berle.

Though I remember little of our vacations to Florida, I have photographs of myself sitting among my mother and her friends, who were all dressed in snakeskin-patterned bathing suits with huge sunglasses and hair turbans. My nanny, Boovie, was also there, still in her white uniform despite the hot sun.

She was also with us when we abruptly moved to California when I was four years old. We lived in a big rented house in Beverly Hills and then moved to another one nearby. I never understood why we moved across the country for more than a year and then returned to Chicago until I read about it in a newspaper story dated June 4, 1964:

What Happened to Manny Skar?

Did you ever wonder what became of Manny Skar, the dinky dandy of Mannheim Road?

He is living in Beverly Hills, Cal., home of the movie stars.

Here's Skar's version of what he is doing out there:

"I am just picking oranges. I am unemployed. I live in a little house out here, and I like it very much."

Chicago police haven't seen him since he disappeared in a snowstorm of unpaid bills in April, 1963, leaving the

Sahara Inn to the courts, to the creditors, and to movie cowboy Gene Autry, and having them all believe he was impoverished.

Let's take a look at him now, with the help of the files of the Los Angeles and Beverly Hills police departments, whose detectives have been watching Li'l Manny.

Skar's "little house" is an $80,000, eight-room stucco and glass dwelling with attached swimming pool and cabana, a few blocks from the homes of Jack Benny, Jimmy Stewart and Lucille Ball.

Investigators' reports show that Skar is living as high on the hog as his 5-foot 5-inch, 140-pound frame can lift him.

Police watching him say his attire ranges from tailor-made Bermuda shorts at pool side, to white linen suits and expensive straw hats in the afternoon, to continental-cut Italian silk suits at night. Sipping rum drinks and conferring with dark types in a booth in the Luau restaurant in Los Angeles, owned and operated by Stephen Crane, ex-husband of actress Lana Turner. Doing a dance called the watusi at a way-out nightspot in Los Angeles called the Whisky-A-Go-Go, which actress Jayne Mansfield frequents. Hanging around with a former Chicago detective named Elmer Valentine, who operates Los Angeles night spot called PJ's. The spot is said to be a favorite of West Coast hoodlums. Gobbling spaghetti and downing Chianti at a Beverly Hills restaurant called La Scala.

I remember little of my relationship with Manny other than what my mother has told me. I do remember, though, that his flamboyance made him seem larger than life, or, at least from my perspective as a little girl, taller than he really was.

One day while we were shopping in Beverly Hills, my mother and I saw a battery-operated toy car at FAO Schwartz and I instantly wanted it. My mother said it was too dangerous and I was too small for it. She left the next day for a trip back to Chicago. A few days later, Manny took me to the Luau restaurant that I used to refer to as "Daddy's dark office." Sitting at the bar, we called my mother. "Daddy bought me the red car," I boasted. Ignoring her objections, I told her about how I had driven the car up and down the sidewalk on Rodeo Drive.

My mother may have been secretive about Manny's business dealings, but she wasn't shy about dropping the names of celebrities they had crossed paths with at the Sahara and in Los Angeles. I had always assumed she was exaggerating a few brief encounters when she mentioned the names of famous singers or comedians as though they were close chums. So it surprised me when, deep in one of the boxes of newspapers, I found several copies of a page featuring two photographs. The top one was of Debbie Reynolds, with her arm draped around Mae West's shoulder. Below it was a picture of Eddie Fisher and my mother. The photo caption read, "Debbie Reynolds calls, Eddie Fisher performs. But Eddie, with Lynn Skar, looked one way. Debbie another."

While Manny may have gone to California to lay low for a while, his presence there sounded anything but restrained. A huge layout in the *Los Angeles Times*, headlined "Sin and Glamour Pave Sunset Strip," talks about how the famous street was a playground for vacationing gangsters from the East and Midwest.

> It's got everything calculated to appeal to hoodlum greed—tourism, beautiful women of slender morals; the night life; entertainment and restaurant industries, which so often are susceptible to mob infiltration and that old green magic, money.

The article said police were checking everyone worthy of their attention who arrived in town, sometimes right at the airport. The strangest thing about the story was that the only visiting underworld figure named was Manny Skar. It was as if he was the Forrest Gump of mobsters.

∽∞∾

Only a few weeks after we moved back to Chicago, Ruth was returning from walking me to school a block away when she slipped and fell on the icy sidewalk and broke her hip. I was not allowed to visit her in the hospital and she never returned to our home. My mother believed that the best way to sever the bond between us was abruptly and completely.

It was only nine months later that my father was killed. When I returned to school in the chaotic weeks following his death, the other children confronted me in the direct, honest style of first-graders.

"Did your dad die?" they asked.

"No, he's in the hospital," I answered.

According to my mother, the school recommended that she take me to a psychiatrist to sort out whatever emotional problems I had lurking beneath the surface. I sat across a big desk with the doctor on one side and my mother and I on the other.

"Debbie, do you know that your father is dead?" the woman asked me in the slow, deliberate manner adults use when talking to children. My mother remembers me leaning my elbow on the edge of the desk, cradling my head in my hand and saying, "Of course, I do. It just hurts too much inside to say it."

The truth of it was that Manny's death magnified the pain of losing Ruth. Somewhere in the back of my mind, exposed only after I began to explore my adoption, was a realization that both of their sudden departures were echoes of the day my birth mother handed me through a car window to people she did not know and walked away.

In September of 1965, there was little dwelling on feelings. A swarm of government investigators and news reporters descended on our lives after Manny's murder. A police car with its blue light turning in circles sat parked day and night across the street from our building. For ten days we couldn't even leave the building through the front entrance because of the reporters camped out front.

That's why I found it so strange that in all of the newspaper clippings in my mother's boxes, there wasn't even one article about his death. I asked my mother where they were, but she remained as obscure as ever on the subject, saying they had probably been lost.

While it was easy to assume that Manny's murder was the predictable end of a fast and furious life, I wanted to know all of the details behind it. So I called my editor at the *San Francisco Chronicle*, who told me I could find archives of the *Chicago Tribune* dating back to the 1800s at the nearby University of California at Berkeley. At the center of campus, in the basement of the Bancroft Library, I found drawers of microfilm rolls and spent several hours scanning every *Tribune* published in the weeks following Manny's murder.

The day my father was killed, September 11, 1965, the Indians were retreating against the attacking Pakistanis and a powerful hurricane named Betsy had wreaked havoc on Louisiana. But those front-page stories were overshadowed by one big, bold headline:

HOOD MANNY SKAR SLAIN

Mandel (Manny) Skar, 42, ex-convict pal of Chicago mobsters and a former owner of the plush Sahara Inn in Schiller Park, was gunned down in gang-fashion early today behind the 17-story apartment building in which he lived at 3800 N. Lake Shore Dr.

A volley of gunshots rang out as he stepped from the garage and he was hit in the right eye, left cheek, chest and right knee. His body was taken to the morgue.

Witnesses said he was assassinated by three dark-skinned men in an "old, beige-colored" auto which then sped away into the darkness. He was killed shortly before 1 A.M.

The shooting occurred shortly after Skar and his wife, Lynn, 41, returned home from a restaurant at 50 E. Oak St. in their leased Pontiac convertible. Skar dropped his wife off in front and then drove to the garage in the rear. Mrs. Skar started for their 15th floor suite.

Two attendants were in the garage when Skar entered, but they were busy, so Skar left his auto to be parked and started through a courtyard to a rear entrance to his apartment building.

The bullets cut him down 30 feet from the garage. Mrs. Skar, who heard the shots, raced to her husband. She screamed, "They've killed my Manny."

A large photo showed Manny's body lying on the pavement next to an ambulance with detectives circling around. It turned out that Manny's real name was Mendel Skovunack. Nine months before his death, he was arrested for evading taxes. Shortly after, he was subpoenaed by a federal grand jury investigating organized crime in Chicago. Any doubt about why he was killed was answered on the *Tribune*'s front page on September 12, 1965. The banner headline screamed the truth behind his murder:

SKAR SLAIN FOR SQUEALING

Mandel (Manny) Skar was murdered because he was in the process of spilling gang secrets to the federal government, *The Tribune* learned yesterday.

The 42-year-old mobster had reportedly been talking to several federal agencies for some months on topics ranging from the framework of collectors and musclemen the crime syndicate uses to shake down night clubs and restaurants to who really benefitted from the ill-fated $7.6 million dollar financing of Skar's Sahara North motel.

The gangster was jockeying for a favorable position in his pending trial on charges that he evaded more than $1 million in income taxes on money which he allegedly diverted to his own use from the multimillion-dollar construction loans.

Skar reportedly approached federal agencies last spring, shopping around for someone to listen to the information that he hoped would keep him out of the penitentiary.

The pint-sized hoodlum, who got his start as a small-time burglar, was still in contact with authorities when five .38 caliber slugs slammed into his head, chest and right knee about 1 A.M. yesterday. . . .

The name Skar repeatedly mentioned to investigators, it was reported, was that of Rocco DeStefano, a onetime Capone gang mobster who was Skar's business associate beginning in the mid-1950s when Skar embarked on a meteoric rise in the apartment building, private home and motel construction field.

There were also indications that Skar may have been ready to talk about his associations with Sam (Teetz)

Battaglia, one of the crime syndicate's toughest gangsters and a west side gambling and loan shark boss.

Skar had reportedly promised investigators that he would reveal in due time the names of his mob financial backers. He spoke with pride of his relations with Phil (Milwaukee Phil) Alderisio, a terrorist and reputed mob killer whom Skar always referred to as Philly.

There were also reports that Skar was ready to talk about the mysterious $30,000 that was wired to him in 1963 at the Cal-Neva lodge in Lake Tahoe, Nev., a gambling joint then half owned by Frank Sinatra, the crooner.

The cash was sent to Skar about the time Sam (Momo) Giancana, the Chicago mob's operating boss, threw a temper tantrum at the gambling joint and overturned tables in a fight during one of two weekends Giancana got the red carpet treatment at the lodge. Sinatra later lost his gaming license and had to sell out his interest.

But the major piece of information that Skar was reportedly prepared to peddle in his attempt to escape federal prison was the names of the mobsters whom he claimed got the money diverted from the Sahara North motel construction loans.

Skar maintained that if the doors of a federal prison loomed before him with certainty, he would tell how the diverted millions did not stick to his fingers, but instead slid through them to higher-ups in the mob . . . Skar said he only served as the "conduit" for the stolen cash.

In the months that Skar sought to use his information to best personal advantage, he gave his hoodlum friends perhaps too many clues to what he was up to.

In a number of near northside joints favored by the high-living mobster, Skar repeatedly threatened to subpoena as defense witnesses at his tax trial next month a number of top hoodlums starting with his old business associate, Rocco DeStefano.

Often as Skar's favorite drink, scotch and soda, flowed, he told everyone within earshot, "I'm going to have subpoenas all over town."

Skar, through his braggadocio, left his mob associates a clear trail to his intentions—stay out of jail at any cost.

If one thing was certain, it was that Manny paid a high price for the life he led. On the day of his death, he had to borrow $100 from a tavern owner to take my mother out on the town. Later the federal government put a lien on his estate to recover back taxes, all part of Attorney General Robert Kennedy's campaign against organized crime.

Having witnessed these events first as a young child and then from the distance of thirty years, I felt like an actress who had played a cameo role in a dark drama. The newspaper stories helped to explain the dramatic turn our lives had taken in 1965, when my mother forsook her glamorous lifestyle to sell corrugated cartons and I was sent into Siberian exile in Minnesota to live with my grandparents.

By the time I finished reading all of the clippings, hours had passed and my eyes burned. Yet I had a sense of satisfaction at having found out what no one had ever been willing to tell me. It made me realize why I had become a newspaper reporter instead of a lawyer as my mother had wanted; I had always felt a need to blow the lid off of secrets and let the truth fall on my head and around my feet, no matter how messy.

I felt more ready than ever before to unravel the story of my adoption.

chapter FOUR

As a child, I never really understood the difference between an orphan and an adoptee. For me they were the same.

My mother once took me to an orphanage in Chicago to donate some old clothes. As we walked toward the faded-white stucco building, which had once been a church, my eyes gravitated toward the giant cross over the front entrance. The old edifice cast a large shadow over the cement yard where the children were playing. They seemed like any other children then: jumping and screeching, playing hop-scotch, chasing one another, seemingly unaware for that moment that they had been abandoned.

We entered the building and handed our bags of used clothes to the nun at the front desk. She thanked us, but I couldn't look her in the eye. I was embarrassed, even ashamed. It was as though I was paying a debt; after all, I could have been one of those children. Instead, I felt like an impostor standing there in my nicely tailored clothes, knowing I would never have to wear someone else's hand-me-downs.

Looking back on that day, I think of those bags as containing not only all of the expensive clothes I'd outgrown, but also all of the expectations my mother had of me. My mother seemed more like my benefactor, in the same vein as Miss Havisham in *Great Expectations*; our story lacked the sentimentality of *Annie* or *Oliver Twist*. Each year as I was growing up, I felt less like that unique, chosen child I had been told I was and more like an orphan, one my mother wished to transform into the child she would have conceived had she been able.

I was the understudy for a leading actress who never showed up. From the costumes she chose for me to the polite and restrained way I was supposed to act, my mother had carefully written the script. The problem was that I did not always play my role very well.

My mother knew there was something different about me when I was very young. I didn't speak, she said. So when I was about three years old, she took me to a doctor, thinking I might be deaf or even mentally retarded.

"The doctor asked you to throw a piece of paper in the garbage can and you did. Then he asked you to turn on the radio and you did," my mother recounted. "He told me there was nothing wrong with your hearing, that we just anticipated your needs and you had no reason to speak. He said you were spending too much time with adults and suggested that we put you in a sandbox with other children and you would begin to talk. So we did. But when you finally did begin to speak, no one could understand you. You had your own language. You even had your own imaginary friend who you talked to. Once we were going on an airplane and you insisted that we buy her a plane ticket and you refused to get on until we promised we had."

The silence of my youngest years evolved into a speech impediment that made me substitute some letters for others, twisting my words and garbling their meaning. "S's" became "K's," "R's" turned into W's" and some words were just beyond my ability to pronounce.

"Does Debbie come from a foreign country?" a playmate once asked my mother. I felt like I did.

I was teased and imitated by my classmates, who found great entertainment in echoing my strange-sounding words.

"Do you go kimming in the kimming pool?" they taunted and laughed when I was in first grade. "Do lions roar or do they wor?" It became easier to just not talk at school, and to speak only in private, sometimes into the mirror in the bathroom, to my invisible friend whom I named "Sis."

I was sent to speech therapists, off and on, from the time I was four years old until I was about eleven. Long, arduous sessions of repeating letter combinations and blowing spit through my rolled tongue eventually improved my ability to communicate, like the painstaking construction of a bridge I had to build to reach the people around me.

My fantasies of orphanhood were confirmed when my mother abruptly sent me to stay with my grandparents in a small town in Minnesota for the summer after my seventh birthday. The summer stretched into two years.

At the time, my mother told me it was for my own good, to shield me from the confused aftermath of my father's murder. My brother, Howie, was already away at college in Boston.

I only learned much later that while I was living with my grandparents, my mother was busy marrying and divorcing her second husband. Whatever reasons were truly behind my move to Minnesota, I could only sense that I had been left again in a strange place with people I hardly knew.

The small town, surrounded by farms, offered an entirely different life from the one I had left behind in Chicago. The streets were lined with simple two-story homes, meticulously maintained white churches and parks with neat rows of maple and elm trees. The winters were harsh and the summers sweltering. Like many of the houses on the block, my grandparents' home was white clapboard with a small lawn in front.

My grandparents were in their sixties and totally unprepared for the task of caring for a young child. Together they worked twelve-hour days at their small grocery store on the town's Main Street. Neither of them knew how to drive, so they were shuttled the five blocks from the house to the store by their delivery boy in an old, white station wagon.

I was left with their housekeeper, Francine Keeler, who was extremely high-strung. She talked fast and frequently, most often to herself, and it was difficult to follow her train of thought. Mrs. Keeler was the most serious person I ever met. I can't recall her ever laughing or making a joke.

I remember watching Mrs. Keeler barrel through the house, her tall, thin frame slouched forward, taking huge ducklike steps that reminded me of Popeye's Olive Oyl. She was probably in her late forties, but appeared older. Her long black hair, streaked with thin strands of gray, was pulled into a bun at the back of her head so tightly that you could see her scalp. She wore oversized glasses that magnified her small eyes and overwhelmed her pale, freckled cheeks.

According to my grandmother, Mrs. Keeler had been a secretary to the governor of Minnesota several years earlier. After her husband was electrocuted while working on a utility pole, she had a breakdown and was sent to a state-run mental hospital. When she got out several months later, she found out that her parents had put her young daughter up for adoption.

"She went from one organization to another for information about the little girl and all they would tell her was that her daughter played the violin, nothing else," my grandmother later recalled. "She never recovered. But she worked like nobody ever worked."

Mrs. Keeler did her best to take care of me, but she clearly resented the duties that had been added to her job description.

My mother had sent my brother's schnauzer with me to Minnesota. At times, Mrs. Keeler responded to the dog's constant barking with a frantic edge to her voice: "That's Ruffie the dog," she said. "The added responsibility from Chicago who's been here one year, four months, five days, twenty-one hours and thirty-two minutes." Every time she repeated that phrase, the numbers changed. I wondered whether she was really keeping track, like a referee checking his stopwatch, or was some kind of weird math genius.

When Ruffie became too much for them to handle, my grandmother, ignoring my pleas, gave him away to a poor family, along with a case of dog food from the grocery store.

At night Mrs. Keeler sat in her small bedroom, mending her checkered housedresses and aprons. Once, I went crying to her room with a horrible earache. She told me to put my ear to her breast, that the warmth would make it feel better. I sat on her lap and she stroked my hair with rare tenderness that made me miss my nanny, Ruth. Maybe, at that moment, she was remembering her own daughter.

In the morning, she got up before dawn to prepare my school lunches at the insistence of my grandmother, and the smell of fried chicken wafted through the house. Several hours later, I would defiantly trade the chicken for peanut butter and jelly sandwiches with other children at school.

Each Sunday, Mrs. Keeler left for church wearing the same dark, tweed suit and brown hat pinned to the crown of her head. "I'll pray for you, Mrs. Goldman," she would tell my grandmother.

"You do that," my grandmother would answer, with a sarcastic laugh, as though she didn't care what Mrs. Keeler's God thought of her.

The two of them fought constantly over housekeeping details like how the linens were folded or how long the meat should be cooked. My grandmother frequently fired Mrs. Keeler.

"I'm going to throw all of your clothes out of this window if you don't leave right now," my grandmother would threaten when Mrs. Keeler challenged her directions.

"You can't do that," Mrs. Keeler shrieked. "I'm a ward of the state and I'll call the governor."

Mrs. Keeler never left. The truth was that my grandmother needed her because she worked hard, did all of the cooking and watched over me while my grandmother was bound to the grocery store.

My grandfather ignored all of us. He was a humorless, impatient man whose body had begun to give out after many years of chopping meat and waiting on customers for long hours. The only contact I had with him was when he yelled at me to keep quiet or stuck his cane out as I ran through the living room, both to slow me down and strike out at me.

He was a very religious man. Twice a day he would wrap leather straps around his arms and fix a square black box to his forehead, rhythmically bowing forward and backward as he chanted Hebrew prayers at the dining room table. On the Sabbath, we joined the town's sixteen other Jewish families at a small synagogue across the street from a large Catholic

church. Because of the dwindling Jewish population, the synagogue had a high turnover of rabbis who left the moment
they found another job with a larger congregation elsewhere.

Like my grandfather, my grandmother had little toler-
ance for the spiritedness of a child and often dealt with me as
though she was trying to tame a wild animal. If I refused to
practice the piano or follow another one of her orders, she
took out the leather belt she kept in a small wooden cabinet
in the living room and chased me up the stairs, swinging it
out in front of her. She would usually catch me on the landing of the stairs and hit me across the back, making my skin
burn. The lashing continued after I fell to the ground, my
hands shielding the back of my head.

"Why are you so rotten? I can't take this anymore," she
screamed, the anger in her voice rising with each stroke of
the belt.

The whipping would stop only when I laid perfectly still,
feigning unconsciousness. Several minutes later, when I
thought it was safe, I would run up the stairs to my bedroom
and lock myself in.

My grandmother often pointed out that she was only taking care of me for my mother's sake. "She has her own life to
lead," my grandmother would say disdainfully in her Russian-
accented English. "She can't take care of you too." Sometimes
I wondered whether she would give me away like she had
Ruffie the dog.

On the few occasions when my mother came to visit us,
she would greet me at the airport with a shrill "Debbieeee!",
her face animated by an exaggerated smile and her arms out-
stretched. I refused to say hello and ran away from her and
the pain of knowing she would be leaving in a few days without me.

I found refuge across the street from my grandparents at
the home of my friend, Mary Holden. Her house was modest
and comfortable, with crucifixes and pictures of Jesus and the
Last Supper on the walls. There was always an aroma of bak-
ing dough coming from the kitchen. At her home I could run
around and play without fear of instant reprimand. Eating dinner with Mary's family was particularly special because I loved
the way they all sat down together. I soon came to feel like just
another of the six Holden children. When Mrs. Holden made
dance costumes for her daughters, she also made one for me.

The moment after I came home from school, I dropped
my books on the kitchen table, said good-bye to Mrs. Keeler
and went to visit the Holdens. I was so excited I would run
across the street without looking both ways. Once a car same
to a screeching halt just inches away from me. I stopped just
long enough to see the look of terror on the driver's face, and
then continued my single-minded escape to the Holdens'
front door.

Mary, who was my age, became more than a best friend
to me. In the fanciful world of seven-year-old girls, she was
my sister. She had the blondest hair I had ever seen and was
always cheerful. With her, I never felt angry. Together we
went to school, took tap dance classes and secretly vowed we
would become nuns when we grew up.

The Holdens took me along on family outings, whether
it was to the hardware store or the park. Often I would
accompany them to church on Sunday. My grandmother
allowed me to go but warned me never to take the Eucharist
from the priest. Once I got there, though, I would stand in
line for the Holy Communion with the rest of the kids and
have the wafer inserted in my mouth. As it dissolved, I imagined that I was becoming more Catholic with each swallow.

I secretly wished that the woman who had given me up for adoption was Catholic. Maybe the Holdens would adopt me and I would never have to live with my mother or grandparents again.

Like my mother, my grandmother often admonished me never to tell anybody that I was adopted. The message I got was that whomever I told would not think as highly of me if they knew my background was uncertain. Better they should think I came from a "good Jewish family," my grandmother would say.

She was always trying to get other people to take care of me. Once I heard her asking her brother-in-law Morrie to take me fishing at his cabin on the lake.

"I don't know what else to do with her," my grandmother said.

"You've got a lot of nerve," he said.

Uncle Morrie took me anyway, and all I remember about the trip is hours of silence, staring at my reflection on the lake's surface, waiting for the fish.

My grandmother's friend from the synagogue, Doris Feldman, often pitched in to care for me. Doris was much younger than my grandmother. She picked me up from school and took me to Hebrew and ballet classes. She had three sons and I grew close to the youngest boy, Jonny, who was my age. We played tag in his backyard and he taught me how to ride a two-wheel bike.

I could tell that Doris really liked kids. Unlike the grownups in my family, Doris played with us, laughed at our jokes and was never too busy to answer our questions. She was a small woman—not a lot taller than we were—with short dark hair, who looked just like her sons. In my fantasies, I imagined she really wanted a daughter and would offer to adopt me one day. I suspected that Doris not only knew how unhappy I was, but understood why. My complaints and willfulness never seemed to bother her. She would often tell me, "You know your own mind."

Although Doris meant it as a compliment, I knew I was difficult. My grandmother often reminded me of it and I wore my designation as a badge of honor. I clearly remember willing myself to be strong when I arrived in Minnesota. It was as if I knew that if I were to survive in the cold, old-fashioned household of my grandparents, I would have to mask any vulnerability.

Nobody ever told me when I was going to return to my mother, and I never asked. After two years of living in Minnesota, I had gotten used to it and didn't remember Chicago very well. I may not have liked living with my grandparents, but I loved Mary and her family, and Doris and Jonny.

A short time after I finished third grade, my grandmother told me my mother was going to be visiting us with a man she was planning to marry. I was confused by that, but didn't ask any questions. The truth was that I no longer knew my mother. She was a stranger to me yet, at the same time, I felt angry at her.

When she arrived with this new man, she announced with satisfaction and pride, "Debbie, this is Jim Levi."

From the moment I saw him, I liked him. He seemed older than my mother. He had a big, round face and blue eyes that had a playful glint when he smiled.

He sat down next to me and said, "Debbie, I'm so happy to meet you. Tell me about what you've been doing here in Minnesota."

Jim was different from the others in my family. When he talked to me, he looked into my eyes and he paid attention to what I said. I showed him my room and took him across the street to meet the Holdens.

Several days after they arrived, he sat down on the sofa with me and told me he loved my mother and was going to marry her. "If it's all right with you, I'd like to be your dad. I have another daughter. Her name is Barbara and she will be your sister."

At that moment, all I could think about was how much I wanted a sister. I imagined she would be like Mary and we could play together and I wouldn't be lonely anymore. Nobody told me at the time that she was twelve years older than I was, already an adult.

"Jim wants to adopt you and take you back to Chicago," my mother chimed in.

Although I was happy to leave my grandparents, I couldn't imagine saying good-bye to Mary. The day I left, we both cried and promised to write, but I knew I would never see her again.

I realized then that adoption was never a choice made by a child. No matter how much I might have wished to be adopted by the Holdens or the Feldmans, my fate would always be decided for me by others.

⚮

Ten years after leaving Minnesota to return to Chicago, I went to see my grandmother. I was nineteen years old and attending college in Los Angeles. My grandmother had retired there and lived in an apartment building in the San Fernando Valley.

As I sat at a table next to the pool with my grandmother and several other elderly residents, one woman asked me, "Debbie, are you going to have children?"

I responded brashly, without thinking: "I don't think so. I would rather adopt a child."

My grandmother, in her most critical tone, said, "That's ridiculous. You should never adopt a child. You never know what you're going to get."

chapter **FIVE**

It was raining hard on the day in mid-January 1992 when I drove to my first adoptee search workshop. Though the meeting was being held in a church not far from my house, I kept checking the written directions in my lap, worried that I would make a wrong turn and miss the start of the meeting. I couldn't shake a lingering sense of betrayal and I wondered if it was because I was looking for my other mother or because I was about to go public with what had so long been a very private secret.

Despite the frantic beating of the windshield wipers, the rain was obscuring the road ahead. When I finally found the church, I parked in a small lot next to it. Tightly grasping my umbrella against the wind, I followed a trail of signs reading "ALMA—Adoptee Liberty Movement Association" that led down some stairs to a social hall in the basement. I took my place in a long line of people waiting to get in and nervously browsed through brochures and fliers about the organization that were laid out in neat piles on a long table alongside us. When it was my turn, I was greeted by a friendly woman who asked if I was a member.

"No, I'm not," I said. "This is my first time attending a workshop. I'm thinking about searching for my birth mother, but I haven't really started."

"Of course, I understand," she said. "When you become a member of ALMA, you can attend these workshops and receive help from one of our trained search assistants. Our registration fee is sixty dollars. Let me give you this packet of forms you can take with you."

I wrote her a check and took a seat at a vacant table off to the side. Looking around, I saw women and men, some very young, others much older. They could have been at any meeting, anywhere: Alcoholics Anonymous or the PTA. Some were standing and talking, while others were sitting on folding chairs staring straight ahead, waiting for the meeting to begin.

The room was huge, practically the size of a gymnasium, with a stage at the front and tables spread throughout the front half. A giant quilt hung across one wall, declaring the "100th Anniversary of the First Lutheran Church." In the center of the small squares of fabric were two stitched appliques of churches—one old, the other new. I looked around and saw that the other walls were bare except for some forgotten Christmas tinsel dangling from a wooden beam.

I felt awkwardly alone and found myself fumbling through my purse to look busy. I took the papers the woman at the front desk had given me out of the envelope and began to leaf through them. There was a thick booklet called the *Official ALMA Searcher's Guide*, forms to fill out and a sheet that read "The Eight Great Fallacies of Adoption." The first one on the list practically jumped off the page at me because it sounded so familiar:

Adoptive parents make better parents than ordinary people because they wanted a child so badly, and went to so much trouble to get one.

My mother could have written that, I thought. I read on.

Actually, adoptive parents are no better and no worse than any other parents. The idea that just wanting a child makes anyone into a good parent is shallow. It's the amount of time, thought, love and labor that goes into raising a child that distinguishes the good parents from the poor ones. To expect parents to be extra good at parenting simply because they adopted is to burden them with impossible standards to live up to, and this can place a strain on the relationships in the family. They may, in fact, feel unsure of themselves, because they had to go to so much trouble to get a child. They may also transfer a portion of these unrealistic expectations to the child.

That too sounded familiar. I scanned down the page to Fallacy Number Five:

An adoptee belongs to his or her new family forever—and owes them something more than the ordinary offspring owes his family. Correction: an adoptee will be a part of the people who love him or her forever, but belonging is a term used for property. An adoptee owes his or her parents nothing more and nothing less than any son or daughter actually born to them. To insist otherwise is to put the adoptee into a special class. It is to transform adoption into a charitable institution, and to make the children who are "benefited" by this service into objects of charity. It is actually a self-pitying plea for gratitude. . . .

The din of conversation suddenly quieted and a woman standing in the front of the room began to speak. She made announcements about adoption conferences being held in the coming months and about lobbying efforts underway in Sacramento and Washington, D.C., to reform adoption laws, and then she invited those who had completed their searches to get up and tell everyone else their stories.

A woman sitting at a table off to the side eagerly raised her hand and was invited up. She looked as if she was in her forties, with a head full of buoyant, brown curls. She seemed anxious and excited, nearly unable to stand still as the other woman pinned a badge on her jacket that declared "Found" in big, black letters. Everyone clapped and the woman began to talk.

"Hi. My name is Laura Simmons. I was born in San Francisco and relinquished on September 16, 1952. I began to search for my birth mother eight years ago, but gave up a short time later out of both fear and frustration. I started up again several times over the years but never seriously until I joined ALMA last year. With the help of my search assistant, Elaine, I received my nonidentifying information from the agency that handled my adoption. I learned that my mother was nineteen, unmarried and came from a large Catholic family in Michigan. She got pregnant while she was in college and came to San Francisco during her pregnancy. After months of writing to different agencies and poring through records, I found out her maiden name was Doris Kramer. I called about ten Kramers in her hometown before I found her uncle. I told him I was organizing a college reunion and he gave me her phone number and her married name, Doris Schecter. I spent days just staring at the piece of paper, too scared to dial the number."

Laura paused for a moment, shifting her weight from one leg to another, still smiling while her eyes became glassy with tears.

"One night I just sat down and forced myself to call. A woman answered and I asked to speak to Doris. She said

'This is Doris.' I said, 'My name is Laura Simmons. I was born on September 16, 1952. Does that date have any significance to you?' There was a pause and then I heard her gasp. She said, 'Oh my God, is this who I think it is?' I said, 'I believe you are my mother.' Her voice became louder and the questions just poured out. 'Are you OK?' she asked. 'Are you happy?' We ended up talking for more than an hour. She told me that she thought about me all the time and prayed that I had a good life. I assured her that I had, but that I just needed to find her and learn about my background. She told me that she got married five years after I was born and had told her husband about the adoption. She has two other children, who she wants me to meet.

"That was two weeks ago and since then we've spoken almost every day, as if we've been making up for all the years we've missed. She still lives in Michigan and has invited me to come visit. I'm hoping to go there next month. I feel so lucky, so happy. It's really overwhelming."

Everyone in the room began to clap and the woman leading the workshop hugged Laura, who was wiping tears from her eyes with the sleeve of her sweater. I envied her elation. It was as if she had opened a secret door and found a whole new world to explore on the other side.

When the excitement over Laura's speech had died down, the woman leading the meeting asked a man named Harold to stand up. I could see that he was hesitating. A few people sitting at his table were whispering encouragement to him. He stood up slowly and walked forward. He appeared to be in his late sixties, perhaps even seventy.

"As many of you here have heard before, I began searching more than ten years ago," he began after a few moments. "I guess I got kind of a late start. Just last month, I finally reached some cousins. My family comes from the West Texas area. It turns out my mother died about fifteen years back."

Some people in the audience uttered a collective groan.

"My cousins told me they had heard about me," he continued, unfazed. "I guess my mother had mentioned it to her sisters. Anyway, they all seemed happy to hear from me. I've talked to a number of them. We had a lot of catching up to do."

He stopped and the audience gave out a sympathetic chuckle and clapped. The woman up front pinned the "Found" button on Harold's shirt pocket.

In the meantime, people began talking in half whispers to one another. A woman at my table said to the woman next to her, "Wow, you've got to admire him. He waited a long time, but he didn't give up."

Shortly after, we were divided into small groups to meet with a search assistant. Mine was a woman named Delores, a birth mother. She told us how she had searched for and found her son five years earlier. We took turns talking to her. The others who went before me showed her old phone directories, marriage licenses, hospital records and written notes they had taken. She helped them piece together their fragmented evidence as if they were amateur detectives. I listened, trying to remember each detail for my own search. When my turn came up, I felt embarrassed that I had nothing to show her.

"I did ask my adoptive mother to send some documents, but they haven't arrived yet," I explained.

"Well, did she tell you what they are?" Delores asked.

"She told me she has my final adoption papers and my original birth certificate."

"Are you sure she said the original birth certificate?"

"Yes, I think so."

"That's very unusual. Most people only have their amended birth certificate with the names of the adoptive parents. The original is usually sealed by the court. But if what you say is true, you might be way ahead of the game. The certificate should have your birth mother's name on it."

"My mother has always said her name was Helen," I hesitated for a minute, then continued. "I should probably tell you that knowing what I do about my adoptive family, I expect my adoption may be a little different than some of the others you've heard about."

I recounted the stories about Helen handing me through a car window, the lawyer, and my mother using political connections in Chicago to pull my birth certificate from the court file.

"It sounds like a gray market adoption," Delores explained patiently. "It was probably done by a lawyer who was a baby broker. We've heard about some of them who operated at that time in Chicago. What year were you born?"

"1959."

"First, you need to request your nonidentifying information," Delores said. "That's the family history your birth mother gave to the social worker at the time of your adoption. Ethnic background, ages, sometimes even the circumstances of her pregnancy and your relinquishment. By law, you are entitled to all that information, but without any names being given. You can begin by putting in a request for that information to the county social service agency in Chicago."

My head was spinning as I thought about all of that family background she mentioned. It was exciting to hear that I might find out so much before I even searched for my mother. Up until then, it was like I had been a lone figure in a black and white photograph; soon the picture would be enhanced with shades of color.

"In the meantime," Delores continued, "once you receive your adoption papers, you can fill out this birth information form and send it in to ALMA's New York headquarters. We have a computerized reunion registry there and if your mother is searching for you, your names will be matched electronically. It usually takes about six weeks; if there's an ALMA match, they will contact you with your mother's name and address."

Delores gave me her home telephone number and address. She invited me to attend a monthly rap session at her house where people gather to talk about how they feel about their searches and reunions.

I walked outside to my car and stared up at the sky. The rain had stopped and the air felt washed clean. Light gray clouds were scattering to reveal blue sky and sun to the north.

As I began to drive, I thought about the computer in New York and the promise that it held. I knew, with a certainty that comes from raw emotional instinct, that my mother was out there, somewhere, looking for me, or at least wanting to be found. All of the elaborate searching that others had to do to find lost relatives would not be necessary once she and I were matched in the computer.

When I arrived home, I found my husband in the downstairs office and told him about the meeting. He looked up at me several times as I spoke but otherwise stared at the computer screen. His black hair was wet but already beginning to form its natural curls on the top of his head. A few gray hairs were sprouting along the edge of his mustache.

"It all sounds very exciting," he said reticently. "But I hope you'll be careful. You never know what you're going to find."

His cynicism annoyed me. He reminded me of a parent warning a child about all of the dangers of wild animals and poison oak just as the child is discovering wildflowers on a nature trail. Even worse, it echoed what my grandmother had once said.

Being adopted could not have been further from Steve's experience. He was raised in the same home his father had grown up in. During his childhood, Steve's mother was a young housewife and his father was working hard to build a closet-accessory business. Even after finding some financial success, they never left their firmly middle-class neighborhood. Unlike my parents, they had no need to flaunt their prosperity. They didn't seem to have any skeletons in their closets to hide from their children or anyone else.

Steve was filled with nostalgia for every sight, smell and taste that reminded him of his youth in Yonkers, New York. He loved to repeat the same stories about his Hebrew school teacher, his newspaper route and his family's summer vacations in the Catskills.

Steve's mother's family was a close-knit network of cousins who all lived in New York and whose parents had all immigrated to the United States from Germany just months before the Jews began being deported to the death camps.

My family's extravagant lifestyle, on the other hand, alternately amused and disgusted Steve. Though my mother respected Steve—more for his résumé than anything else— he had no such admiration for her. Like others, he was at first taken in by the charm and flamboyance of her Auntie Mame approach to the world. He laughed at the parade of people she hired to do everything from my father's laundry to watering the plants. But as with any comedy routine, he grew tired of it and came to scorn her shallowness. The darker side of her personality, the one that desperately sought to blame others for her own mistakes or misfortunes, repelled him. But that didn't stop him from using her as a weapon against me.

When he was mad, he liked to tell me, "You're acting just like your mother" or "It figures considering the family you grew up in." He knew his comments were certain to hurt or make me angry.

The differences in our backgrounds created a wedge between us, often blocking our ability to understand or empathize with one another. I suspected that, like my parents, Steve secretly wished I would keep my adoption neatly locked away and not repeat Pandora's mistake.

But for me, it was too late. I had already begun to open the box and there was no turning back.

⌒∞⌒

I checked the mailbox several times a day during the next week. When the papers didn't appear, I worried that my mother had decided not to send them or, worse, had destroyed them. I decided to wait until the end of the week before I called her again.

One afternoon, I hurried to check the mailbox before it rained. It was a cold California day but I ran outside barefooted anyway. I opened the mailbox and saw a large manila envelope rolled around a stack of letters. It was addressed to me in my mother's handwriting. I tried to yank the envelope out, but the other mail came with it and dropped to the ground. Ignoring the mess, I frantically tore it open.

Inside there was a bundle of documents. On the very top was a birth certificate. I read the words, feeling an odd sensation as though I were reading about somebody else. The noises on the street all came together in a steady hum in my ears like the muffled sound you hear when you're underwater.

The baby's name on the birth certificate was not mine, but Shirley Jane Dunne. "Shirley Jane?" I repeated the name out loud several times. It sounded so funny to me, wholesome yet completely foreign. I read on:

Date of Birth: 8:39 A.M. May 14, 1959
Name of Hospital or Institution: Mount Sinai Hospital
Father's Full Name: William Robert Dunne
His Age: 30 years
His Birthplace: New York City
His Usual Occupation: Salesman
Kind of Business or Industry: Machines
Mother's Full Maiden Name: Helen R. Jones
Her Age: 24 years

The words were flowing into a deep, empty hole in my chest that was much deeper than I ever imagined. A moment later, my eyes fixed on the small typed letters beneath the heading "Mother's Birthplace" and all I could think of was a trip I had taken twelve years earlier.

chapter SIX

Hitchhiking across the country was not something I had ever envisioned myself doing—at least not until I met David in the summer of 1979. If I knew then that my experiences with him that summer would reverberate through my life more than a decade later, I probably wouldn't have been surprised. I knew from the moment I met David that he was no ordinary college kid who just wanted to have a few wild times before settling down. There were no white-picket fences and suburban ranch houses on his horizon.

David was a psychedelic cowboy. He walked with a bow-legged stagger, his long legs taking slow strides as though he was never in a hurry to get anywhere. You could tell by looking at him that he considered getting dressed in the morning one of life's absurd requirements. He would wear an old flannel shirt unbuttoned over a tie-dyed T-shirt, and his faded jeans fell haphazardly in and around his untied hiking boots. His dirty-blond hair lay in thin strands over his wide, smooth forehead.

But it was his blue eyes that attracted people's attention, pulling them in and keeping them in a playful trance. They were the eager eyes of a child and the prophetic eyes of a sage, enabling him to see the wonder in what others viewed as ordinary. Sometimes I would catch him staring off into the distance, grinning and, every once in a while, laughing silently to himself, as if he were seeing pictures the rest of us could not.

While most of the students at our small Southern California college had rejected the hippie lifestyle in favor of surfing and beer-keg parties, David still lived as though it were 1968. He experimented with a wide variety of drugs, followed the Grateful Dead like a religion and played Frisbee barefoot on the parched pavement as his own unique brand of meditation.

We were both attending a few classes that summer— David to catch up after transferring schools a year before and me to avoid going home. The days were lazy on our nearly deserted college campus under a canopy of thick smog, trapped in place by the persistent Los Angeles heat. We had been introduced by friends shortly before the summer began. David needed a place to stay, and I had an extra bedroom in my apartment since my roommate had gone to the East Coast for the summer.

Our relationship quickly fell into an easy rhythm as if we had known one another for a long time. There was little of that awkward maneuvering through words and manners that occurs when two people are getting to know each other. I never felt self-conscious around David. Together we could be just as happy sitting in silence as we were making each other laugh in hysterical bursts.

By late June, David had begun taking short trips up to San Francisco. At first, I figured he was just going up to visit friends and escape the heat. Then one Sunday in July, he returned shortly after midnight. I heard the door open and shut, and a few moments later I heard a thump, thump, thump down the stairs that led up to the apartment. I ran out of my bedroom and saw David lying at the bottom in a crumpled heap, his backpack on top of him. I rushed down the stairs and knelt beside him, cradling his face in my hands.

"Are you OK? What happened?"

His eyes looked glazed, the whites splattered with red and yellow. He seemed half asleep.

"Wake up, David," I said, trying to lift him up.

"I'm all right," he said weakly. "Can you help me upstairs?"

I took his backpack off, put his arm around my shoulder and struggled to get him to his feet. We stumbled up the stairs, practically falling backward a few times, until we made it to the bathroom. He lunged toward the bathtub and vomited, then he collapsed onto the floor. He lay there while I rinsed out the tub, checking every few seconds to make sure he was still awake. Finally he got up and seemed more alert. I cleaned him off and helped him into the living room. He sat down on the couch and I went to get him some water.

"What happened?" I asked, as I handed him the glass.

"I guess the stuff I took wasn't so good," he said, looking sideways at nothing in particular.

"What stuff?"

"I took some heroin I got up north," he answered casually.

Suddenly I felt anger rise up from my stomach and settle in my throat like a hot coal. "I can handle anything else, but I can't handle heroin," I said. My voice came out slow and quiet, but I felt like shouting. I walked over to the window, stared into the darkness and then turned toward him.

"Do you realize my brother died of a heroin overdose? You could have died right here."

There was silence. My eyes were filled with warm tears and he was looking at me and blinking like a balloon had just popped in front of his eyes. I got up and went to the kitchen, grabbed a paper towel and wiped the wetness from my face. I leaned against the counter and just stared at a discolored spot in the sink. The tears kept rolling down my cheeks as the anger burning in my throat was released by deep, silent sobs. I calmed down enough to catch my breath and went back into the living room. I fell back on a chair across the room from David.

"Tell me about it," he said. His face was filled not so much with pity as with real interest.

"Howie lived away most of the time. First at boarding school, then at college. He was a lot older than I was, twelve years older. He was my parents' natural child. They adopted me because my mother couldn't have any more children."

As I spoke, I alternately stared out of the window and at the carpet, unable to look into David's face.

"Howie was eighteen when our father was killed. He got hooked on heroin when he was in college in Boston. He got busted for possession and distributing. My mother and her new husband bailed him out and brought him back to Chicago. I don't think he ever got any treatment. I guess my mother thought that just by their putting up a lot of money to get him out of jail, he was going to stop using heroin. Like some magic wand had erased all of his pain."

I grabbed a cigarette off of the table and lit it.

"I was ten years old the night it happened. My parents were in Arizona, and Howie was in their bedroom with one of his friends. I was asleep when the paramedics arrived, but the loud noises woke me up. I ran out to the hallway and saw these men rushing Howie out of the apartment on a stretcher.

The housekeeper who was taking care of me, this very bitchy German woman, pushed me back into my room. It was the last time I ever saw him."

"Wow, that's a lot for a little kid to understand," David said. His voice was quieter than usual.

"My parents lied to me and said Howie died because he hit his head on the bedpost. A few years later, when I found out the truth and was old enough to understand it, I wondered whether or not he had intentionally taken an overdose, whether he really wanted to die. But I don't think so. It must have been an accident. He just took too much."

I inhaled some smoke, forcing it out in a few different directions, and then ground the tip of my cigarette into the ashtray. I remembered how when I first tried drugs, I thought that Howie must have been so weak and unhappy to let a drug control his life. Maybe my own drug taking was partly to prove to myself that I was stronger than him.

"David, don't you see? That's why I would never even try heroin. Don't you see what can happen? Heroin is a fucking death sentence."

David was looking down at his hands, which were nervously pulling small strings from a rip in his jeans. "Yeah," he said, looking up into my eyes. His were glassy and wet.

"Are you addicted to it?" I asked him.

"I've only tried it a few times. I guess I like the high. Too bad the trip is such a bummer."

⟡

As far as I know, David never took heroin again while I was around. But the experience made me realize that he had come to feel like a brother to me. I didn't realize how deeply I missed Howie until then. Although I was always aware that

I wanted an older brother, it was not Howie in particular who I imagined missing from my life. His death erased my memories of him—of all the times he took me ice skating and to children's plays, or how I used to talk to him on the phone when he was at boarding school. Even though I was only ten years old when he died, I sensed that an important part of my life had been irretrievably lost. Maybe I was trying to find it again when I hooked up with David.

On the surface, Howie and David couldn't have been more different. While David didn't make any effort to conform, Howie tried desperately to fit in with my parents and their friends. My sister, Barbara, who was the same age as Howie when her father married our mother, remembers him appearing straitlaced on the outside—a "nerd." But David, and I imagine Howie too, were both self-destructive and had a certain melancholy about them. Maybe I was wrong, but I believed David was using drugs to expand his mind while my brother took them to anesthetize his pain. I had come to believe that if I had only been older, I could have saved Howie. David might not have needed my protection, but by secretly offering it I was making good on an old promise.

It seemed natural when David and I began our trek across the country that we would pretend to be brother and sister, instead of just friends, so men on the road would be less likely to hassle me. We even resembled each other in the coloring of our straight golden brown hair, blue eyes and pale skin. It never occurred to either of us to act as though we were a couple, because that would have involved a kind of intimacy that didn't exist between us.

David was going home to New Jersey, and I wanted to visit some friends in New York before school started again. One hot August day, we began our journey in Berkeley on the University Avenue entrance ramp to Interstate 80. It was there that we initiated our ritual of my standing on the shoulder of the road with my thumb pointed toward the highway while David sat a safe distance behind me on our knapsacks. David said we would be more likely to get a ride if the driver first saw a woman.

It seemed to work because only twenty minutes passed before a car pulled off the road toward us. We scrambled into the old white Cadillac, throwing our gear into the huge back seat. The driver was a middle-aged man who claimed to be the manager of the Pointer Sisters. For hours David asked him questions about the music business and listened with rapt attention as the man recounted stories that seemed far-fetched, but were entertaining nonetheless. I sat in the back seat, alternately listening to the conversation and watching the highway ramble through golden hillsides and then, after about two hours, climb into the verdant Sierra Nevada.

As the sun began to set, we reached Reno, our driver's final destination. David said camping out there wouldn't be a good idea, so we stood on the highway on-ramp at twilight and waited for what seemed like hours for a car to stop. Finally, a beat-up old Chevrolet pulled over, and a seedy-looking guy with long, stringy hair and wild eyes motioned for us to get in. I whispered in David's ear that we should wait for another ride, but he quelled my protests, eager to get back on the road.

I sat in the back seat, crammed between our knapsacks, with my feet on top of a small pile of garbage on the floor. The car sped through the Nevada desert and up mountain ranges. Stars lit up the black sky, often providing the only other light on long stretches of highway.

"You travel much?" David asked the guy, who had introduced himself as Bill. I secretly nicknamed him Wild Bill.

"Yeah, I like the change. I have friends scattered around Montana, Wyoming and Colorado. I stay with them for a while, lookin' for work. Carpentry jobs here and there. Then I move on."

"Yeah, I know what you mean," said David. "The road is a cool place. Staying in one place too long can definitely get stale. Hey, you want to smoke a joint?"

"That'd be great," Wild Bill said.

We shared the joint in a revolving triangle. Each time I inhaled I felt my body relax and my mind wander. I watched David talking to Bill but could no longer hear their words. I thought about how David was like a chameleon who could change to fit whichever circumstances he found himself in.

Suddenly I felt David's arm pressing against my knee as he reached into his knapsack and took out a plastic bag. He took out a small sheet of paper and ripped off a tiny square, handing it to Wild Bill.

"What are you doing?" I asked incredulously.

"It'll help him stay awake," David explained calmly as if he was giving him a cup of coffee.

"But he's driving!" I said, my voice rising. "He can't take acid and drive at the same time!"

"It's cool. I can handle it. I'm not taking much," the guy said, ripping the square of paper in half and putting one of the pieces in his mouth.

For the next few hours, I sat with my eyes fixed on the road, my body too tense to sleep. Wild Bill talked constantly, in a rambling monologue with no punctuation, about his friends and their reckless lives. Most of his stories were too disordered to follow, and soon his voice receded into the background like the muffled blare of some awful radio station.

As the sun began to rise, the gray light made me feel more secure. We came to a row of fast-food restaurants in northern Utah and stopped for the first time in many hours. I crawled out of the back seat, like a liberated pretzel, and my muscles ached as I straightened them to stand. We went into a truck stop for breakfast. I didn't speak as I wolfed down some eggs and toast, my first real meal in more than a day.

"He's a pretty funny kind of guy, isn't he?" David said with a chuckle, not so much laughing at the thought as laughing at himself for thinking it. Bill had gone to the bathroom, leaving us alone for the first time.

"And crazy too. David, we could have been killed!" I looked around, suddenly conscious that I was shouting, and lowered my voice to a near whisper. "David, he drove hundreds of miles tripping on LSD! Let's just get our stuff out of the car and get another ride here."

"Listen, he's stopping somewhere in Wyoming to visit friends. He told me he'd leave us off at a campsite and pick us up tomorrow morning."

"Yeah, right. He's never going to come back and get us. And who knows where he's going to leave us. C'mon David, let's get out now."

"It's only a few more hours and who knows if we'll get another ride soon," he said. "Besides, it's really hot out there. Let's just go as far as we can." David slid next to me on the vinyl bench seat, put his arms around me and kissed my cheek.

I agreed to go on the last leg of the trip with Wild Bill, more out of exhaustion than anything else. Once we got back on the road, I fell asleep instantly. I woke up when the car came to a jolting stop.

"Well, here we are. You guys are really going to like this place. It's called Green River," Wild Bill announced. We grabbed our backpacks out of the backseat and got out of the car. I carefully scanned the cluttered car to make sure we weren't leaving anything behind.

I'll pick you up sometime tomorrow morning," Wild Bill yelled out of the window as his car screeched away in a 180-degree turn.

"Yeah, right," I said, swinging my pack over my shoulders. I looked around. I had no idea how far we were from the highway. On one side of the road, set far back, were a few scattered houses and down the other side was a forested gulch surrounding a river. I hadn't asked any questions because I was happy just to get out of the car.

As we hiked down to the river's edge, I reminded David several times that Wild Bill was never going to come back. David half-heartedly disagreed, and I knew he had his doubts too. Anyway, it didn't seem to matter. There we were, all alone in a secluded gorge. The sounds of the rushing river and birds crooning in an off-key serenade were a welcome change from the noise of cars and trucks on the highway.

In a small, flat clearing we unpacked our sleeping bags, took a swim in the river and lay naked in the sun to dry. As the sun began to lower itself toward the hillside, we got dressed, took some LSD and climbed up a rocky slope to watch the sunset. As I was beginning to feel the lofty sensation of the drug taking over my body, we stopped on a wide ledge and just sat there watching colors jump off the river and hillsides like lasers. For long moments we sat in silence, our senses soaking in the sights and sounds of a place that seemed so at peace with itself. Then, in energetic spurts, we talked and laughed and sang songs.

"Just look at what Wild Bill is missing," I said. "Too bad we can't go all the way to New York with him and listen to more of his interesting stories."

It was easy for me to make David laugh; my sarcastic sense of humor was so different from his own that he seemed constantly amused. He would slap his knee, his body shaking in quiet giggles as he looked up at the sky and then down at the ground again.

As the sun began to dip below the hillside, we climbed down, tripping a few times and then laughing hilariously like two kids. The air grew cool and we collected branches and built a campfire. We stared at the flames as they danced against the dark sky, and we traded sips of wine from a suede flask.

The fire began to die out and David moved close to me. We put our arms around each other for warmth and before we could think about what was happening, we were kissing—inviting in a passion neither of us knew existed until that very moment. As we pulled each other's clothes off and crawled under the thick softness of a sleeping bag, our bodies gave in to an attraction that may have been unforeseen but now refused to be held back.

Later, as we lay staring at the stars in the vast Wyoming sky, there was no need to question what had happened or how it would fit into our lives. We were content to let our feelings flow as freely as the currents in the steadily rushing river beside us.

When I woke the next morning, the sun was beginning to rise and causing ripples of light to move in a snakelike dance along the water's surface. We packed up and waited, but Wild Bill never came. Despite the miles we had to hike to get back to the highway, I was happy to be free of him.

The heat was sweltering as we climbed up the steep hill and followed roads toward the highway.

We must have walked three miles before we reached the highway on-ramp. We were hungry, tired and dusty. My hair fell in oily clumps, the pores on my face felt tight with dirt and my body was coated with layers of dried sweat under my jeans and T-shirt. Yet I had never felt so exhilarated.

Within an hour, we were picked up by a large tractor-trailer. The driver's name was Jack. He was a big, jolly man who hauled Idaho potatoes to the Midwest a few times a week. Everything about Jack seemed oversized—his truck, his laugh, the baseball cap he wore.

He would often say whatever popped into his head, eager, I imagined, to have someone to listen. "The road captures you, sharpens your instincts," he said. "It's like life with all its twists and turns. But it's got a life of its own, a kind of courage that anyone like me who has spent any time traveling down it has got to respect."

As the miles disappeared behind us, we quickly grew to admire Jack and feel safe with him. Except for his bulk, Jack did not fit the image of the gruff, macho trucker. He had the kind of wisdom that comes from years of being alone with your own thoughts.

The first night, he let us doze in the truck's sleeping compartment. Later, while he slept, we watched over his truck and ate at a truck stop along the highway. The next morning, he arranged for us to take showers at a motel where he knew the manager.

The dramatic landscape of the West had given way to flat, geometric vistas of farmland in Nebraska and Iowa. The vast stretches of road gave us time to both talk and daydream.

"You two aren't really brother and sister, are you?" Jack asked, shortly after we had crossed the Indiana state line. David and I looked at each other and smiled.

"Why don't you think so?" I asked.

"Because it's easy to tell that there is something else, something kind of special between you," he said.

"It's true . . . we're not . . . brother and sister, I mean," I said, fumbling my words. "We're really just friends." I looked at David, but he was just staring out of the window. "Maybe," Jack said. "But I think it's a little more than that."

Our travels with Jack came to an end the following night at a truck stop just outside Gary, Indiana, because he was heading north toward Michigan and we were continuing east. It was hard to say good-bye to him, knowing we would never see him again and not knowing what to expect next. Jack asked a bunch of truckers he knew there whether they could give us a ride, but no one was heading our way. So we camped out in a field behind the truck stop. The constant grinding noise of truck engines made it difficult to fall sleep, but the warmth of David's body next to me in the sleeping bag relaxed me. I buried my face in his hair and kissed his neck softly. He had a sweet outdoors smell, like sweat mixed with pinecones. A light mist began to fall and we covered ourselves with a plastic tarp.

"I don't care about going to New York anymore," I said. "I just want to stay like we are here now."

He hugged me tight. I couldn't see his face. A few minutes later, he whispered, "I love you. You know that."

"I do. . . . You know too."

A loud horn woke us at dawn. We gathered up our things and walked to the truck stop for breakfast. Afterward we took up our position on the highway and within a short time, a pickup truck stopped. Two men and a woman were in the front seat and offered us a ride as long as we were willing to sit in the open air of the truck bed.

The wind blew our hair with frantic twists. We took some LSD and soaked in the warmth of the hot Ohio sun. Our drivers stopped briefly at a Howard Johnson's where David and I roamed around like amazed children at a carnival. We stared at the flashing light bulbs on popcorn machines and rows of multi-colored ice cream barrels that all seemed to mesh and resemble the paintings of Peter Max. The people's faces in the crowd started to look like caricatures and we both ran outside, afraid of laughing too hard and making a spectacle of ourselves.

I was happy to return to the road, where my mind could roam the scenery. Some time later, with no warning, the pickup truck came to a stop. The sky had turned to twilight.

"We have to let you guys out here," the driver said as he put down the tailgate.

"Where are we?" I asked. David just stared straight ahead, seemingly oblivious to his surroundings.

"We're in a small town in Pennsylvania," the driver answered.

I saw a restaurant nearby and suggested we get some coffee. There were pies in a case near the front door and waitresses dressed in Dutch dresses. Walking in under the glare of the restaurant's florescent lights, I realized how bedraggled we looked. David was staring up at the ceiling and his eyes looked like they were glued open. It seemed as though everyone there was staring at us, so I quickly directed David to the closest empty table. His walk was unbalanced. I knew that I had to take control of the situation. I ordered us each a cup of coffee and some toast and told David to just sit there quietly.

I went to the bathroom and couldn't believe what I saw in the mirror. My eyes looked like David's: black pupils the size of dimes with just a little blue surrounding them. My hair was a scraggly mess. I splashed cold water on my face and ripped a comb through my hair.

When I sat back down at the table, the coffee was sitting in front of David untouched and he still looked like a lost little boy. I drank my coffee and felt its warmth throughout my body. I forced myself to eat a piece of toast, even though I wasn't hungry. As my stomach began to fill up, I felt more aware of my surroundings and my mind seemed clearer.

Suddenly, out of the corner of my eye, I saw four Highway Patrolmen walk into the restaurant and sit down a few tables away from us. Panic overtook me as if someone had grabbed me from behind. I reached for my knapsack, took out a five dollar bill and laid it on the table.

"David, we have to get out of here," I said, reaching across the table and pressing his arm. "There are some cops over there. Just look toward the door and follow me."

I held my breath until we got outside, trying to keep my feet pointed in a straight line and walking toward a small parking lot behind the restaurant that couldn't be seen from the front door. When I finally stopped and put my knapsack down, David began anxiously pacing back and forth.

"I think it's OK now," I said. "We better decide what we're going to do."

David was mumbling to himself. I walked up to him and put my hand on his arm. He jumped back.

"What's wrong?" I asked.

"I'm afraid," he said.

"Don't worry, we're out of the restaurant and everything's OK."

"I'm afraid of you," he said, staring into my eyes, taking a few unsure steps back.

"What are you talking about?"

"You're a witch . . . "

"I'm a what?"

"You're a witch, and there are other witches out there," he said, pointing to a wooded area across the highway. "They have a coven in the forest, and they are going to come and get you. They want you back."

I realized that David was having a bad hallucination and that there was no way I could talk him out of it. Better just play along with him and try to reassure him, I thought.

"David . . . " I moved toward him but he jumped backward again.

"They're going to come get you and they're going to hurt me," he said, nearly crying.

"David, I won't let them hurt you."

"I don't want you to leave me," he said.

"I won't leave you. I promise. I won't go with them."

"But what if they cast a spell on me?"

"I won't let them."

"They want you back. They think you belong with them," he said, beginning to shiver.

I moved closer and put my arms around him. "I love you David, and I'm going to stay with you. I won't let them hurt you."

We stood silently in the parking lot for what seemed like a long time. I stared at the dark forest, the tall pine trees on the outer edges illuminated by the highway lights appearing more treacherous than beautiful.

For the first time since leaving California, we checked into a motel. We ate dinner in the motel's restaurant and then sat outside by a small swimming pool, never again discussing what had happened. As I was putting a cigarette out in an ashtray, I noticed some writing imprinted on the black plastic bottom: "New Haven, Pennsylvania."

⋘⋙

The words on my birth certificate read: "Mother's Birthplace: New Haven, Pennsylvania." My mother was born in that *same* little town where David had sensed the presence of witches, witches who wanted me back. If it was a coincidence, it was an uncanny one. Of all of the small towns we could have found ourselves in, how did we wind up there?

I looked down again at the birth certificate, thinking that I must have imagined what I had seen. But there it was again, in white letters on a black photocopied document, along with other facts of my birth. The mystery of that night in Pennsylvania reinforced my belief that someone was out there waiting and wanting to be found.

chapter SEVEN

My search for my birth mother immediately became an obsession.

Since my daughter's birth, I was no longer writing for the newspaper on a regular basis, so I was able to steal moments each day to seek clues while my son was in preschool and my daughter was napping or playing quietly by herself.

One of the first things I did after receiving my birth certificate was to call the Cook County Department of Supportive Services in Chicago. That's where Delores, my search assistant, had said I could request the official records of my biological background.

I gave my birth date and some of the other information on my birth certificate to the caseworker who took my call, then waited nervously for several minutes while she checked her records.

"You struck gold," she said. "We have a record of your case file. We'll need you to send a written request for any and all information on your biological background. Include your present name, your adoptive name, your date of birth and your mother's name. We can give you her year of birth, her nationality and other information she may have given us about her siblings, religion, education and job."

"Thank you so much," I said, feeling an outpouring of gratitude to this faceless bureaucrat.

"Well, you are entitled legally and ethically to this information," she said, her voice softening.

"Thank you," I repeated. "How long do you think it will take?"

"Maybe two weeks from the time we receive your request," she said. "We have to make a special trip to the warehouse where our records are stored."

I thought about how all of those intimate details of my mother's life, and of mine, had been laying around in some big metal filing cabinet in a huge, drafty warehouse all of these years, probably wedged up against those of so many other adoptees, just waiting to be discovered.

That day in late January I also wrote to the Department of Health in Pennsylvania, asking for a copy of Helen's birth certificate. But I made sure to use the maiden name she had given on my own birth certificate, Helen R. Jones. Her own birth information would give me more knowledge than I had now, maybe even the names of my grandparents. With each new piece of information, I would be one step closer to having a history.

In some ways, the search was a lot like the work I did as a journalist. I was used to dealing with public agencies and uncovering facts. This time, though, I was determined not to miss even the smallest detail along the way.

The first batch of letters I sent off included the form necessary for putting my name on the computerized ALMA registry. A part of me felt certain Helen's name would be listed, especially after learning of the convergence of her birthplace and my trip to Pennsylvania. I imagined her patiently waiting for the phone to ring, assured that one day I would call.

I had often thought about how she must have felt on my birthdays. I wondered if they were sad days for her, mourning the loss of years between us, or if, wherever she was, she was celebrating too.

As a teenager, I walked down busy streets and fantasized that my mother was nearby, observing me, to see what I looked like and whether I was all right. Even as an adult, I've found myself occasionally scanning the faces of strangers on the street, looking for any hint of a resemblance or trace of a memory.

⤬

After sealing the envelopes that night, I climbed into bed. It was past midnight and Steve was already asleep. My mind was leaping from one thought to another, but my body was weighed down with fatigue. It was pitch black when I woke up suddenly, minutes or hours later, with the strange sense that I was in the middle of a dream that was as much a part of my waking as my sleep. I closed my eyes again, willing the dream to continue.

I am at a museum. Every wall is filled with impressionist paintings. I stand inches away from each painting and all I can see are chaotic and jumbled brush strokes, blended and overlapping colors yet no discernable picture. Then I step backward and the farther away I get, the clearer the image becomes. Suddenly each brush stroke has a purpose, adding to a complete view of a garden, a river or a park full of people. It is as if every time the artist made a dot or a line, he was in the midst of a search for his own unique view of a landscape or a person.

As I stand in the middle of the huge gallery, each painting becomes a small video screen acting out its own story. The lines of color begin to swirl around in celluloid movements. The images are moving so fast that I feel my head spinning and I lie down on the nearest bench, staring at the stark white ceiling.

When I lift myself up again, there is someone else in the room. I can only see her back as she stands motionless before a painting of a mother washing her baby with a red cloth in a glistening basin of blue water. I walk to the side of the woman to get a better glimpse, but she does not move. She is like a statue frozen in place with her hands clasped tightly together against her chest as if in prayer. I stare at her profile. She has a short, thick bob of brown hair framing her pale face. Her dark eyelashes do not blink; her eyes are fixed straight ahead. The longer I watch her, the more I sense a startling familiarity in her long, oval face. I move a few steps closer to her and suddenly she turns her head toward me and smiles. It is then that I see my own face, older perhaps, not with wrinkles but with a ripened sophistication. As I look closer, I see the face is as smooth and clear as a porcelain pitcher pouring warmth through lips curved like the very center of a perfectly blooming rose.

Again I awoke, this time aware of the distance between my body lying in bed and the dream already beginning to slip away.

More than two weeks later I still had not received any responses to my requests for birth information.

"These things take time," Steve said, as he watched me pacing around the kitchen. "You've waited thirty-two years to do this, and it's only been two weeks since you mailed out those letters."

"I'm just getting frustrated because every time I call that social service worker in Chicago she promises she is going to the warehouse to retrieve my file in the next few days and when I call back she still hasn't done it."

"Just wait a couple of weeks and then call her again," he said. "If she hasn't done it by then, ask to talk to her supervisor." His patience frustrated me, since I had so little of my own.

"There must be other things I should be doing in the meantime," I said, placing the last of the breakfast dishes in the sink. "Maybe I'll make more calls today."

"I understand that you have to do this and I think it's important," said Steve. "But you have other things to pay attention to, like the children and the stories you're writing. This can't take control of your life."

"It's easy for you to say that," I snapped with too much anger. "You've taken for granted all your life who your parents are, where you come from. I've waited all of these years to do this, and now that I've decided to go through with it, every day counts."

I studied the ALMA search handbook looking for ideas of whom else I could contact. Most of the instructions were written for people who had no birth certificate and no real clues, those who were beginning their searches from scratch. I had names and places but no story, no details—like the grainy black and white pictures in the newspapers piled on my desk.

I pored through the envelope containing all of the birth records my mother had sent me. A faded sheet from Mount Sinai Hospital read: "Instructions in the Care of Baby." On a blank line underneath, it says "Girl Dunne." It set out feeding times and a baby formula recipe and included lists of necessary supplies and equipment.

"The newborn baby does not require a great deal of fancy or stylish clothing. He asks only for cleanliness and warmth. Thus, the more simple your layette, the more time you will have to enjoy the company of this precious newcomer."

The envelope also contained the Decree of Adoption, a court document dated January 6, 1960. In formal legal writing signed by the presiding judge of the county court, the document seals my fate:

> . . . That Helen R. Dunne, the mother, is unable to maintain her said child, and she abandoned and surrendered her said child to the petitioners herein; and the said mother consents to the adoption of her said child by the petitioners herein. . . . That the petitioners are reputable persons of good moral character with sufficient ability and financial means to rear, nurture and educate the said child in a suitable and proper manner. . . . IT IS THEREFORE ORDERED, ADJUDGED AND DECREED that from this date, Shirley Jane Dunne, a minor, shall be to all legal intents and purposes the child of the petitioners, Manny Skar and Lynn Skar, his wife; and for the purposes of inheritance and all other legal incidents and consequences, shall be the same as if she had been born to them in lawful wedlock. IT IS FURTHER ORDERED that the name of the said child shall be changed to DEBRA MICHELLE SKAR. . . .

An attached letter from the lawyer declares that the final adoption decree "closes the matter."

Without even thinking, I picked up the phone and dialed the number listed on the lawyer's stationery. The man who answered had never heard of the lawyer. I called directory assistance in Chicago, but there was no listing for him. I even called the Chicago Bar Association, but they had no idea who would have his legal records. I presumed he must be dead by now.

I looked at my birth certificate again, reading each line anew. At the very bottom was a signature that I did not remember seeing before: *Leonard Feldman, M.D.* I picked up the phone and called directory assistance in Chicago. I was surprised when the operator gave me a phone number and I wondered if it was the right doctor. How could he be in practice after so many years? I dialed his number.

"Hello, doctor's offices," said a woman.

"Hello, my name is Shirley Dunne," I said, using the name of the baby on my birth certificate. "Is this the office of the same Dr. Leonard Feldman who was an obstetrician thirty years ago?"

"Yes, it is," she said. "My name is Margaret, how can I help you?"

"Dr. Feldman delivered me on May 14, 1959, and I need my medical records for some reproductive problems I'm having."

"If you can wait a moment, I'll check."

As the minutes passed, I thought about the paradox of using lies to uncover secrets, but knew I had no other choice. I had been warned at the ALMA meeting never to admit up front that you're adopted because doors could be shut in your face.

"I'm sorry," she said. "We have no records left from before about nine years ago."

"Perhaps I could talk to the doctor," I said.

"May I ask, were you adopted?"

I hesitated and decided to try the truth. "Yes, I was. But I already have the name of my birth mother, I just need the medical records. I know it was a long time ago, but could you just ask the doctor if he remembers? My mother's name was Helen Jones. Her married name was Helen Dunne."

"Hold on," she said. When she returned to the phone, her voice had changed from that of a busy office worker to a sympathetic friend. "Dr. Feldman said he could not remember your particular case, but that he handled many cases like yours in those years. He suggested you contact the hospital."

With that door closed, I felt compelled to try another. I called the hospital where my birth certificate said I was born and requested my mother's medical file. I told my story about reproductive problems and said my doctor suggested my mother's labor and delivery history might help to solve them. I didn't mention I was adopted, figuring I might be lucky and get someone who wasn't paying close attention.

The woman I talked to in the medical records department appeared nonplussed. She simply told me to send a $10 money order for copies of the records. At that point, maybe what I was really looking for was evidence that a Helen Dunne actually existed. Even the smallest detail about my birth, no matter how technical, seemed important now.

About a week later, there was an envelope from the Pennsylvania Department of Health in the mailbox. I ripped it open. Inside was a single white sheet with big block letters at the top that read: "No-Record Certification." At the bottom it said, "This certifies that a record of the birth of Helen R. Jones has not been located in the Vital Records files of the Commonwealth of Pennsylvania."

I futilely searched the envelope for other sheets of paper, thinking there had to be more. I walked over to the breakfast table and sat down to regain my balance. I felt the kind of sensation that comes when you walk into a chair or the corner of a wall when your mind is not watching what your body is doing. This time, however, I had walked into a wall that was blocking my view. Any images I once had of this woman began to fade from my mind, as though she had just stepped into a large shadow.

❧

As Steve suggested, I waited another week before calling the caseworker in Chicago again. I had tried hard to put the search out of my mind, but it always came back, whether I was at the park with my children or shopping for groceries. Life was going on as usual; meals had to be cooked, dishes had to be washed. I was going through the motions of a normal life, but my thoughts never stayed in the present very long. It was almost like I was leading a double life, or having a secret love affair on the side.

"Hello, Mrs. Gleason, this is Debbie Levi. I called several weeks ago about my nonidentifying adoption information and I wondered if you had a chance to get my file from the warehouse."

"Let me look, hold on." It took nearly five minutes for her to return. "Hello. It appears that your file was destroyed in an explosion and fire we had in the warehouse ten years ago. I'm awfully sorry, but we lost most of our records for that year and some of the following one."

For a moment I just stared straight ahead and remained silent. "I can't believe that," I said, drawing out each syllable and holding my breath. I imagined the flames eating up the piles of papers, their edges curling slowly and then being consumed into a mass of black smoke.

"Listen, I'm not supposed to tell you this, but I did find a Rolodex card that lists your mother's name. It says Helen Rose Dunne. The father's name was left blank."

Helen R. Dunne. That was the name she used to sign my birth certificate, I remembered.

"Well, that does help," I said. "I didn't have her middle name before."

"Ms. Levi, it wouldn't hurt to contact the court," she said. "An amendment to the Illinois Adoption Act last year says you can petition the court to have a confidential intermediary appointed if there is a medical or psychological need to find members of your biological family."

As she was talking, I could hear her words but no longer pay attention to their meaning. All I could think about was how the fire had begun. I flashed on a wild idea: just as my mother had invaded the court records for my birth certificate, had she also hired some gangster friend to burn this file so I would never learn the truth about my adoption?

I called Delores to tell her that what had seemed like an easy ride was becoming an uphill trek through the wilderness.

"I'm sorry about that," she said. "I was worried that might happen. I've heard about that fire from other adoptees born in Chicago at that time. Maybe what you should do now is get the phone book from New Haven, Pennsylvania, and start calling every Jones listed. There can't be that many in such a small town."

That night, I slipped into my children's rooms as they slept. My son was lying on his back, his arms stretched out to each side, his head turned gently to the right. His face looked serious, as though he was deep in thought. I put his favorite stuffed animal under his arm and smelled his just-washed hair. I walked into my daughter's room and found her curled in a ball in the far corner of her crib. She was grasping her pink blanket up to her cheek. Her lips were gently curved into a satisfied smile. As I pulled a quilt over her shoulders, I thought how lucky they were that they would never have to struggle to learn the truth about themselves. They would never have to look very far to know exactly where they came from.

chapter EIGHT

Collecting the mail each afternoon became an anxious ritual. I would make my pilgrimage to the mailbox at the bottom of the driveway with a strange blend of excitement and dread. The rectangular, metal box with its curved roof was covered with a painted scene of a house on a grassy hill that had begun to crack into jagged squares. I rushed out, but I always hesitated before opening it.

One day in early February, I approached the mailbox under a sky tense with gray clouds threatening rain. I hadn't put on my coat, so I stood shivering on the street as a cold wind scattered dead leaves around my feet. I opened the little metal door and slid my hand inside to grasp the pile of mail. Then I peered inside to make sure I didn't leave any behind. As usual, I couldn't wait to get into the house before I began shuffling through the letters. I noticed the familiar bills, unwanted solicitations and other junk mail. But I stopped suddenly when I noticed the ivory envelope with my mother's handwriting. She almost never wrote letters, preferring the telephone. Birthday cards usually came in express mail packets because she would wait until the very last minute to send them, making the sentiment seem like an expensive afterthought.

I sat down on a step outside the front door. As I poked my finger though a small opening in the corner of the envelope, the paper ripped in several directions. I pulled out the folded papers, straightened them and read the first page:

> *Dear Debbie,*
>
> *When I sent you your adoption papers several weeks ago, I did not include this letter. I had thought it would be better for you not to see it, but now I realize that you insist upon continuing your search for this woman.*
>
> *As I told you, I only saw her once—when she handed you to me in the car. But a few weeks later, we had our lawyer contact her to write this letter. You have to understand, in those days such issues were important to people. I had heard about a Catholic family who found out the child they had put up for adoption was going to be raised by a Jewish family. They reclaimed the child after that. I could not let that happen to me. I had to cover all bases.*
>
> *I'm sending you this so you'll better understand that adoption is what this woman wanted for you.*
>
> *Love,*
> *Your Mother*

I turned the page over and found two photocopied sheets, each with a smaller paper superimposed on it with handwriting faded in spots. The first time I read through the letter I did so in a mad rush to consume the meaning of it. The second time, I read slowly and deliberately, not wanting to miss a word or nuance of the language she used.

To the Adopting Parents of My Child

Having this day signed a consent to the adoption of my child by you in the county court of Cook County, I wish to thank you for taking my child into your home and raising her as your own child.

I was informed that both of you are of the Jewish faith and intend to raise the child as a Jewess. I completely approve of this.
May God bless you.
Helen Dunne
June 1, 1959

My skin, which had felt so chilled just moments before, now felt flushed and hot. I walked back into the house, barely taking my eyes off the letter even to climb the stairs, and fell back into a chair at the breakfast table. I read the letter over and over again, each time noticing something new. This was the closest I had ever felt to my birth mother, as if her very handwriting breathed life into someone who had long been an apparition floating over my world, without earthly concerns.

I looked for similarities between my writing and hers, but found none. I noticed the way her letters curled and swayed with an idiosyncratic artistry: symmetrical, formal, graceful.

But what struck me the most, and more intensely with each reading, was how she used the words "my child" three times on the first page. It was as if she wanted everyone to know that I was a part of her.

That she wasn't Jewish came as no surprise. For much of my life I felt that I was posing as a member of a club to which I did not belong. While my parents rarely attended synagogue and never lit candles on Shabbat, almost every one of their friends was Jewish, they belonged to a Jewish country club and gave annual donations to Hadassah and B'nai B'rith.

My mother, the child of religious Jews and perhaps a little guilty for not being observant herself, was determined that I understand our Jewish heritage. Beginning when I was five, she sent me to a parochial elementary school attached to a conservative synagogue a block away from our apartment building. A giant Star of David on the stained-glass double doorway greeted me each day, a biblical reminder of who I was supposed to be.

It was there, at Anshe Emet Day School, that my own feelings of being different took firm root. From as early as I can remember, people would say, "Debbie doesn't look Jewish." It became a common refrain. I secretly wished that my light brown hair was darker; that my blue eyes were brown; that my complexion was olive, instead of pale and freckled.

The school seemed to grow smaller each year as the same twenty-two children traveled from one grade to the next and secrets were impossible to keep. My father's notorious death made me a target of ridicule for the other children, who acted out the prejudices they heard at home. When I returned to the school in the fourth grade after two years in Minnesota, my role as social outcast had become permanent.

"Look at that statue. Doesn't it look real?" the kids would taunt me. "Stop it," I'd say. "Is that statue talking?" they would respond, laughing and whispering to one another as they walked away. Often I would walk into a room and a group of girls would all look at me and then turn toward each other, giggling as if I was their own private joke.

I never let them see me cry. I would run into a bathroom stall, cover my face with my hands and weep silently. Afterward, I would rinse my reddened face with cold water and emerge, not with a pout but with an angry edge. Unlike those earlier years when my speech impediments made communication so difficult for me, now I learned to use language as a weapon. But I soon found that mean-spiritedness, even when used as a defense, has a ricochet effect. Any insulting comments I made to one person about another could backfire suddenly in the constantly shifting alliances of such a small, insular group. While I did have friends, they changed often depending on whether those girls who were most vindictive toward me held a position of popularity at any given moment.

One of those girls, Rachel Zimmerman, was short and pudgy with a freckled, doughy face framed by dark brown bangs. Desperate to be accepted, she would do whatever it took to rise up the social ladder. She regaled her friends with stories she had heard from her parents about my family, purposely amplifying her tales if I was within earshot.

"Did you know that Debbie had to go live with her grandparents because her mom didn't have any money to take care of her after her dad died?" she asked a group of girls. "And Debbie's mom had to move out of her building because her daddy was killed there."

"Really?" the other kids said in unison.

Sometimes I would catch Rachel staring at me as if she was trying to figure out what other dark secrets I might be hiding.

I never told my mother about my problems with other children at school. By then she was fully immersed in her new marriage and social circle. She spent her days shopping and her evenings going out to dinners and parties, striving to rebuild her social identity and put the shame of her first marriage behind her.

She and my new father, Jim, traveled a lot after their marriage, leaving me with transient housekeepers with names like Ingebord Flaskamp and Raginheld Poulson. It was during one of their trips that Howie died. To this day, I find it difficult to travel away from my own children without a cloud of guilt hanging over me for the time I've stolen from them to be by myself. Or worse, I'll have horrifying flashes of accidents happening to them that I could have prevented had I just been there.

My brother's death only a year after my return to Chicago from Minnesota further set us apart as a family tainted by tragedy. I remember my mother crying in her bedroom and on the phone with her friends, but I don't recall her ever talking to me about him or making sure I was all right. As with Manny's funeral, my mother did not allow me to attend my brother's memorial. That may have been part of the reason that he never really died in my mind: he just disappeared one night carried out on a stretcher by paramedics.

My mother successfully hid the actual cause of Howie's death from me for months. I learned the truth one day on the school bus. Jane Weinstein was a year older than me and her family had been friendly with mine when we were very small. I still have pictures of the two of us playing on a beach in Florida and on a swing set dressed in identical polka-dot dresses with white anklets and sneakers. She was the only other child I knew who had known misfortune worse than my own. Her father had abandoned his family when she was a baby, and her mother committed suicide in the bathtub when Jane was six. Raised by her aunt, Jane became even angrier than I did as we grew older. Her voice was like an out-of-tune violin that made me cringe. She usually pretended she

didn't know me, perhaps because I was younger or, more likely, because she suspected that I knew more about her family
secrets than anyone else.

As I sat down on one of the vinyl bench seats near hers
that day, Jane taunted me, her voice even more shrill than
normal: "Debbie, do you know how your brother died?"

I turned around, embarrassed and surprised, and
answered without thinking: "He hit his head on a bedpost."

"No, you're wrong," she said with a short, malicious
laugh, shifting her eyes around to make sure everyone could
hear. "He took a bad drug."

I didn't understand what she meant, but I could tell by
the looks on the other children's faces that it was bad. I told
her she was wrong, but I knew she wasn't.

Whenever I mustered the courage to ask my mother
about Howie as the years went by, she would say, "I don't
understand why you are so interested. It was a long time ago
and you didn't even know him for very long." I looked for
solace in Howie's collection of Beatles albums, listening to
them over and over again.

I never told anyone I was adopted. It was just one more
difference I couldn't bear anyone knowing or teasing me
about. I don't remember ever meeting anyone else who was
adopted, or at least not anyone who admitted to being
adopted, so I remained silent. My experiences at Anshe Emet
taught me that there were secrets worth keeping.

Years later when I met Steve, he was in search of the perfect Jewish woman with whom to have children. He was
thirty-five and already divorced twice; continuing his family's
traditions was important to him. Prior to our meeting, he had
joined a Jewish singles' group, but hadn't been attracted to
most of the women he met there.

A few months after we began dating, I asked him what had drawn him to me the day we met at a music festival.

"I thought you were pretty, and I liked your last name," he replied.

When Steve was in his early twenties, he married a Jewish woman from an orthodox family. That lasted less than a year. Soon after, he met "the shiksa of my dreams," as he described his second wife. She was a thin woman with long blonde hair who claimed she was going to convert to Judaism but never did. Their marriage lasted just under five years and Steve blamed its failure, in part, on the difference in their backgrounds.

I feared that if I told Steve I was adopted he would discover that I wasn't really Jewish, and our relationship would fall apart. But one day not long after our engagement, my secret burst out like a tiger having paced too long in a small cage.

"I have something important I have to tell you," I said as we were reading the newspaper one Sunday morning. I waited until he looked at me and I was sure he was listening.

"I was adopted."

Steve didn't speak for a minute, but his expression remained surprisingly unchanged.

"Why didn't you tell me before?"

"I was afraid . . . afraid that you would consider my background uncertain, that you might wonder if I'm not really Jewish."

"C'mon, you're more Jewish than I am," he laughed. "Anyway, do you know that you're not?"

"No, but just by looking at me you can tell that I'm not."

"Well, that's true. I always figured by your upturned nose that you must have had a great nose job. Anyway, you were adopted into a Jewish family and according to Jewish law, that makes you a Jew."

Historically I had much in common with the Jewish people. Like Israel, surrounded on all sides by people different and distrustful, I had felt isolated and constantly under attack. My birthday fell on the same day that Israel declared its independence. And just as the Israelites were chosen to receive God's revelation, I too had been chosen to fulfill someone else's vision of whom I should become.

chapter NINE

The street address my birth mother listed on my birth certificate was that of a building on Dearborn Parkway, in an upscale neighborhood just a few blocks west of Chicago's lakefront. It turned out to be a residential hotel where people took short-term leases of six months or a year, suggesting images of anonymous drifters and social outcasts with nowhere else to go. If my birth mother had chosen to live in a place that others choose for a life unfettered by permanency or possessions, I thought, she must certainly have been in Chicago just to wait out her pregnancy.

By telephone, I reached a woman who worked in the building's office who told me that she doubted any records remained from the late 1950s. She offered, though, to talk to two residents who had been living there for more than thirty years. I was hopeful that some elderly man or woman with an unusually sharp memory would remember a pregnant woman named Helen.

But I found out a week later that moving quickly is essential, even when digging through more than three decades of history.

"I realize the timing couldn't be worse," the woman said apologetically. "But the one man who could have helped—he lived here for forty years—passed away this week. The other resident I mentioned to you has no recollection of a Helen Jones. And there are no records left. I'm so sorry."

I hung up the phone and sat for a while just staring at a stain in the carpet. Were all of these dead ends bad omens? Adrenaline pumping through my veins, I ignored them and moved on.

I ordered a phone book from New Haven, Pennsylvania, so that I could look up people with Helen's family name and start making random calls. The phone company said it would take ten days for it to arrive. That seemed too long to wait so, in the meantime, I called the library in New Haven. I figured a librarian in a sleepy little town would be eager to look through the phone book for me or maybe even search through old newspapers for marriage or birth announcements that included the name Jones.

The reference librarian was a middle-aged woman with an encyclopedic knowledge of her hometown and an enthusiasm to match. She said that the library's collection of *The New Haven Progress* newspaper only dated back to 1976, but she knew for a fact that there were a lot of people with the name of Jones in the area.

"Everyone in the entire world has passed through here," she said, exaggerating the allure of the area. She explained that a great influx of people settled in New Haven between the 1820s and 1930s for lumbering, farming, brick making and coal mining. As some of the industries began to die out, many people moved on, leaving the small borough with just over eight thousand residents.

I told her my reason for calling was that I was putting together my family tree. She recommended a man named Ryan Barrett who was known in the area for his interest in genealogy.

For fifteen dollars an hour, Ryan agreed to check out local marriage records and sift through old newspapers at the historical society. He said it would take between one and two weeks.

By then it was mid-February, when winter slows down the passage of time and weeks begin to feel like months. I found myself unable to sit still and do nothing, so I called the hospital again about getting Helen's medical records. Since I hadn't heard from the hospital, I knew there was a chance that while looking for my mother's file, they had discovered it involved an adoption and dropped my request.

A different woman took my call this time. She put me on hold to check the file's whereabouts and returned to the phone about ten minutes later.

"The roll of microfilm that contains your mother's medical records seems to be missing," the woman said without a hint of apology.

"It can't just be missing," I said, remembering the disappearance of my adoption background information. "I mean did someone just take it, or are other rolls lost too?"

"No, actually, it seems that your microfilm roll is the only one we can't find," she said matter-of-factly. "We don't know what happened to it."

It was becoming difficult not to feel paranoid. At that moment, I was certain that there was some sort of conspiracy going on, and that it probably involved my adoptive mother. Instead of confronting her about it though, I asked for her help. She told me she knew someone on the hospital's board and would call her. The only answer I ever received was that the woman was told the same thing that I had been; the roll was mysteriously missing.

Next I called the Department of Vital Records in Chicago and asked for a copy of my birth certificate, claiming I was Shirley Jane Dunne. My own copy was a rough photocopy and I could see that at the very bottom there was a section titled "Supplementary Medical Report." I could make out a few questions like "Length of pregnancy," "Weight of child at birth" and "Legitimate?" But the answers written beneath were cut off. If I got another copy, I thought, maybe they would send me the whole certificate and there would be more of the kind of information I needed.

I expected a quick response since they let me pay for an express mail return over the phone by credit card. When it did not come in a few days, I impatiently called back. A woman who sounded like a bored receptionist at an empty self-storage facility said, "There is no record on file. If the name was changed, the original certificate was sent to Springfield and impounded."

She explained that I would have to petition the court if that was the case. I hung up feeling like a stolen car whose original owner could not be found. Petitioning the court seemed like a monumental task that would have to wait until I was desperate.

The next day I heard from the adoption registry at ALMA headquarters in New York. The letter kindly explained that while I had no match in their data bank—meaning my mother had not submitted her own name—I should not give up hope. ALMA encouraged me to keep up my search and offered a list of locations of support groups that I could attend.

I called Ryan Barrett back in Pennsylvania. He didn't have anything to offer that would change my stubborn streak of bad luck. He had checked the marriage records for New Haven County between 1949 and 1963 and hadn't found my mother's name. The historical society was closed until spring, he said, but he would check local elementary and high school yearbooks. In a last-ditch attempt, I suggested he look for a Shirley or Jane Dunne—after all, maybe I was named after someone my birth mother knew.

When I did finally receive the New Haven phone book, I was staggered by the long column of people named Jones because, even though it was one of the most common names, it wasn't as if I was looking in the New York directory. But among the many Jones, there was no Helen. I prepared myself for calling every one of the Joneses listed.

"You know," said Steve, after looking at the phone book for a few minutes. "Maybe you've been looking for the wrong name. After all, she named you Dunne and she signed the birth certificate Helen Dunne. And look, there's only a few Dunnes listed here."

"I've been looking for the maiden name all this time because I doubted she was actually married when I was born," I explained.

"Well, it's just a hunch," he said.

As I looked at the phone book myself, it made sense. Maybe I had been careening down a dead-end street all this time. There was something about the name Jones that had never felt right. It was time to change direction.

chapter TEN

There was no Helen Dunne in the New Haven phone book. But there was a Robert Dunne. Since the name listed under "Father" on my birth certificate was William Robert Dunne, I decided to start with him.

I held my breath as I dialed the number. "Hello, is Robert Dunne there?"

"Yes, I'm Robert," he said.

"Hello, my name is Debbie Holtz," I said, lowering my voice a little to sound older. "I'm an old friend of Helen Dunne and I'm trying to look her up. I was wondering if she is related to you?"

"Oh, yes," the man said. "She's my cousin. But I haven't seen her in years."

I couldn't believe what I was hearing. Finally, Helen was becoming a living person instead of just a name.

"Did she ever get married?" I anxiously blurted out.

"Yes. She was married for a while sometime in the '60s and lived in New York for a few years."

"Does she have any children?"

"No, I don't think so."

"Do you know anyone named William Dunne?" I asked, deciding to go for broke since he seemed to believe my story.

"Well, there's another cousin named William Dunne in Maryland."

Oh, great, I thought, she had a baby with her cousin.

"How old is he?" I asked.

"Oh, he's got to be over seventy by now," he said.

I felt relieved. My father's age on the birth certificate had been given as thirty years old, thirty-two years ago. Simple math would make him too old. It struck me that Helen might well have combined the names of two cousins to create a husband for the sake of legitimacy on the birth certificate.

"You've been very helpful," I said. "Does Helen have any other relatives?" I was hoping there was someone out there who was closer to her, closer to me.

"Well, she has a brother named Michael, Michael Dunne. He lives in a nearby town."

I quickly searched the phone book in front of me for Michael Dunne. "Is that the Michael Dunne in Lockhart?"

"Yes, that's right."

"So, do you know where Helen is now?"

"Last I heard she was in California, I think in Los Angeles."

I thanked him profusely and hung up the phone. My mind was working so quickly that my hands could barely keep up as I scribbled all the information I had just learned on the closest piece of paper I could find. Then I picked up the receiver and dialed directory assistance in Los Angeles. There was no listing for a Helen Dunne.

Maybe, I thought, this guy got Los Angeles confused with San Francisco. I called the San Francisco operator and asked for a listing for Helen Dunne. Suddenly a computerized recording was giving me a phone number. Unable to fully grasp what was happening, I called another operator and asked for Helen's address.

It was almost impossible to believe. There she was, living across the Bay, only twenty minutes away from me. It had to be more than a coincidence. Maybe she knows I am here and wanted to be close. Even if that wasn't true, I couldn't help but take it as a sign that this was the time for us to finally come together.

I stopped myself from picking up the phone again and dialing her number. I may have been stalling, but I had to be certain that she was the right Helen Dunne. First I'll call her brother in Pennsylvania, I decided. But by then I was too nervous.

It was getting late and I was planning to attend my first ALMA rap session that night. The timing was perfect since the whole purpose of the meeting was supposed to be to gain the support of strangers who were living through similar experiences. Deciding to wait until the next morning to make the phone calls, I carefully laid the paper with my notes and the phone numbers in the center of a crystal dish on the dining room table and went to get dressed.

✑

The rap session was at the home of my search assistant, Delores, just a ten-minute ride from my house. It was getting dark outside when I walked up the brick stairs to Delores's Tudor-style house. There was an ALMA sign on the door instructing people to just come in. Once inside, I scanned the unfamiliar faces to find Delores. She was standing with several women in the living room, where chairs and couches had been moved around to form a circle. She suggested I put my purse down on an empty chair and then showed me around.

We snaked our way around small clumps of people scattered throughout the first floor of the house. Articles about searches and reunions and ALMA brochures lined the nearby dining room table. Brownies, coffee and tea were neatly laid out in the kitchen.

I poured myself a cup of coffee, sat down to wait for the meeting to begin and watched the others trickle in to the room. Most of them were women, but of all different ages.

The room grew quiet when Delores sat down and welcomed everyone. She explained to the group that the evening was to be devoted to sharing our stories and feelings about our searches and reunions. Specific questions about how to conduct searches should wait for the group's monthly search workshop, she said.

Delores, who I took to be in her fifties, was very gracious. She always seemed to be smiling, which ignited her strawberry-blonde hair and blue eyes. When she listened to other people talk, her attention never wavered and she looked straight into their faces.

Delores suggested that we take turns introducing ourselves. "My name is Delores Thom and I am a birth mother," she said, as if to illustrate the proper introduction. "I relinquished my son in San Francisco in 1962 and found him two years ago. He lives nearby and we now have a good relationship."

Each person took a turn, some saying just a few words, and others recounting their adoption adventures in great detail. It impressed me how the birth mothers in the room used words like "relinquished" and "surrendered," while the adoptees almost always said they were "given up" for adoption.

One woman told of finding her birth mother married to her birth father. After giving her up for adoption, the parents married and went on to have eight other children. Yet, instead of believing and welcoming her, they asked her to submit to DNA testing to make sure she was really their daughter. To make matters worse, they didn't want her to contact her siblings because they weren't ready to tell them about the big sister they didn't know existed.

The middle-aged woman sitting next to her, who hadn't been able to find her own daughter, was sympathetic. She had kept her maiden name in the phone book for the past thirty years in case her daughter ever searched for her.

Another woman, about my age, told the group how she hadn't been told she was adopted until she was twenty-four years old, despite years of looking and feeling different from her adoptive family. After searching for two and a half years, she found an aunt who told her that her birth mother had been killed in a car accident. The aunt assured her that her mother had wanted very much to find her before she died. Eventually she met her birth father and younger brother and sister. It seemed clear to me from the way she talked that all those relationships somehow could not make up for never having had the chance to meet her mother. I felt sorry for her—the way she told the story by laughing to keep from crying; the way she seemed to believe that if she repeated the story enough times, as time went on, the pain might diminish.

I noticed that the mood of the room kept fluctuating between humor and somber concern, as if every few moments people needed to release their tension by laughing.

One of the only men in the room told a story that was both touching and hilarious. He was a good-looking man in his thirties and you could tell right away that he enjoyed performing, particularly in front of a room full of women.

With flamboyant gestures, he recounted the day he flew to a small town in Nevada to meet his birth mother for the first time.

"I panicked when I got off the plane, afraid that I wouldn't recognize her," he said. "But in a sea of faces I saw her standing there. It was like she was glowing, like she was wearing a neon halo around her head. All I could think of was, 'This is Planet Mommy.'" It was a description he would repeat often.

When he talked about the following days, his description of their budding relationship sounded more like a love affair than a mother-son reunion.

Changing the mood drastically, a birth mother told the group how she found her daughter in a mental institution, mildly retarded and emotionally disturbed. She recounted how she took the twenty-four-year-old daughter to the library and had to check out books for first graders.

"Part of me wonders if she is the right daughter," she said, her eyes downcast. "I'm so disappointed."

Another woman, who appeared to be in her mid-twenties, and her birth mother sat on a sofa holding hands as they told of their reunion four weeks earlier. Their resemblance was unmistakable and they laughed every time one of them finished the other's sentence. As it turned out, both of them were hairdressers who shared many similar interests.

There were several others in the room like me who were either considering a search or were right on the brink of finding who they were looking for. It surprised me that even those who had been disappointed by what they found still encouraged the rest of us to go forward. Everyone in the room seemed genuinely excited about my planned call to Helen the next day and made me promise to return the following month to tell them what happened.

By the time I got home, I was so anxious to make the call I couldn't sleep. I just lay in bed thinking about how my life was about to change. When Helen came to visit, I imagined her sitting on the floor to play with my kids and even offering to change their diapers. I would have a mother who was also my friend, in whom I could confide without fear of judgment and without the subject shifting abruptly to her problems. She would come over for Sunday dinners and we'd have profound conversations because she would have no patience for superficiality. And she would always offer to do the dishes because she doesn't care about her nails.

The last time I looked at the clock that Saturday morning it was about 4:45 A.M. My son came in around seven and jumped between Steve and me. I didn't even need my usual two cups of coffee to become fully conscious. Instead I felt like I often did when I was nervous—as if a ball of pressure was rising from the center of my chest and bursting through the top of my head and out of my fingertips. I spent the next hour feeding the children and dressing them. Steve offered to take them to the park so I could have time alone to make the calls.

I stared at my notes from the previous day. In red ink at the bottom of the page I had written "Call Helen's brother first." I would stick to the story about being Helen's long-lost friend, I thought, because she should be the one to tell them the truth about me. I did regret, though, that my first conversation with a close relative would have to begin with a lie. I dialed the number slowly so I wouldn't make a mistake.

A woman answered.

"Hello, is Michael Dunne there?" I said in a polite yet purposely mature voice.

"No, he's not. This is his wife, Sylvia. Can I help you?" She had an accent I couldn't place. It sounded almost Southern.

"My name is Debbie Holtz and I'm an old friend of Helen Dunne's. We lost touch years ago and I thought her brother might be able to help me find her."

"Goodness, we haven't spoken to Helen in more than a year," she said. "She's a traveling person. She doesn't keep in contact. She likes to go her own way. You know she travels so much on vacations and the like."

There was a pause. She was giving me very little specific information, but I sensed it was more out of confusion than suspicion.

"Do you know where she is living now?" I asked.

"She moved to San Francisco a few years ago," she said. "I think she's still there. She's hard to keep track of."

I imagined Helen as a sophisticated artist, exhibiting her paintings in one city after another.

"You know, it's strange," she said after a few moments, "but you sound like her. When we first started talking I actually thought it was Helen playing a trick on us."

"Wow, that's funny," I said, laughing nervously. I thanked her after she gave me the same phone number I had been given the day before. It was startling to hear our voices sounded alike. It was my first biological connection to anyone—no one had ever before said I sounded or even really looked like anyone else until my children were born. It gave me the confidence I needed to pick the phone right back up and call Helen Dunne.

She answered the phone on the third ring.

"Hello, my name is Debbie Holtz. Is this Helen Dunne?" I gripped the phone with both hands, worried that my trembling fingers might drop it.

"Yes, it is." She sounded friendly.

"I was wondering if May 14, 1959, is a significant date for you?"

"No," she said without hesitation.

Struggling to find the right words, I said, "I was adopted in Chicago thirty-two years ago and I have reason to believe you are my birth mother."

"You must have the wrong person," she answered in a monotone.

Refusing to give up, I asked her a few identifying questions.

"Were you born in New Haven, Pennsylvania?"

"Yes."

"Is your middle name Rose?"

"Yes."

"Well, that's strange because your name is on my birth certificate," I said.

"You have the wrong person," she said flatly.

Confused and disappointed, I apologized for bothering her and said good-bye. After hanging up, I felt as though the world had stopped spinning and all other life had dropped off the planet.

For a few moments, I believed her. Then I realized she was lying.

chapter ELEVEN

I woke up with the same dream running through my head over and over again, yet no matter how hard I tried, I couldn't remember what it was about. An image was dancing out in front of me, but every time I tried to grab it, it moved farther from my reach.

As I moved my body to the edge of the bed to get up, I felt like I had drunk a pint of whiskey and fallen off a roof. I gave up and fell back down on the pillow. For the first time since my kids were born, without the excuse of a 103 degree fever, I just lay in bed. I wasn't aware of how much time was passing because I couldn't bring myself to look at the clock. I heard Steve's voice before he opened the door.

"Do you remember that my mother is coming to visit today?" he asked, handing me a large cup of coffee. "I have to pick her up at the airport in two hours."

I had forgotten. My mind was stuck in neutral, unwilling to think back to what happened the day before or what I should do next. Time seemed crippling and perverse.

"You know, my mother might be able to help you with this. It's the kind of thing she gets really interested in."

It sounded as if he were talking about a hobby I'd just taken up, like needlepoint. I took a sip of the coffee and then buried my head deep beneath the comforter.

Suddenly I heard my daughter crying and it brought me to my senses. I ran full speed into the kitchen and made an exaggerated gesture of sympathy over what turned out to be a recalcitrant Donald Duck pop-up toy.

It was time to pull myself together. I was never comfortable with self-pity and I was determined not to wallow in it now. Short of confrontation, writing had always been a good way for me to gain control over difficult experiences. I would write Helen a letter, I decided, to help her understand my intentions while keeping myself a persistent presence in her mind.

I went downstairs to my office, closed the door and wrote:

March 1, 1992

Dear Helen,

I am so happy to have found you after so many years. I do understand, though, that this may be a shock to you and a reminder of a painful memory.

My decision to search for you was inspired by the birth of my two children and a need to know about my origins. My adoptive parents support my decision. It was particularly special to find out how close we live to one another. I live in Oakland with my husband and children.

Meeting you would mean a lot to me. I am not trying to disrupt your life. I am only seeking answers about my heritage, both for my own peace of mind and for my children.

Please call me. My phone number is ....

Sincerely,
Debbie Holtz

At the last minute, I decided to enclose two photographs of myself and the children, hoping they would make me more than a disembodied voice on the telephone or some phantom from a forgotten past.

I mailed the letter, and began my vigil of waiting for the phone to ring.

∞

When I told the story of my conversation with Helen to friends outside of the adoption group, the response was often, "Are you sure she's the right one?" It was as if mistaken identity was the only possible excuse for her behavior.

Although my instincts were sure she was the right person, I couldn't stop doubts from taking over. Not knowing what else to do, I set out to prove, once and for all, that this woman in San Francisco was the same Helen Dunne who had given birth to me. I decided to go to the San Francisco Registrar of Voters and get a copy of her voter registration affidavit. That way I could compare her signature on that document to the one on my birth certificate.

My mother-in-law, Carol, agreed to go with me the following day. Steve was planning to be out that night and I had already scheduled a babysitter so I could take her out for dinner.

The registrar's office was in City Hall, a large domed building I knew well from working as a news reporter. After finding Helen's name on microfilm, a clerk pulled the card and handed it to me. I stood for a moment with Helen's voter registration in one hand and my birth certificate in the other, my eyes darting back and forth from one signature to the other. It took only a few seconds for me to be sure.

"These signatures are identical, Carol," I said. "I can't believe it hasn't changed in all of these years."

I paid the clerk a quarter to make a copy. As we were walking out of the building, I suddenly stopped and turned toward Carol. "Would you like to stop and see where this woman lives?"

"Wouldn't it be something if we saw her?" my mother-in-law said with uncharacteristic enthusiasm. "I'd just love to see what she looks like." Carol loved hearing about the dramas in people's lives, whether they were real or the plot of a television mini-series.

We parked the car across the street from the apartment building. It stood on a hill near Golden Gate Park. The pale blue building was two stories high and stretched around the gentle curve of the street, with a garage underneath the far end of it. Rows of silver mailboxes lined a wall in front of the building's entrance. Maybe she would receive my letter today, I thought. I ran over briefly to see which mailbox belonged to her in case she appeared to collect her mail. Though I believed I would know my mother the moment I saw her, I wanted to be sure.

We sat in the car for more than an hour. Many women came in and out of the front door. Some were easier than others to dismiss as candidates. They were either too young or too old, or looked so different from me that Carol and I burst out laughing. We joked about how conspicuous we looked—two women on surveillance in a Volvo station wagon.

"It's possible she's just shocked," suggested my mother-in-law. "She may have never imagined you could find her and didn't know what else to do when she heard your voice but deny it."

"If it was me, though," she said after a pause, "I would have been so happy to hear my daughter's voice."

At about 5:30 P.M., just when we were about to give up and leave, a woman emerged from a dark green sedan in the garage and walked up the street carrying a small bag of groceries. She was striking—tall, in a long, black raincoat, with dark hair cut above her shoulders and a face that seemed pretty in a taut, angular way. I could tell she was someone you had to really study before appreciating her unusual beauty. Yet she appeared almost too young—more like a woman in her late forties, not fifty-seven.

"Could that be her?" I uttered in a loud whisper, clutching my mother-in-law's arm.

"I'm not sure," said Carol. "She doesn't really look like you."

The woman stopped at the mailboxes, bending over toward the same lower right-hand corner where I had found the box that said H. Dunne. I couldn't help but stare at her every move, like the way she shifted her bag to her left arm to open the mailbox with her right hand. As she was removing the letters, she suddenly looked right at us with an icy glance. At that moment, I was certain she knew exactly who I was.

When I returned home, I studied her voter registration card. She had signed it *Helen Rose Dunne* in October of 1989. Her birth date perfectly matched the age of the mother on my birth certificate. She wrote *accountant* for her occupation. As her political party, she checked Libertarian. What was that again? I tried to remember my political science classes in college: Libertarians don't believe in many laws or taxes. They distrust government and are out there on the political fringe. Helen listed her prior registration as a Republican, which meant she probably voted for Ronald Reagan and George Bush, then perhaps later thought better of it.

The registration card also gave her former address in Pasadena. That would mean she lived there during the 1980s, I thought. I too had lived there, probably just a few miles away, until I left in 1981. Was she there then? I cringed at how strange it was that we ended up living in two of the same places. Normally I would think of it as a striking coincidence, but under these circumstances, coincidences seemed unlikely.

The next day, to be absolutely sure, I asked my editor to run Helen's name through the Department of Motor Vehicles. She had the same birth date, brown hair, hazel eyes (like my daughter's), and was 5 feet 6 inches tall and 132 pounds (bigger than me), with a clean driving record.

∽∞∽

Ten days went by and I received no answer to my letter. I tried to distract myself by hanging new wallpaper in Jake's room, exercising and writing an article for the *Chronicle*. The silence was hard enough to tolerate, but it was my inability to do anything to change it that was nearly suffocating.

On the following Saturday morning, I decided to go to San Francisco and confront Helen. While I knew deep inside that it was something I had to do, I dreaded the very idea of it and was in no hurry to get there. I drove slowly over the Bay Bridge, thinking about all of the well-intentioned advice people had been giving me over the past week. "Give her time" was the common refrain. But I felt like I had already given her as much as I could.

I was going there to beg her to change her mind. If I were her, just seeing my daughter for the first time would be enough to erase my fears. Perhaps more than talking to Helen, though, I wanted to see up close the face I had tried to imagine all these years, even if only once. When I started the search, I really believed it was to fulfill my genetic curiosity, an intellectual pursuit of facts and history. Now, though, I felt driven by sheer emotion. Was I really looking for a new mother? Was I trying to fill my own emptiness?

I kept going over all the possible reasons in my head for her refusal to acknowledge me. She felt overwhelming guilt. She was ashamed to explain why she had given me up for adoption. She never told my father she was pregnant and doesn't want him to find out now. Or, she has no desire to know me at all.

I had grown up learning to expect the worst so, as I wound my way through the streets of San Francisco, the grimmest scenarios began playing out in my mind. What if she sees my face and feels nothing? What if she continues to deny she is my mother even after I show her my adoption papers? What could I possibly say to change her mind? Could I give up and walk away?

Hope stubbornly resides in the hearts of even the greatest cynics. I fantasized that the moment she saw me, she would begin to cry and hug me close, whispering in my ear how happy she was that I was there, how she had secretly wished I would come back.

As I got closer to her building, so many possibilities were swirling around in my head that I was distracted from figuring out just what I was going to say to her. I parked my car down the street, out of sight of the building. Gripping my adoption papers tightly against my chest, I walked slowly to the front door. People were walking in and out of the building, and I noticed that the glass door never really closed completely. I walked in and searched the apartment doors for her number. I found it quickly on the first floor. In a moment of panic, I considered leaving but couldn't let myself. I knocked on the door. Once, twice, three times.

There was no response. I thought I saw a shadow cover the peephole for a second. I could smell the aroma of food cooking, but couldn't be sure it was from her apartment. I sensed that she was inside, so I sat for nearly an hour on some nearby stairs, never taking my eyes off the door. It didn't open. Young people with backpacks who looked the age of graduate students kept stepping around me.

Finally I walked outside and looked into what I was almost sure was her window. The drapes were open and a light was on. A huge bookshelf covered an entire wall.

I got into the car and called her phone number from my car phone. There was no answer.

When I returned to the building, the front door had locked, so I sat down by the entrance as a light rain began to fall. Soon I saw a woman walking up the street. She stole a glance at me, and I realized it was Helen. She must have left the building through a different door, I thought. I followed her to the garage and watched her approach the same green sedan she had gotten out of on my previous visit. I walked right up to her. There was no time to lose.

"Excuse me, I'm looking for Helen Dunne," I said, louder than intended.

"Yes?" She seemed extremely nervous, drawing the word out too long.

"Hello, I am Debbie Holtz and I have been waiting a long time to talk to you."

"I said all that I have to say on the telephone," she said, no longer looking at me as she opened the car door.

"But you lied on the phone," I said, trying to be forceful but not harsh. "I have some documents I'd like you to look at."

She refused to even glance at the papers I was holding out to her and instead placed her purse and a small bag in the car.

"I hate to be rude, but there's nothing I can say," she said.

"I don't want to disrupt your life," I said in a desperate tone I had never before heard in my own voice. "But I've spent my whole life needing to know where I came from."

"There's nothing I can say," she repeated, turning away.

Shocked at her indifference and grasping for the words, any words, to change her mind, I studied this woman who was my mother. She doesn't really look like me, I thought. She was unlike anyone I had ever met, yet she seemed oddly familiar. I wanted to soak in her presence, knowing how important it would be to remember later. But even as I tried to memorize her features, there was something about her that seemed elusive, otherworldly.

She sat down in the driver's seat.

"You gave birth to me," I pleaded, kneeling down to get closer to her. "Can't you just talk to me for a few minutes? Can you at least tell me who my father was?"

My pleas were silenced as she shut her car door and started the engine. I stood there completely still as she pulled out of the garage and drove down the street, feeling more alone than I ever had before. As I walked toward my car, I thought I might choke from holding back the tears. I fumbled with my keys and then forced the right one into the lock as though I was in an anxious rush to get somewhere. The second the door shut I began to cry, not in quick sobs, but in long, mournful groans like some helpless newborn.

chapter TWELVE

Only a week after confronting Helen I went away with my family on a long-planned trip to Hawaii. Watching the pulsing waves and listening to their steady rhythm seemed like a perfect way to quiet my mind and find some perspective on all that had happened. Once we got there, though, I realized the irony of people leaving home to forget about their problems; vacations only give you more time than you usually have to put a magnifying glass to your thoughts.

I sat on the beach, watching my children playing happily in the sand, and wrote, hoping pen and paper would lead me to answers my mind alone could not:

> *When I thought about searching for my birth mother, my greatest fear was that I would never find her. I never imagined that she would be living twenty miles from me with the same name she had thirty-two years ago when she gave me up for adoption. And I never once thought she would reject me. But she did.*

I no longer have to fight the courts or public agencies for information. Now my greatest challenge is to understand the heart and mind of a woman who is an absolute stranger to me. She is so close to me, but couldn't be farther away.

As each day goes by, the pain of her silence grows deeper in me. It is such a profound loss, so much greater than the bewildering sense I grew up with of not knowing who or where she was.

I wonder if she ever held me right after I was born—ever felt the intense attachment I did the moment I saw my children's faces. I always believed that she chose adoption because she thought it was best for me. But I wonder if then, like now, she only considered herself.

So many people I know have speculated about her reasons for lying to me. My own attempts to empathize with her do not ease the pain I am feeling. I have no reason to believe she is overwhelmed with guilt or paralyzed by shock, although it may all be true.

I am not sorry that I decided to search for her. The mystery of my origin would always have been there, only made more intense by my lack of effort to unravel it.

Soon after I returned home, I attended another ALMA rap session. I recounted the story and announced that I had decided to call Helen's brother and tell him the truth. Some of the people there, mostly the birth parents, urged me to give Helen more time to come around. She is probably in a lot of pain, they argued. One woman suggested I write a second letter asking specific questions about my biological background and give her the opportunity to respond in writing. The cautionary approach won out. I wrote the letter:

March 28, 1992

Dear Helen,

It is clear from our last two conversations that you either don't want anything to do with me or have emotional reasons to deny my existence. I understand that the circumstances of my birth may be very painful for you. Maybe this has been a secret you had hoped to never have to face again or perhaps you have reasons for wanting to withhold the true name of my father.

I decided to search for you out of a need to know facts about my heritage that most people, including yourself, probably take for granted. I have no access to any biological background information from the public agency responsible for my adoption because of an unfortunate fire. My parents, who have given me a good life and are supportive of my search, have very little information to offer me.

If you still refuse to talk to me, I would appreciate it if you could just answer a few of my questions in writing and return them as soon as you can.

1. What is the ethnic and religious background of your family?
2. What is the family's medical history?
3. What is your educational level and occupation? And that of my father?
4. Do you or my father have any special talents or interests?
5. Do I have any siblings?

Of course, I would appreciate any other information you are willing to share with me.

Also, I received a postcard six years ago that may have been written about you. I am enclosing a copy. Could you tell me who wrote it and why?

Sincerely,

Debra Levi Holtz

Three weeks passed and there was no response. It no longer surprised me. I was coming to realize that making contact with her brother was the only way I was going to find out anything about Helen and my birth family. I had to do it, even if it meant betraying her.

"Hello, this is Debbie Holtz. You may remember me. I called you about two months ago and told you I was an old friend of Helen's."

"Why, yes, I remember." I recognized Sylvia Dunne's voice from my last call.

"Is your husband home?"

"No, he's not."

I decided to rely on the kindness I could hear in her voice. "Oh, I see. Well . . . uh . . . this may come as a big surprise to you. I want to apologize, but I didn't tell you the truth the first time we spoke. I'm not really an old friend of Helen's. I am her daughter. She gave me up for adoption almost thirty-three years ago."

"Oh, my goodness," she gasped.

"I just want to assure you that I am not asking for anything. I'm a newspaper writer and I'm married to a doctor. I have a comfortable life. I just need to know where I come from. Did you know Helen had a baby?"

"No, I didn't," she said. "Did you ever get a hold of her?"

I told her about my conversations with Helen, the letters, all of my evidence, her denials.

"I'm surprised Helen had a child, but I'm not surprised she would lie about it," said Sylvia, with polite exasperation. "She's not a family-oriented person."

"I hope you can understand my need to know about my biological family after so many years of wondering," I said. "Now that I have a son and a daughter, I want them to know too."

She asked me about Jake and Sarah. As I talked about the children, I could tell she was growing more sympathetic.

"Let's see," she said. "Your grandparents are both dead. Helen's dad died in, oh I think it was either 1960 or 1961. Her mother died eleven years ago. They were Protestant. Twins run in the family. Two of our grandchildren are twins . . . "

The facts just spilled out and I couldn't get enough.

"Helen's separation from the family is of her own making." Her voice became strident. "How can she have a relationship with you when she doesn't have one with us?

"She is very, very intelligent. Intelligence runs in the family. My grandson is in the first grade but he is studying at a fourth-grade level. He is very advanced. But Helen is a very self-centered person. Maybe that runs in the family too. My own daughter rejected her children, and now we have them."

As she paused for a moment, I kept trying to imagine how to paint myself into this picture.

"My husband is a deeply religious man and I know he would want to talk to you. Before I say anything else, could you send us copies of your adoption papers and maybe a few pictures of you and your children? We just need to be sure. Is that all right?"

She gave me her address and I repeatedly thanked her before I said good-bye.

It was the first time in months that I felt like some light was shining on this dark corner of my life. Listening to someone else talk about Helen made her less illusive. While Sylvia's descriptions of her were disturbing, Helen's rejection of me was beginning to make an odd sort of sense.

I sent an overnight express envelope to Sylvia with copies of my adoption papers and the same photographs of myself and the children I had sent to Helen. I included copies of the letters I wrote to Helen and a chronology explaining the various incarnations of my name from Shirley Jane Dunne to Debra Michelle Skar to Debra Levi to Debra Levi Holtz so I wouldn't just appear as some impostor with a lot of aliases.

The phone rang the next day.

"Well, I can see a lot of Helen in you," Sylvia said right away. "I think you look like her . . . very much so."

Her words validated me. I wasn't some kind of criminal, burglarizing these people's lives.

"Debbie, your uncle is a truck driver and he's on the road a lot. He called yesterday and I told him about you. He said it wouldn't surprise him that you would be her daughter. And after I saw the pictures, good God, your nose, chin, cheeks— they're all Dunne. But it's that bump on your nose, that's a distinctive Dunne characteristic. Helen has it, so does Michael. And that picture of your daughter, Sarah. If I didn't know it, I would say she was my own granddaughter!"

She paused for a few moments and I stayed quiet, just absorbing it all. I found myself reflexively reaching for a pen and paper, knowing I must write it all down so that I would never forget any of it.

"Debbie, when we talked on Monday I didn't want to get involved," Sylvia admitted. "But you have every right to know about your family history. Let's see, what can I tell you? There's a high life expectancy in the family. Your great-grandma lived to be ninety-nine and still had her mind. She was very intelligent and well known in the community. Your great-grandfather, Henry Schmidt, painted houses and churches."

She continued speaking and I struggled to capture every detail.

"Michael and Helen are completely different people. Michael worries about the other person. He's soft-hearted;

he would give a nickel to someone who needed it. Helen would say, 'I'll go out and take the person's last nickel.'"

I could hear in Sylvia's voice that her disdain for Helen went back a long way.

"Helen was pampered. She loved to look in the mirror. She was a model for a while. Her parents married late in life. Her mother—your grandmother Emma—was very stern and intelligent. She taught school for fifty-four years. Helen made a career out of college for awhile. She didn't visit her mother like she should have. The only thing that was important to her were her cats. She treated them better than children."

I flashed on my own cat, Eliza, living in the garage and the crawl space under our house, to whom I barely paid any attention. She had been dumped in my lap by a college friend who hadn't known what else to do with her. I had taken care of her the past fourteen years out of obligation, not out of love.

"Your grandmother built a Baptist church near here," Sylvia continued. "They donated the land to the community."

After a momentary pause, she said, "Debbie, I believe everyone in the world has a right to know who they are. If you would like to talk to your Uncle Mike, call on Sunday. That's the day he's usually home. In the meantime, do you think you could send some full-length pictures of yourself and some copies of your newspaper articles?"

I was surprised by this sudden request, assuming she was looking for more proof that I was who I claimed to be. But I agreed. After all, she was being very generous by sharing all of the family history that my birth mother refused me.

Four days later, I was finally able to talk to my uncle. His voice was low, with an accent that struck me the way Sylvia's had—part Southern and part New Jersey.

"Well, hello there," he said, sounding friendly but a bit reticent.

"I apologize for not telling you who I really was the first time I called, but I wanted to speak to Helen first," I explained.

"I guess I talk to her every couple of years," he said. "I hadn't talked to her in a year when you called. She's a very private person. Her having a baby surprises me. But nothing else about it surprises me. I would kind of expect that."

"You would have expected her to lie to me?" I asked incredulously.

"She's the kind of person that takes and the rest of the world can do whatever," he said sadly, but without a hint of bitterness.

"She left home after grade school. She stayed with our aunt and uncle in New Haven so she could attend a better high school. My mother was a schoolteacher all her life. My father was in the coal business and was a farmer on the side."

He paused for a moment.

"Helen got all the brains," he said with resignation. "She has a very high IQ. She went to a teacher's college not far from here. My mother always wanted her to become a teacher, but then she went into the service in 1954 and did secretarial work."

"Where was she based?" I asked.

"Fort Monmouth, New Jersey, in the women's army corps."

My mother, a soldier. I didn't know very much about her life, but it was a piece that nonetheless struck me as incongruous, like putting stripes on polka dots. I had never before known any woman who voluntarily joined the army and couldn't imagine doing it myself.

"She was also a model for a while," he continued. "I think she lived in Miami, New York and the state of Washington. I can sure tell from your picture you got the Dunne bump, on your nose, I mean." He laughed for the first time.

"I think Sylvia could probably give you a better rundown on the Dunne family tree than even I can." It was a self-effacing remark, partly intended to remove himself from the conversation.

"Thanks for everything, Mike," I said. "I hope we can meet someday."

Sylvia's voice came on the phone. It was easy to tell that she liked to talk as much as Mike disliked it.

"Well, you can probably see by now we're a little country family," she said. "We're good people who are well known in our little community. We're Pentecostals, you know. Michael wasn't raised that way, but my family is. There are two churches here with two hundred people, but for now we don't attend either one. The preacher we liked moved away, and we're waiting for the right one to come along."

As she talked about her deeply held religious beliefs, I scanned my memory for what I remembered about Pente-costalism. Fundamentalist Christians, I thought. Don't they speak in tongues? I wasn't even sure what that meant.

"I've been looking through some of Grandma Emma's old papers and address books to help me remember things you might want to know. I had a stroke a couple of years ago, a small one, and my memory's not so good anymore.

"Anyway, Helen married John D'Lorio on November 22, 1962 in Flushing, New York. They were married for a few years before we even knew it. She brought him home about three times. Once they even brought his mother. She was a friend of Helen's. That fella had big eyes, I remember."

Could John D'Lorio be my father? I counted the years in my head. They were married three and a half years after I was born. Was it possible?

"Mike and Helen had dark eyes until they got into their forties, then they got lighter, turned hazel," she continued. "That fella John was a tall, thin man. He was in the service for a while during their marriage. They went to the state of Washington for a short time. He was based at Fort Lewis."

"Why did they get divorced?" I asked.

"I remember Helen told me: 'I had to keep him, even down to buying his cigarettes. He put all his money in the bank and I had to take care of him. And I got married for someone to take care of *me*.'"

Sylvia ran down the listings for Helen in my grandmother's old address book. In 1965, Helen and John still lived in New York. Then there was an address in Los Angeles on Beverly Boulevard. In 1972, the address changed to Pasadena.

"She was so hard to keep track of that when her mother passed away we couldn't even get a hold of her," said Sylvia, sounding a bit exasperated any time she spoke of Helen.

"Finally my mother called her and told her that Emma had died and Helen said, 'Well, does it really make any difference if I come home? She's already dead.' My mother said, 'Yes, it matters. Your brother needs you.' So she came.

"I'll never forget how she went out for dinner and only came back just in time for the funeral. She wanted to make sure she got her nose in everything, especially whatever was left for her to take. They owned some land near here. She still owns a part of it. Michael looks after it for her."

Helen was starting to sound like a real mercenary.

"Anyway, you should probably know this: Helen's parents both died of cancer. Her mother was in her eighties. Her father hurt his back and his health deteriorated from then on. He died when he was sixty-six. But, like I said before, your great-grandmother Schmidt died at ninety-nine and your great-granddad Dunne was close to one hundred. Another aunt lived to ninety-seven. The family has long life spans.

"Grandma Dunne's maiden name was McIvers. They were Irish. Her mother was Rose. All the girls in the family, including Helen and my own daughter, have been given that middle name ever since."

Not me, I thought.

"Her husband, Geoff Dunne, came from Maine. His great-great-granddad was a horse thief who was forced to move there from England."

By the time Sylvia began running down the German side of the family tree on my grandmother Emma's side, I had lost track of the direction of the branches. The names seemed more like stars in a distant constellation, of which I did not yet feel a part.

I started laughing and told her it was a lot to take in all at once.

"When you laugh, you sound like Helen," she said. I was no longer sure that it was a compliment.

chapter THIRTEEN

I laid out my evidence before the handwriting analyst: the anonymous postcard, my birth certificate, the letter Helen had written to my parents approving my Jewish upbringing, and her voter registration affidavit. I figured that if this man had consulted with the San Francisco Police Department on difficult cases like the Zodiac serial murders in the early 1970s, he would be able to handle mine.

Ed Wilton's office was in his house on a hillside in San Francisco's Twin Peaks neighborhood. Neat stacks of paper covered much of the oversized dining-room table. He offered me a seat and immediately began looking at my documents.

Ed, who appeared to be in his early fifties, exuded an air of confidence about his expertise. Graphology, he said, can compare signatures but it can also tell quite a bit about the personality and even the physical health of the writer.

I told him what each piece of paper was, careful not to give too much information for fear of influencing his analysis. First he considered the two-page letter by Helen, dated June 1, 1959.

"She has not developed her own style of writing," he explained. "We're all trained in the Palmer style. This is all Palmer. Many women don't change from Palmer."

He stared silently at the first page for a few minutes.

"Her writing indicates neuroses. She has difficulty expressing her true personality. This monotonous kind of handwriting shows a person who is hiding her personality. At the time she wrote this, she was not happy with herself, maybe had already given up on herself. She tends to be unrealistic. She isn't down to earth. I'd say that she has a Don Quixote syndrome."

"What does that mean?" I asked.

"She gets caught up in the romance of ideals beyond her reach, perhaps she's even looking for someone to save her," he said. "You see, she's not practical. She has a strong lack of flexibility. She's headstrong, stubborn and unrealistic. A bad combination."

He delivered his opinions unequivocally, never wavering. And he rarely took his eyes off the paper he was discussing.

"This writing shows someone being repressed," he continued. "On the positive side, she is a friendly person. More extroverted than introverted, yet often afraid to express herself. She is very secretive."

I listened closely, wanting him to be right.

"From the short time I've talked to you, I can tell you have a higher IQ than this person, at least in this letter," he said. "She shows distrust in people from a young age. The right person coming along may have pulled her out of this. She desperately wanted closeness but was unable to seek it out herself. She was not given positive reinforcement in her childhood. Sometimes she puts herself in a cocoon. It's extremely difficult for her to show emotions, especially on a one-to-one basis. She's looking for things in people she's not going to find. And she's not flexible enough to roll with another person in a relationship because she's not capable of enough give-and-take.

"There's a small amount of depression in the letter, not a great deal. This person is not really a mean person or one with a terrible temper, but she could develop one later because of frustration."

It felt as if I was interviewing Helen's psychiatrist.

"She was not a vindictive person in 1959. But her outlook on life and on herself is distorted. There are all kinds of signs of extreme secretiveness. I wouldn't trust everything she says. When you have an inability to express anything, then you get a liar. All of her problems are caused by her parents."

Aren't everyone's? I thought, laughing to myself.

"So it sounds like the person who wrote this letter is a very screwed-up woman," I said.

"There's no question," he answered, as he picked up the postcard and held it up next to the letter.

"I tend not to think this is the same handwriting as in the letter."

He put the letter down and examined the postcard closely.

"I'm 95 to 98 percent sure this was written by a woman," he declared. "All the writing on the postcard is done by the same person. An older person, probably past the age of fifty, with gastrointestinal or abdominal problems."

"How can you be so sure?" I asked.

"I can tell from a handwriting sample if someone has AIDS or predict even fifteen years before they get cancer," he said, leading me to now wonder if this man was just too confident of his abilities to read someone's past, present and future from a small handwriting sample.

"AIDS, cancer and lupus can be confused, however, because they all attack the immune system. For example, I think the Zodiac Killer was gay and later developed AIDS. I think he's probably dead, which is why we haven't heard from him recently and the police were never able to solve the case."

He sounded credible, but I couldn't help but have some doubts.

"If the postcard and letter were written by the same person, the handwriting on the postcard shows a person who is far more in charge of her own life or has better fulfilled their potential. The person in the letter is too rigid to change," he said.

"I was afraid of that," I thought out loud.

"There's a disturbance in here." He drummed his index finger on the postcard. "It could be a psychological or neurological problem, although I don't think it's Alzheimer's disease or some form of dementia. More likely a problem in the abdominal area, probably on the right-hand side such as the liver, gall bladder or ovaries. I've seen this kind of problem with dyslexia, although the letter of 1959 does not show this."

He paused for a few moments, which he hadn't done until now, sitting back against the chair and taking a deep breath.

"One other possibility is that the person may have a speech impediment. The postcard appears to have been written spontaneously. Although it's written with the same pen, different parts could have been written at different times, as if the writer left it on the desk and came back to it. While I don't see a high IQ in the letter, the person who wrote the postcard is well above the average IQ."

Maybe Helen isn't as smart as her brother said she was, I thought.

I asked him what kind of personality disorder was evident in the letter. Schizophrenia? Multiple personalities, perhaps? I was grasping for a really good excuse for her behavior.

"The woman who wrote the letter could have hysterical outbursts, but the letter indicates more of a tendency to be an introverted schizoid. Someone who could withdraw from society and become very self-centered, which is true of people with a lot of problems."

Anxious to figure out who wrote the postcard and why, I brought his attention back to it.

"The postcard could be more sarcasm than for real," he said. "For example, the 'H' in Helen is smaller than the other capital letters, which could indicate a lack of regard for the person."

"If I give you a sample of my handwriting, could you tell me whether the person who wrote the letter and signed my birth certificate is my mother?" I asked.

"No, I doubt it," he said. "Handwriting does not appear to be genetic."

"Unlike voices," I said, remembering how Sylvia Dunne got my voice confused with Helen's.

"That's right," he said.

He called the signatures on the birth certificate and voter registration card "amazingly similar," but refused to commit to any absolute certainty because, he said, the darkened photocopy of my birth certificate was not a good sampling.

I left that day wondering if, without Helen's word, there might always be a lingering suspicion that I had not found the right woman.

꧁

It was early May, and I was getting the same peculiar feeling of dread I get every year as my birthday approaches.

Unfortunately my birthday comes right around Mother's Day—some years it even lands on the same day. In the past, this struck me as ironic. The year I found Helen it seemed almost cruel.

My own children, though, gave Mother's Day new meaning. Steve showered me with Hallmark cards, while Jake and Sarah competed for my attention and a place on my lap.

My daughter has a book about a young Inuit girl in Alaska who asks her mother, "Mama, do you love me?" After being reassured, the girl tests her mother's love by giving examples of things she could do that would make her mother sad, angry or worried. By the end of the book, the mother's answer remains the same: "I will love you forever and for always, because you are my Dear One."

Each time I read that story to my daughter, I am reminded of myself as a child and even as a teenager. But unlike the Alaskan girl, I found myself asking my own mother the same question over and over again without the same confidence in her answer. Instead of comforting me like the mother in the book, my own mother used to say to me in obvious annoyance, "Debbie, why do you always ask me that?"

Perhaps because I never want my children to have to even ask me this question, I am constantly kissing their impossibly soft cheeks and declaring my love for them so that they will take it for granted. That's the way it was that Sunday morning of Mother's Day as they sat on my lap at the breakfast table and helped me open my cards and presents. With Sarah only eighteen months old and her brother, Jake, nearly four, any celebration was bound to turn into their own. They laughed, tried the bows on their heads and then got bored.

As they moved on to their own toys, I picked up the phone to call my adoptive mother. I told her how I had found Helen, right here in the Bay Area, and how she had denied any maternal responsibility, first on the telephone and then in person.

"I hope you're going to stay as far away from that woman as possible," she said. "You found out what you wanted to, now let it go."

I knew it was her way of protecting me but, at that moment, what I really needed was some empathy.

"It's not that easy," I tried to explain. "I guess I'm still hoping she'll change her mind. It's not like I want or need her to be my mother, it just hurts that she won't admit the truth. I want to understand why she's lying."

"I wouldn't want to have *her* genes," she said. "You should be happy she gave you up. You've had a very sheltered and a very good life. Look at all the opportunities you've been given. You had a wonderful education, beautiful clothes to wear. You lived well. You should be grateful."

When my thirty-third birthday arrived a few days later, I walked around like a jilted lover waiting in vain for a phone call or card. I couldn't help hoping that my birthday coming so soon after I had found Helen might soften her and weaken her resolve to hide from the truth. I also mistakenly assumed I would hear from my aunt and uncle in Pennsylvania, but I came to realize that maybe it was too much to expect—I was still little more than a stranger to them.

Knowing it was a particularly hard year to celebrate, Steve took me to a restaurant I had always wanted to go to in San Francisco. I told him over dinner that I thought this man who was once married to Helen, John D'Lorio, could be my father.

"I hear stories all the time from adoptees about unmarried couples who give their children up and then later marry," I said. "It's not so far-fetched."

"You'll only know if you call him," said Steve.

⌇

I tried to figure out how to best approach this man who may or may not have known I existed. The only answer was to go for broke; I decided to tell him everything outright. It all poured out in the minutes after he answered the phone.

"Wow, I didn't even know about this," he said, genuinely surprised. "I can't believe this, she never even mentioned it. I didn't even meet Helen until 1962."

That year definitely put John out of the running as a candidate for my father. But I could tell right away that he was anxious to talk.

"Let's see, what can I tell you? We got married shortly after we met. She was living in Manhattan. She was very attractive. I was only twenty-two. I had just gotten drafted and I was really off balance, really mixed up. She was working at a radio station after studying home economics in college. I don't think she ever finished though."

His voice was gentle, thoughtful and passionate all at once.

"She's an extremely bright lady, unbelievably intelligent. A nut about reading. I thought she was the smartest woman I had ever met and I found that very attractive," he said, echoing what Helen's brother had said, but more fervently.

"She had been in the army. She was stationed at Fort Monmouth, New Jersey. It was while she was there that she first discovered New York City and fell in love with it. I don't know how much you know about her background."

I told him that I had some impressions of it from talking to Helen's brother and sister-in-law.

"The place she came from, Lockhart, is a little poor Appalachian town. She worked very hard to break from it, to have nothing to do with it. She was romantic, idealistic. She wanted to see the world, become a sophisticated woman. Part of her attempt to become a new person was to leave that town—as well as the people and the culture—behind."

I found myself admiring Helen as an intellectual renegade. When I was young, I fantasized that my birth mother had exceptional talents that made her stand apart from other women. Yet I could never have dreamed up this character. It felt as if someone was holding a door open for me and letting me peer into Helen's secret world. Unlike Sylvia and Mike Dunne, John intimately understood Helen. It was even more significant to me that he was willing to share it all without once questioning that I really was her daughter.

"Do you know if she ever married again?" I asked.

"No, she never did. I haven't seen her in many years, but I have a friend who is still in contact with her. She has had problems with guys. She's a very, very mixed-up lady," he said.

"Why did you divorce?" I asked.

"We were living off post at Fort Lewis, near Tacoma. She was extremely emotional, screaming and hysterical a lot. She was unstable. I remember saying 'I'll give it a year after I get back to New York, or I'll leave.' And that's what happened. I said to myself, 'I still love her, but I can't live with this person.'

"I went into a deep depression. It sent a message to my subconscious—I will never fall that deeply in love again if it hurts that much. You see, I was supposed to save her. I was supposed to be her knight in shining armor."

I remembered at that moment what Ed Wilton, the handwriting expert, had said. "She's looking for someone to save her. . . ."

"Did she ever mention anyone she was involved with before she met you?" I asked John. "Someone who could have been my father?"

"She had a boyfriend in the army," he said. "She described him as a very sweet, boyish second lieutenant. She never mentioned his name. But for two or three years before I met her, she was seeing an older man. He sounded dangerous. She even drove across the country with him in 1962 to meet me in Washington. He was a con man and she was very much in love with him. He was probably already in his fifties then."

He stopped to think for a moment.

"I think it would be one of those two. They were the only two people she ever described as being romantically involved with. But I have to warn you," he said, interrupting himself, "She's a very screwed-up woman. She has heavy psychological problems, mostly of her own making. It's as though she was always searching for peace, but was her own worst enemy. She always stridently attacked so many people, so many things. She was very mistrustful, never able to value anything. Yet she was always able to hold down a job."

I asked him whether he thought she would ever reconsider and acknowledge that I was her daughter.

"I know you don't want to hear this," he answered. "But once she makes up her mind, she doesn't go back."

We were both quiet for a moment.

"I remember now," he said suddenly. "The con man, his name was Frank, Frank Harlett. He was extremely important to her. She had broken up with him when I met her. In 1962 she bought his car and drove with him to Washington. I was so screwed up. I thought I was madly in love with her, and I believed her when she said she was never going to see him again.

"Frank was on the edge of the underworld. They used to do drugs, heroin together. That was pretty strange back in 1962," he said, trying to keep pace with his memories.

The coincidences no longer seemed accidental. They seemed downright bizarre. Heroin, I thought. Howie, David, the underworld, Manny. Now, this Frank.

"Anyway," John continued. "Frank eventually moved to Pasadena.

"Just like Helen did," I pointed out.

"That's right, but I don't know if they kept in contact. By the time she moved, I was just so happy she was out of New York City. We separated in 1965, but still weren't divorced by 1968. I was in art school. She threatened my life once when she saw me out with another woman during the separation. She was hysterical, yelling at me. She said, 'You know I could kill you and I have the guns to do it.' She was still holding on to the belief we would get back together. For a long time, she refused to agree to the divorce, but eventually she consented. The only grounds for divorce in New York was adultery. It was very difficult if not impossible to get at that time. So I went and got a Mexican divorce. I paid for everything."

"She sounds even crazier than I had thought," I said, hoping he might disagree.

"I think she is," he said. "In the early '70s, she was living in West Hollywood with a friend of mine. He says she's still unstable. I met her again in 1974. I thought we could be friends. We drove up to San Francisco. It was horrible, the fighting. It was a nightmare. She threatened at one point to drive us off the Pacific Coast Highway."

At that moment, I didn't want to know any more about that side of her.

"Are you surprised she didn't tell you about me?" I asked.

"We never even talked about kids. I never thought about that with her. But I am surprised she didn't tell me. Even then she must have been repressing it."

I told John about the postcard with the Matisse painting and my adoptive mother's story about Helen's interest in art.

"Yeah, she was always interested in art, but she wasn't that much into modern art. She was into classical art." His voice took on a conspiratorial tone, the way people get when they are about to divulge someone else's secrets.

"I'll tell you what she is obsessed with—she is fanatical about looking, seeming and acting younger than she is. She once went all the way to Hungary or Romania for some kind of special beauty or health treatments."

That's why I wasn't sure it was my mother the first time I saw her, I thought. She seemed younger than I had expected.

John and I went on to tell each other about ourselves. He's a sculptor who teaches art at a college in Manhattan. He's been living for several years with his current girlfriend, a former student. We promised to get together when I visited New York the following November.

"You are the one person who has the right to find out who she is," John said. "After all, she is your mother."

John called back a week later, surprising me with his eagerness to share more information about Helen.

"I forgot to tell you the last time we spoke how I met Helen. In the early 1960s, we were part of this philosophy group. Ayn Rand, the writer, was at the center of all of these people's lives and at the center of Helen's life. She was a hundred percent immersed in that philosophy. I think she was trying to find a new way to look at life that would make it acceptable to her. Ayn Rand appealed to people who really didn't feel like they fit in. One of the reasons she fell in love with me was our shared belief in Ayn Rand."

"What was the philosophy?" I asked.

"It's about having the strength to stand alone and confront cultural values you're opposed to. The whole movement was sort of blown apart in the late 1960s. Eventually one part of the group moved to Los Angeles and the other stayed in New York. But back in 1962, when I met her, Helen's message was, 'Judge me for what I am now.' She never allowed me to ask her questions about her past. I let those questions go unanswered because you knew there were mistakes in her past. I accepted that then. Now I would see it as a red flag."

"I guess I was one of those mistakes," I said.

"All I know is that she wanted more out of life than she saw as a child," he continued, sidestepping what I had said. "That's why she got into reading romantic novels about foreign lands. The big joke was that she left this small town to travel around the world by joining the army, and wound up in a small town in New Jersey. Monmouth was known for its military base and its racetrack. Helen knew a lot about horse racing; it was Frank Harlett's specialty. I remember she told me how they traveled around the country, to Florida and other places, after she got out of the army. She said she was a tout, someone who gets people to bet on certain racehorses to change the odds."

I was quickly losing the ability to be shocked by anything I learned about Helen.

"You seem so different from her. What do you think she saw in you?" I asked.

"I guess in a kind of offbeat way I represented purity to her—an honest, angelic figure to remove her from her embarrassing and messy past."

"Why didn't you ever get married again?" I asked him.

"The experience with Helen crushed me. It was so painful. She was my dream lady. I was very naive and limited. It was the first time I ever fell deeply in love and she turned out to be a wacko."

chapter FOURTEEN

Almost everyone I told my story to over the next few months was certain Helen had forced my birth out of her mind many years ago and was suffering some form of emotional amnesia. While her rejection might be painful, they would say, it didn't have anything to do with me personally.

"She is crazy enough to have cut herself off from the experience and convinced herself it never happened," Steve repeatedly insisted.

But that theory brought me no comfort.

As if drawn by a gravitational force, I kept coming back to the belief that Helen was deliberately lying. After all, she had a history of swindling people. Even my adoption appeared to have been a self-serving scam from which, I had learned, she walked away with ten thousand dollars—a lot of money in 1959. My own experience with my adoptive family taught me that people will lie if they have something worth hiding.

Like many other adoptees, I grew up feeling I had no control over my life and I spent many years trying to call all of the shots, often at the expense of others. Anger was the vehicle I chose for careening my way through life, careful to avoid the deep potholes of despair along the way. So I found it less painful and infinitely safer to be angry at Helen than to feel sorry for her.

I couldn't help thinking it had been her decision to give me away as a baby, and now she was controlling my fate once again by refusing to tell me the truth. Blaming her decisions on an abstract force like madness meant that no one had any control, and that was a notion too threatening for me to accept.

Going to Pennsylvania was the only way I could think of to recapture some control over the situation. I was driven to learn as much about her as I could. Visiting the place where Helen and several generations of her family had lived might even reveal something about myself. For despite the vast chasm that divided Helen and me, I couldn't shake the idea that every cell of my body contained thousands of genes from her, genes that determined who I was. I could have been raised in an entirely different adoptive family and I might still be the same person.

For several months now, the Dunnes had been saying they wanted to meet me, so I decided to visit them in late July, the time when Steve and Jake take their annual trip to Lake Tahoe with Steve's brother and twin nephews. Helen might be writing me out of her own life story, but it was up to me to claim my role in the family legend. I wouldn't allow Helen to make history, as Napoleon once described it, "a set of lies agreed upon."

I wanted to bring Sarah along since she had been the spark that ignited my search, and I hoped that her presence would create an image of myself as a baby in the minds of my aunt and uncle.

The town of Lockhart was so small it wasn't even on my
map of Pennsylvania, leaving me to rely on written directions
provided by my aunt. New Haven, which *was* on the map,
appeared to be the largest town in the area and probably the
only one with a hospital, where Helen was born. Sarah fell
asleep in the back seat of the rental car shortly after I navi-
gated my way out of the Pittsburgh airport on a northeast
course toward Lockhart. She was only twenty months old,
barely walking, and far too young to understand the significance of the journey we were taking.

I was grateful for the nearly two hours it would take to
drive there. Even though we had already flown overnight and
most of the morning to travel from California to Pennsylvania, I still needed more time alone to prepare myself for
meeting my new family.

The towns I passed through on the road to Lockhart were
surrounded by dense forests, conjuring up memories of my
trip through Pennsylvania with David years before when he
imagined a witches' coven in those very same woods. Yet in
the bright sunshine that day, they no longer seemed foreboding. The trees stood still and proud, providing a lush
backdrop to trailer homes and white houses with red-brick
chimneys.

Sometimes cornfields popped up in the middle of mead-
ows. The summer air was thick with moisture and mosqui-
toes. I stopped briefly just a few miles before Lockhart to
walk around the car. My muscles ached from apprehension
and sitting too long. When I got back in the car and started
the engine, Sarah woke up and began to cry.

"It's OK, honey," I said. "In a few minutes we'll be getting
out of the car and you can play with cousins you've never met
before. It will be fun."

I watched her from my rearview mirror as her eyes slowly closed and she drifted back to sleep. I checked my directions for the tenth time in five minutes and tried hard to breathe slowly.

A small sign informed me I was entering Lockhart. An auto-body shop, a garage, a post office and a rundown hotel lined the two-block center of town. Careful to veer left at the fork in the road past town, my eyes searched for the white house with the big red fence and the gray Oldsmobile parked in front that Sylvia had described.

I parked the car across the street and glanced at my face in the mirror, nervously pulling at my bangs so they would fall into place. Before I opened the car door, I looked toward the house and saw a side door opening and a man and woman rushing out. Leaving Sarah asleep in the car, I got out and walked across the large lawn to meet them.

"Even if it wasn't for your unfamiliar car, I would know it was you," the woman exclaimed. She put out her arms and hugged me.

"She looks like Helen, doesn't she, Mike?"

My uncle just stood there, hands in his pockets, appearing unsure of what to do.

I walked up and reached out to hug him. He was tall and had to bend over to reach me. I could feel his stiff frame. His hair was mostly gray, receding high over his tall forehead, and a blanket of gray stubble covered the bottom of his face. His nose was long, like Helen's, but he didn't seem to resemble either of us.

Sylvia was a small woman, with a short salt-and-pepper hairdo, and a sweet smile dominating her small, round face. She wore an apron over her shirt and pants.

Together we walked over to the car. I picked Sarah out of

her car seat and she looked up drowsily at the unfamiliar faces behind me and then buried her head in my shoulder. My uncle offered to carry our luggage to the house.

I followed Sylvia through the screen door and into the kitchen, where a neatly set table held a plate of cold cuts, a basket of bread and small bowls of salad.

"Sit down," said Sylvia, as she motioned toward the table. "We thought you two would probably be hungry after the long trip. Mike normally comes home late on Saturday nights, but he wanted to be here when you arrived."

Sylvia was the kind of person who filled up any possible moment of silence with words, and right then I appreciated that quality because my own nervousness made me shy and awkward.

I sat down and scanned the room for clues about these people's lives. Quaint knickknacks gave the kitchen a folksy feeling—appliques of Jack and Jill on the dishwasher, plaques of owls and tea kettles under the cabinets and a cookie jar shaped like a giant cupcake with a cherry on top. From outside the window, I could hear the occasional snapping sound of a bug killer.

Footsteps suddenly stampeded down the stairs and two children ran into the room.

"These are my grandchildren," said Sylvia. "Lisa and Matthew."

Lisa, a tall girl with tight brown curls and glasses, immediately gravitated toward Sarah as if she was a new doll. Sarah seemed to like the attention of an older child and, after lunch, went willingly with Lisa to play with some toys in the living room.

Matthew, whose hair was a dark blond, politely asked if he could play outside after finishing half of a sandwich.

During one of our phone calls a couple of months earlier, Sylvia explained that she and Mike had been taking care of eleven-year-old Lisa and seven-year-old Matthew for the past five years after their daughter, Patty, abandoned them. Their son, Chris, lived across the state with his wife and three daughters.

"Has Patty seen her children since she left them?" I asked.

"No, we don't even know where she is. She's called a few times and talked to Lisa." Sylvia sounded more angry than hurt.

"When someone turns their back on their children, what am I supposed to do, worship their name? The Bible says 'Thou shalt come out from under them.' That's what I've had to do. We've done our best to provide a home for Lisa and Matt. That's why Mike is on the road six days a week. He can't retire now, not with the responsibility we have."

Sylvia stood up and carried some dishes to the sink.

"You know Helen once called me and told me I stole Patty's kids. I said, 'Patty left those kids at a truck stop. She said she couldn't take care of them. Matt was only two years old. What was I supposed to do?' And then I hung up on her."

She turned the faucet on and started washing the dishes.

"Helen and Patty are made from the same mold," Mike chimed in. "They're exactly alike." He seemed sorry about it, but resigned.

"I tell you, Debbie, my mother-in-law, your grandmother Emma was a good woman but she ruined Helen and Patty," said Sylvia. "She took Patty over when she was a little girl and wouldn't let me have a say in it. She put those girls up on pedestals and let them do whatever they wanted. All because she lost a son to diphtheria when he was twelve. She

divorced her first husband and married Mike's dad before
Helen was born."

Sylvia never waited for a response, she just continued
from one subject to another, anxious to get out everything
that came into her mind.

"I don't have a lot of money and all that, but I have what
it takes to be happy. I might have a lot of problems but
they're not my problems, they're God's problems. You just do
what you have to do and you live the best you know how."

Sylvia showed me around the house as Mike dozed off
in an upholstered glider chair in the living room. The house
was dark with a lot of wood paneling and most of the blinds
were drawn across a few small windows. There was a rustic,
country feeling about the decorations. Fabric dolls with
orange yarn hair and others with fragile porcelain faces sat
on side tables in the small living room and upstairs bed-
rooms; plants and artificial flowers hung from macramé
holders.

Lisa was sitting with Sarah on an orange vinyl couch.
Above their heads were wood-framed pictures of Jesus at the
Last Supper and a young girl praying. On the fireplace mantel, photos of myself, Jake and Sarah were wedged between
framed pictures of their five grandchildren.

It was their way of saying there was a place for me in their
family and I was touched by it. I wanted so much to earn
their acceptance—to fit into their world, despite the differences between our lives, so they could connect with me in a
way they never could with Helen.

❦

The next day we took a walk to a nearby park. The streets
were unusually quiet except for the occasional sounds of chil-

dren playing in the distance. The homes were unassuming but not poor. While some appeared neglected because of peeling paint and cracked cement stairs, most were well cared for, with cheerful flower gardens and plaques above the front doors with the family's name.

As we walked through town, it was hard for me to avoid comparing it to the ornate apartment buildings and streets bustling with well-dressed shoppers where I grew up on Chicago's Gold Coast. I struggled with the myth I once read about in an adoption book—that adoption elevates a child from poverty to riches, from a lower class to an upper class. Was where I grew up really *better* than this? Helen would have thought so. Was she thinking about that when she arranged my adoption in a big city, I wondered, or did Chicago just provide the anonymity she needed?

At the park, a creek running through a ravine looked more like a river. Sarah kept reaching for butterflies gliding high above her head.

After Lisa and Matt took turns pushing Sarah on a swing, Mike pointed to a graveyard on a secluded hillside above the park. He asked me if I wanted to visit the graves of some of my ancestors.

I followed Mike as he walked toward the family plots. Along the way, I took quick glances at the gravestones we passed and saw that many of the people buried there were born in the 1800s. Small American flags and artificial flower arrangements decorated some of the graves.

The same names appeared repeatedly on a cluster of headstones in the center of the cemetery—Dunne, Schmidt, McIvers. With each one, Mike offered a brief history of the person and how he or she was related to the others. There was a great aunt who lived to ninety-nine and a cousin who died as a child. But without memories of my own, I found it difficult to connect the dots and visualize a family portrait.

While he spoke, I stared at the names and dates on the gray stones. I had wondered all these years where I came from and here I was—in a Christian cemetery in a backwoods town, far from all that I knew. I had come to see the place where my mother was raised and to try to figure out what she had run away from. Yet I was really groping for a way to connect myself to these people around me, dead and alive. As I smelled the fresh scent of pine trees, I searched my psyche for some primordial memory that would make it all seem familiar. But it wasn't.

That night, Sylvia took out old photo albums and family mementos. There were many pictures of my grandmother, whose face looked long and foreign to me, and my grandfather, who was tall and looked a lot like Mike.

"Did Helen get along with your parents?" I asked, looking at my uncle.

"My mother badgered her about becoming a teacher, but I don't think she ever wanted to," he said. "She adored my dad, though."

Mike hesitated for a moment, looking across the room at nothing in particular and then back at me.

"My mother and dad never told us they loved us," he said. "They just weren't that way."

"They weren't open people," Sylvia quickly added. "They kept everything very quiet."

"My dad was a heavy drinker," Mike recalled. "I remember one Christmas he came home drunk and smashed the

Christmas tree. Helen ran off crying and never liked Christmas again after that."

"Was he abusive to Helen?" I asked.

"My dad wouldn't abuse Helen," he said. "He adored her."

"What was it like between you and Helen while you were growing up?" I asked him.

"We weren't real close. I tried to be a good son, but Helen always came first. She did well in school, never had to struggle. But she was kind of odd. She refused to conform." I was impressed by the lack of bitterness in his voice. It was as though he was always throwing up his arms and silently saying, "That's the way it is."

"Helen used to come home to visit with these special health food drinks and yoga exercises she would do in the living room. She always had to be different," Sylvia said derisively. "She only came back a few times after her parents died to check on the land she inherited. She'd like us to buy it from her, but we don't have the money."

"She didn't like it here," said Mike. "She once wanted us to send Lisa to live with her in California so she could send her to private school. She said, 'Lisa's too bright for this place.' She even told Lisa, 'Don't waste your mind in Lockhart. You should get out of there.'"

I appreciated my aunt and uncle's willingness to discuss Helen, but couldn't help but think that they didn't know or weren't telling me the whole story. Helen's disdain for this small town must have arisen from years of feeling different and alienated from the people here and the simplicity of their lives. Perhaps she was frustrated by the lack of intellectual stimulation, or didn't get the kind of love she needed. She must have felt like I did in my adoptive family—an unwitting transplant unable to fit into the mold created for her. I wondered if she had ever found anywhere she felt like she belonged, or did she just find a way to disappear in a bigger world?

We looked through the photo albums and dozens of loose, yellowed pictures. Both Sylvia and Mike took turns explaining who the people in the pictures were, telling anecdotes about them. I tried to pay attention, but my mind kept wandering. I pondered the reasons why my aunt and uncle were opening up their lives to me. They certainly weren't doing it for Helen—they had to know she wouldn't be very happy about it. Maybe they just thought it was the right thing to do. After all, they were deeply religious people and Mike had so few relatives left. Most of his family was in the graveyard. Perhaps he believed that doing right by his niece was what his mother would have wanted him to do.

After sifting through many photos of unfamiliar faces, pictures of Helen appeared. Mostly in black and white, they showed her in all of her various incarnations: as a baby in her father's arms; a schoolgirl in a Peter Pan–collared dress with a bow in her hair; solemnly staring in full military uniform; an ingenue in black and pearls, smoking a cigarette and posing seductively for the camera; and sitting on the lawn with John D'Lorio when they visited Lockhart.

Sylvia pointed to a picture of Helen dressed as an angel with an aluminum halo taken when she was about three years old. "I can see your little girl's face in Helen, can't you?" she asked.

It was true; I could see a resemblance in the pictures of Helen as a child. But as an adult she seemed nothing like Sarah and me, particularly when I remembered the impervious expression on her face during our brief encounter in San Francisco.

I opened an envelope and inside, along with Helen's army dog tags on a silver chain, there was a photograph of a handsome man in military uniform.

"This must be the second lieutenant," I exclaimed. I explained how John had told me about an army officer Helen was involved with while she was enlisted.

"We knew him as a friend of Helen's," said Sylvia. "Even after Helen was gone, he used to come and visit your grandmother. Maybe he was trying to find out where Helen was."

"Do you remember his name?" I asked.

Sylvia looked at the picture again and then handed it to Mike. They both shook their heads.

"I just remember he was good-looking and Helen's mom was mad that she wasn't interested in him," said Sylvia.

I asked if I could keep the picture and Sylvia said I could keep any picture I wanted.

"Are you sure?" I asked.

"Listen, Helen just left them all here and I doubt she will be coming back or that she even wants them," Sylvia said. Mike remained quiet, with the same reticent look on his face he often had.

I carefully selected some photos of Helen, knowing that they were probably all I would ever have of my mother. I also took her dog tags and several pictures of my grandparents. As I was finishing, Sylvia came back into the room with a few pieces of costume jewelry and three small glass bowls.

"These belonged to your grandmother and I'm sure she would have wanted you to have them," she said. "If she had known about you before she died, she would have gone to the ends of the earth to find you."

"That's true," said Mike. "She loved little girls."

When I thanked them, my gratitude was genuine. Those few modest items had more value to me than any diamonds or expensive Irish crystal ever could. They were symbols that my aunt and uncle believed me and accepted me as their niece, even if Helen would not acknowledge her mother-hood. These were family heirlooms that had belonged to my grandmother, a woman I would never meet and whom I suddenly found myself mourning.

Over breakfast the next morning, the question of Helen's denials came up for the first time since I arrived.

"Mike, I think that after Debbie and Sarah leave, you should call Helen and get her to tell you the truth," said my aunt.

He didn't respond, instead looking nervously at both of us as through he knew he should say something but didn't know what.

"I probably should tell you a little more about my adoptive family," I offered. "The circumstances I was born into." I explained about Manny, his ties to organized crime, his murder. I told them about the way the adoption was arranged and the ten thousand dollars my mother told me they had paid Helen to get me.

"You come from a very different world than we do. We're just a little, small-town family," said Mike in a self-effacing way. "I don't have any reason to doubt you are who you say you are when you have the kind of papers you do. And you sure look like a Dunne."

He hesitated for a moment, pushing his plate away from him.

"I just don't know what to say to Helen. I don't know if she'll tell me the truth or whether I could even change her mind," he said. "She has a way of dominating you with her tongue. You have to be on your guard with her."

He was intimidated by her, I thought, afraid of what she would do if she found out he had invited me into his home. But what did Mike fear she could possibly do to retaliate? The only thing I could imagine was that she might stop talking to him altogether and pull away from the family forever.

"I can understand that you feel a sense of loyalty to Helen," I said.

"It's just that she's my sister," he said, holding back any visible emotion. "It's true, though. She doesn't call very often. Gosh, we have more of a relationship with you and your little girl now than we do with her."

"You're her daughter," Sylvia said with deliberate emphasis. "I feel it with all my heart, my soul, my body. I can tell by the way you move, the way you talk, the way you put words together. You're so similar to Helen."

I knew her words were meant to convince me that they really did believe my story. Yet I couldn't help but feel I still had to prove myself to my uncle—that somehow Helen's refusal to admit that she was my mother stirred within him an ambivalence he couldn't let go of despite all of my evidence.

My uncle left that morning, a day later than he was supposed to. We walked him to his truck, parked a few blocks away. He told me a bit about it: the kind of engine it had, how many people could comfortably fit into its sleeper compartment. He was fumbling for words.

He picked Sarah out of her stroller and placed her up in the driver's seat. The huge steering wheel dwarfed her tiny body and we all laughed.

I told him how much I appreciated how welcome they had made me feel.

"I wish we could do more . . . it's a tough situation," Mike said, shaking his head and staring at the ground. I could hear sadness in his voice.

He kissed Sarah on the cheek. I hugged him and we said good-bye.

⸎

That afternoon, we took a long walk to the next town. Lisa pushed Sarah's stroller along the dirt road, and Sylvia and I talked.

She told me about Pentecostalism, their revival meetings and how her faith gets her through the rough times. Helen, she said, is an atheist and that accounts for her strangeness.

"I know you were raised by a Jewish family. I'm just happy they weren't Catholic," she said. "We believe the Jews are the chosen people. They just took the wrong path."

I laughed to myself, thinking what Steve would say about that.

The road took an uphill turn, but a soft breeze kept us from getting too hot. I could hear the sounds of birds and crickets and little else. I was still amazed by the slow pace life took on away from the tumult and distractions of big cities. People here may be provincial and uninterested in the outside world, I thought, but at least they seem content.

The first building I saw when we came to the small village of Newton was a picture-book white church with a gold cross beneath its steeple. A few neatly kept houses were scattered along the surrounding blocks.

"Look, Grandma, there's Aunt Millie," said Lisa, pointing to an elderly woman on her hands and knees planting flowers in front of a small yellow house.

"Millie is ninety-two," said Sylvia. "She was married to Grandma Dunne's brother. She has lived here since 1922."

Millie looked up as we approached and waved.

"Hello, Millie," Sylvia shouted. We walked closer. "This is Debbie, she's visiting us."

Millie scrutinized me, the way I imagined all people from small towns looked upon strangers. After a few moments, she turned to Sylvia and said, "Whatever happened to Mike's sister?"

I could see the surprise in Sylvia's face. "She's living in California."

"So, who is this?" the woman asked.

"This is my niece," answered Sylvia.

"She's not your niece, she's Mike's niece," Millie declared.

"This is Debbie's daughter, Sarah," Sylvia said, changing the subject and bending down to touch Sarah's cheek. "Isn't she adorable?"

We asked Millie about her garden and her own daughter, and she didn't bring up my identity again.

After we left, I asked Sylvia why she didn't tell Millie the truth.

"It's hard for us to explain who you are because Helen doesn't admit it," said Sylvia. "After you leave, I'm going to talk to Mike about calling Helen and bringing this all out into the open. Maybe she'll tell us the truth if she knows we believe you."

When the time came for Sarah and me to leave, I said good-bye wondering if I would ever return. This much I knew: when Helen found out I had visited her hometown, she would have to realize that her lies were not enough to make me go away.

chapter FIFTEEN

In early August, a week after I returned from Pennsylvania, I received a phone call from my aunt.

"We called Helen and told her you visited us," she said outright. "We told her, 'She looks like you and she talks like you,' but it didn't matter. She denied she was your mother."

My questions poured out. "What exactly did she say?" I asked. I needed to know what words she used.

"You know, the Dunnes are very close-mouthed about everything," said Sylvia. "It was actually Mike who talked to her. He even went in the other room to make the call."

Since my uncle wasn't around to talk to me, I had to rely on Sylvia's translation.

"Helen seemed nervous. It seemed like something was bothering her," she said.

Of course something was bothering her, I thought; she had been caught.

"She seemed like she was scared," Sylvia continued. "And she's not a person to be scared about anything. Mike told her he had a lot of documents showing you are her daughter. The phone seemed to go dead a few times, she was so quiet."

"What did Mike say about my visit?" I asked.

"He told her about Sarah. He said, 'She's a cute little duffer.' Helen even asked him how old your children are. He told her and she made some comment like, 'Well, they're a couple of years apart.'

"The strangest thing was that Helen cried when she talked to Lisa. She told her, 'You were such a beautiful and intelligent young lady. I hope you stay that way.'"

I imagined that Helen must see herself in Lisa, a smart girl being raised in the hinterlands. She has a daughter and grandchildren of her own living just across the Bay, but she's more interested in a grandniece she barely knows, I thought.

"Helen's a real hard one to break. She wouldn't even take your phone number," Sylvia went on. "Mike told her, 'Even if she isn't your daughter, she's such a nice young lady, we wouldn't mind having her again. I did what I did for both of you. If you say you're not her mother, but you are, that's something you have to live with.'"

"Did Mike believe her?" I asked.

"I don't think so. But he's scared for her because she seems so frightened. He said there's something going on here that we don't know about."

Helen told her brother that she would be traveling on business to Washington, D.C., the following month and wanted to see them. I wondered if my visit had somehow provoked this rare impulse since it had been nine years since Helen was last in Lockhart, for her mother's funeral.

While I was anxious to hear every detail, I couldn't stop glancing at the clock; I was already late to pick up Jake at preschool. Before I hung up, Sylvia promised to have Mike call me.

As I drove to the school, I played the conversation back in my mind. Though I wasn't surprised by Helen's denials, I was still disappointed. I had hoped that once she realized I was serious enough to travel across the country to her hometown, she might back down and at least admit the truth to her own brother.

The following day, my uncle called me.

"I couldn't get any response from her," he said. "It's a tough situation. I do think she was affected by the conversation though."

No matter how hard I tried, I couldn't get him to tell me precisely what Helen had said. So, instead, I recounted what Sylvia had told me. It was quickly apparent that his version was not the same.

No, he said, Helen had not asked about my children's ages, he had volunteered them. No, she wasn't really scared or nervous, only "startled" when she found out I had been in Lockhart.

There was a certain detachment in Mike's voice. I could tell he was anxious to get off the phone. He was obviously uncomfortable, caught between Helen and me and not willing to take sides. Her lies cast a shadow that loomed larger than the facts.

That week I sent my aunt and uncle a flower vase and some photographs with a card thanking them for their hospitality. "Sarah and I had a wonderful time and felt so comfortable in your home," I wrote. "No matter what happens, I will always have fond memories of our time together."

Over the following weeks, I couldn't shake the idea that perhaps Helen *was* threatened during my adoption. Maybe she was too scared to admit the truth. If I could just learn more about my adoption, I might find out why.

For months, my adoptive mother had been promising to use her connections in Chicago to find out why all my records were missing. She offered to call some political types to see if she could get my court case opened. Despite my persistent reminders, though, she never made the calls. Her excuse was that she was too preoccupied with financial problems, but I also suspected she just wished the whole issue would go away.

Had my mother used those same political connections more than thirty years earlier to have my hospital file and adoption records destroyed? I knew that if I asked her this point-blank, she might get defensive and angry or, worst of all, refuse to help me at all.

My mother doesn't like to talk about serious issues at night because she often has a difficult time sleeping. So I called her very early one morning, over my first cup of coffee in the kitchen before anyone else in my family was awake, to take advantage of the two-hour time difference between California and Chicago. I repeated many of the same questions I had asked before. This time she told me about a lawyer she knew who helped to arrange the adoption. He was not the lawyer listed on my adoption papers, but the friend she had mentioned once before who drove with her the day she picked me up. The lawyer, Bill Erlich, had had some experience since he and his wife had adopted two children, so he offered to help my parents.

"The adoption lawyer told Bill there was a woman who had come to Chicago to have a baby," my mother said. "I don't know how she found him. He was a dumpy lawyer, not a high-class lawyer. The babies he found were called black-market babies. I later told the judge all of my fears and everything was done according to the law. We were more than generous with her. We paid all of her living expenses while she was in Chicago and the ten thousand dollars after you were born."

"Could Manny have told the lawyer to threaten her in any way?" I asked.

"I know he didn't," she said with absolute certainty. "Manny had a good side to him too. Anyway, Manny wasn't really involved with organized crime at the time you were born. He was still building and selling homes. Manny didn't threaten her; he didn't even know her. We didn't want anyone to know who we were, so the woman was never approached by anyone but the lawyer, and he would never have threatened her."

I could hear growing vexation in her voice, but I could also tell she was trying her hardest to choose the right words to put the matter to rest.

"Listen, Debbie. You weren't an accident of birth as far as this household is concerned. We went through a lot emotionally and financially to get you. You didn't just fall into our laps."

An accident of birth. The words reverberated in my head for a long time after I hung up. She may not have been trying to hurt me, but she did. Not even I had ever put it in such blunt terms. I went into the bathroom and cried hard but as silently as I could so I wouldn't wake my children up. I hadn't cried since the day I confronted Helen and, like then, it felt like my tears had been waiting a long time to burst out.

I didn't tell Steve about the call. I was beginning to realize that no one else could understand why I wasn't able to let this go and walk away—not my husband, not my mother. I could hardly explain it to myself. I only knew that I had to prove beyond a doubt that Helen was my mother, and I needed to understand why she would so adamantly deny it.

I suspected that Bill Erlich would tell me things that my mother was unwilling or unable to say herself. I found his number in Chicago easily enough and called him a few days later. He recognized my name right away, and I briefly conveyed my mother's version of the events.

"I didn't find the lawyer," he said immediately. "Your parents had heard that I was able to find babies through doctors for people who wanted to adopt. They asked me to find them a child. I handled it as a friend.

"You see, I was associated with doctors I played poker with. Women would go to these obstetricians and tell them they wanted to give up their babies for adoption. I got a call from a doctor—I don't remember which one—and he told me there was a baby due. I said if it's a little girl, let me know. The doctor wanted me to meet the mother, get some information, have her sign some papers. I can't remember exactly. We met at somebody's house, in an apartment building on the northwest side."

"What did she look like?" I asked.

"I picture her as a very lovely looking young lady. She was a very vivacious girl, a redhead if I'm not mistaken. A pretty girl, fairly tall."

Sure, I thought, why should he remember her out of the whole parade of unwed mothers he must have met at that time?

"Was her name Helen Dunne?"

"That's not the name I would think of," he said. "That name doesn't ring a bell."

His words alarmed me, even though I knew that more than three decades had passed since then and it was unlikely he could really remember very much.

"Anyway," he continued, "the doctor later called and said she had given birth to a baby girl and definitely wanted to give up the child. Somebody picked her up, maybe it was the doctor, and we met at a specific place. She was in a car, blocks away from the hospital. I went along with your parents to make sure they got the right baby. She got out of the car, we opened our window and she handed you over."

"Wasn't that kind of a strange way to handle an adoption?" I asked him.

"Ordinarily you would go through an agency," he said. "But in your case, a nonagency adoption, that was mostly how it was done."

I grasped for any additional details he could give me. Did she mention anything about my father?

"I have a funny recollection that your father was a sailor. There was something about the military. I don't think he was in a position to get married."

Fireworks went off in my mind. I remembered the second lieutenant Helen was involved with in the army. I thought of the picture of the soldier my aunt and uncle had given me.

While my mind raced, Bill talked about his own son's adoption and how the two of them rarely speak anymore. I couldn't resist asking him whether it was true that my birth mother had smiled as she handed me through the car window.

"She was happy to know her baby would be given to people who would give her a good home." It was a perfunctory phrase, one that could be used on any adoption brochure. But then, as if a clearer image had come to him, he said with conviction:

"She was very happy to part with you."

Helen's birthday came on a day in early September. She was turning fifty-eight. I knew that because the little information contained on my birth certificate had long been burned into my memory. It made me sad to picture her spending the day alone. What would it have been like for us to celebrate together? The day filled me with a sense of lost opportunity and time slipping away.

While I knew I couldn't call her, I decided to call my aunt and uncle to find out if Helen was still planning to visit them that month. To no one's surprise, I was told she had canceled the trip.

"We're disgusted with her," said Sylvia. "She's just not the type of person who is going to do the right thing."

Sylvia explained how Helen had told them a week earlier that her company canceled the trip because of the recession. Maybe she would come for Christmas, she said.

"She backed out for her own reasons. She's too scared to come," said Sylvia. "I think she may suspect we're setting her up, that you might be here waiting when she arrived. She has to come sometime, though, she can't hide from us all her life.

"I tried to talk to her about you but it's like beating my head against the wall. I came right out and asked her if you were her daughter and she said it wasn't true. I mentioned that you had been here and she said, 'I've been told by Mike.'

"I said to her, 'All I'm asking is, am I entertaining someone who is a part of you or not?' She said nothing. I went on, 'This girl has a good life. She doesn't want any money. She doesn't need your love. She just wants you to say you are her mother.'

"'You can tell her no,' is what she said."

A film loop played in my mind's eye. I am speeding down a road, in a hurry to get somewhere, and the red warning lights of a railroad crossing begin flashing before me. The gates come down to block my way and a train darts in front of me. I anxiously wait for the train to end and the railway arms to rise, but it just keeps coming in an unbroken line and I am trapped in one place.

"I wished Helen a happy birthday," Sylvia continued.

"'I don't think about my birthday,' she said. 'I don't want to think about my age.'"

Helen seemed different during the conversation, Sylvia said. She was unusually concerned about her brother's financial problems and expressed interest in their grandchildren.

"She wanted to know whether they looked like her," said Sylvia.

"I dearly love Lisa and I think I would love the others as much, don't you?" Helen said, according to my aunt's account.

I asked Sylvia if I could say hello to my uncle. After a few minutes, she returned to the phone. "He said he doesn't know what else to say to you."

"Doesn't he believe me anymore?" I asked, trying to hide my hurt and frustration.

"Listen, Mike cares about you. We both do. You're here in our lives, and we've accepted you as our niece. You're welcome any time you want to come through our door. We feel bad about what Helen has done, but we're happy to have gained a niece. There's no difference between her being Mike's sister and your being his niece; the same blood flows through your veins. I adore you and I'll do anything in my power to make her your mother. She thinks she can keep this covered up, but it's not covered up anymore. She has to face the truth sometime, even if it's more than she can handle.

"The most important thing to us now is to make you happy," said Sylvia, promising to stay in touch.

⸙

Two months went by without my hearing from Sylvia or Mike again. My conversations with my aunt had started to bring a picture—of me, of Helen—into focus. It was as if I were in a darkroom, peering at the photographic paper in the tray of solution, just beginning to be able to see a vague image emerge from shadows and outlines. But now that image had suddenly frozen again and the picture remained an indistinguishable blur.

Their silence, no matter how hard I tried to justify it, felt like rejection. Maybe it was unfair of me to expect them to make up for the acceptance Helen denied me.

Finally, one day in November, I could no longer resist the temptation to pick up the phone. Right away, I admitted to Sylvia that I was disappointed about not hearing from them.

"Oh, I've been so bound up with everything," she said. "I have a lot of problems."

As she explained her recent estrangement from her son and repeated her ongoing problems with her wayward daughter, I began to suspect that their God-fearing, small-town lives might be more complicated than I imagined.

"I told Mike, 'I don't have a daughter, I've lost a son, but at least I have Debbie,'" she said. "You've been on my mind for the past three days terribly bad, but I feel funny because I don't want you to feel that I'm pushing myself on you. I just have to be sure I don't hurt you. I don't live the same lifestyle you do. We're worlds apart. I fell in love with you when you were here. You were interesting, you were sweet. But I don't feel like you fit in with me. You came from a big world that I did not. I live in a different type of world."

Until then, I'd assumed I must have appeared to them like a hapless orphan looking for a home; it didn't occur to me that they might be intimidated by my big-city background.

"Even my son told me, 'Mom, she must be Helen's daughter or she wouldn't have anything to do with us,'" Sylvia said.

"After my son called, I figured the Lord was telling me this was the time for me to call you. I haven't done my part and maybe I was wrong. I'm just having a hard time with all this. I'm trying to find answers. I just think it's time for Helen to make this right—to tell the truth so the rest of us can get on with our lives and become a family."

chapter SIXTEEN

If Helen had lived in Texas or Kansas, it might have been easier to put her out of my mind. But with only twenty miles separating us, forgetting about her was a much bigger challenge. There were moments when I would look over my shoulder in the grocery store or peer into the rearview mirror as I drove and imagine her watching me, curious but afraid to come too close. With the irrationality of unrequited love, I imagined that she was only pretending not to love me for some mysterious reason I did not yet know.

But if not my heart, then my mind was slowly accepting that Helen was not going to change. If I couldn't have a relationship with her, I would find other ways to learn everything I could about her. Maybe, along the way, I would come to understand her actions.

Our annual Thanksgiving visit to Steve's family in New York gave me the chance to meet John D'Lorio, the person who had the most intimate connection to Helen in the years after I was born.

I took the bus to Manhattan from my in-laws' house in Westchester County the day after Thanksgiving. The bus whizzed down the highway past Yankee Stadium and wound its way through the rundown streets of Harlem before gliding by the sleek high-rises on Fifth Avenue and the lush borders of Central Park. Soon the bus was chugging by throngs of pre-Christmas shoppers in front of Bloomingdale's, Saks Fifth Avenue and scores of designer boutiques. I kept scanning the signs on each corner, being careful not to miss 37th Street, where John lived.

I got off the bus and headed west. Industrial warehouses with smashed-out windows and hulking apartment buildings blocked the late-afternoon sun and created a long gray tunnel of grimy concrete. Fresh scrawls of graffiti, like angry afterthoughts, contributed the street's only color.

This was Hell's Kitchen, John had told me.

I found his name on the pad outside the front door of his building, the best-kept on the block, and pushed the button. Immediately he buzzed me in and I pushed open the heavy door. The elevator, more like an industrial lift, lurched its way up to the sixth floor. I nervously brushed my hair and put on some lipstick before the elevator came to an abrupt halt.

John was waiting for me at the end of a long hallway painted glossy gray. He was tall and very thin, with a salt-and-pepper beard and a kind smile. As I approached him, he gave out a small laugh that broke through the awkwardness of finally meeting in person. I stood on my toes to give him a hug.

"Come in," he said.

The apartment was one large room that looked more like an artist's studio. Rows of shelves, filled with clay sculptures of naked men and women, climbed all the way up to the high ceiling. Several easels containing anatomical drawings were scattered about the floor. All of the room's light came from

huge windows lining the far side of the apartment and overlooking the Manhattan skyline.

John led me over to a small kitchen in the corner and we
sat down on tall wooden stools. He offered me coffee and a
cigarette.

I couldn't help asking him if he noticed a resemblance
between Helen and I.

"No," he said and then hesitated. "Well, yes, I guess there
is . . . but you're much prettier."

Knowing how attracted John had been to Helen, I knew
he was trying to be nice.

"She was always so regal," he recalled with a strange
combination of admiration and ridicule. "She carried herself
almost like royalty. She'd love to hear that." He laughed.

I told him about my trip to Pennsylvania and how my
aunt and uncle had confronted Helen about it afterward. He
listened intently, never taking his eyes off of me except to put
out his cigarette in the ashtray.

"Why is she doing this?" I asked him, knowing he could
not say for sure but must have a better insight than anyone
else.

"She's doing this because she's spent more than thirty
years forcing it out of her mind and pretending it never happened," he said. "Now reality is coming back in and her
whole identity is being threatened here. It's not an attack on
you, it's an attack on the event that she wishes had never
happened. You're bringing it all back.

"But from everything you say about her conversation
with her brother, it sounds like this whole thing is getting to
her," he continued. "Maybe the layers of repression and covering up are cracking open. There's probably a lot more layers to go though. It could take a very long time."

I thought of the layers of an onion, how stripping them away burns your eyes and makes you cry. Most people describe onions as sweet, but their taste has always seemed to me more complex and harder to describe than that.

I opened my backpack and pulled out some papers I brought along to show John. The mysterious postcard, the letter Helen wrote to my parents, the photograph of the nameless lieutenant. Slowly and silently, he looked them over.

"I figure that the only way I have the wrong person is if someone else used her identity," I said.

"No, this is her signature," he said with certainty, holding up the letter. "It's absolutely, totally, completely her style of writing. It's even the same paper she used to use, smaller than regular size. I have no doubt whatsoever that she wrote this."

For the first time, I no longer doubted it myself.

"How strange, though, that she constantly refers to you as 'my child,'" he continued. "She was always concerned with appearances, outwardly looking good. That's one reason she would have written 'May God Bless You' even if she didn't believe in it."

I thought about how similar that made Helen to my adoptive mother—sacrificing everything for appearances.

"But this is really bizarre," he said, now staring at the postcard. "For one thing, it's definitely not her handwriting. And by 1986, Matisse would definitely not be an artist she would have any interest in."

We speculated for a while about the postcard. Could it have been from someone she knew in the army? The person who helped her to arrange my adoption? As always, there were no easy answers.

"I hope it's all right with you," John said. "I talked to a friend of mine in California who still has contact with Helen. I made him promise not to say anything to her. He knows she's kind of volatile, and he knows how much I don't want to have any contact with her.

"His name is Paul Solia. We met him during our Ayn Rand days in the early '60s. He's the only one I know who is still in touch with her. I told him your story and he was stunned. He wondered why she had never said anything to him about it."

"Is he willing to talk to me?" I asked.

"He is. He told me, 'I realize Debbie might be hesitant to call me. Try to assure her that I am in complete agreement with what she is trying to do.'

"But I should warn you, this is a guy no one really trusts. He was born in Lebanon, a Jew who grew up in the Arab world. He went to private French school, but was always picked on as a child and learned to stick up for himself with his mind and his words. He's good at figuring out angles to things. He's legally oriented and somewhat of a wheeler-dealer. I think Helen has always seen him as someone who knew how to handle problems."

"Does that mean I can't trust him?"

"I think you can. He's always been honest with me. He's very sympathetic to your situation, and he has nothing to gain from telling her. When I met Paul, he was studying philosophy at NYU. I was swept off my feet by this guy. Everyone sort of looked up to him, especially Helen. What we all had in common was our devotion to the philosophy of Ayn Rand—it appealed directly to people like us who didn't feel like we fit in. Everybody I know from that time has grown away from objectivism over the years, except Paul."

John wrote down Paul's number and I took the paper, folded it and pushed it to the bottom of my backpack. I wasn't sure when or if I would call him.

We talked for another hour, touching on other subjects but always returning to Helen. Ideas came from John with speed and intensity. I was eager to find out everything he could tell me about Helen, but I was also drawn to his intellectual fervor, tempered by what seemed like a heavy heart.

He told me more about being shipped off to Washington by the army in 1962 and the painful weeks he waited for Helen while she was driving cross-country with her ex-boyfriend, the con artist Frank Harlett.

I imagined Helen and Frank in an old Pontiac, cruising down the interstate and looking for trouble. I could see them eating meals in roadside dives and then sneaking off without paying the bills. Maybe, for old times' sake, they detoured to the racetracks to make a few fast bucks on the horses. It was hard to believe she didn't cheat on John during that trip, and John obviously wondered about the same thing.

"The whole time I was thinking, how can she pretend to be on the straight and honest track, looking for people on the level, and still be connected to a guy like him?"

"With my luck, it'll probably turn out he was my father," I said sarcastically, though I knew it could be true.

"It's hard to know. But I do believe it was either Frank or the lieutenant." John poured himself another cup of coffee. I watched him furrowing his brow, and could tell he was remembering at a furious pace.

"Helen liked to play the devil's advocate," he went on. "She was so provocative in conversations. She would create an argument, step by step, very logically. But if she made a mistake in her logic she would continue even if she reached an erroneous or irrational conclusion. Like when she wanted to buy land in Arizona because Pat Boone was touting it. When we went to see it, it turned out to be barren desert. She bought more anyway."

"That's just stubborn," I said, shaking my head. "That may be the only thing she and I have in common."

"You are so different," he said, laughing at the thought. "You seem so open. If this weren't so personal, she'd like your direct style. That's what she was attracted to in me, I think. But she's another story. She seems to constantly be throwing sand in people's eyes. She likes to disorient people, throw them off track. Sounds like she's still doing it."

Finally I had to leave to catch the bus back. John promised to do anything he could to help me. His friendship, I told him, had been the best thing to come out of my sordid search up to that point.

⌘

By the time I returned to Yonkers, my children were asleep. My mother-in-law was anxious to hear about my meeting with John. Steve, though, lost interest in the story within minutes and returned to watching TV.

The following day, I dug out the rumpled piece of paper with Paul's phone number on it. I sat down in my mother-in-law's small '50s-era kitchen on a yellow vinyl swivel chair on which my children liked to spin around in circles. I had the same uneasiness weighing down on my chest that I got whenever I took my search in a new direction. I jotted down a few questions in case I got too nervous to remember them and then dialed the number.

"Hello," the voice on the other end of the line said. I stuttered a bit, but finally got the words out: "Hi, this is

Debbie Holtz. I think John D'Lorio may have mentioned me."

"Oh, yes," he said. "I'm glad you called. I've thought a lot about this since John told me. Your story is really beyond belief." He had a strong accent that sounded Middle Eastern with a flourish of French.

He launched right in. "Helen is a very strange person. I've known her for more than thirty years, and I'm not surprised that she didn't tell me about this. I know nothing of her private life. We have a great respect for each other's intellect. We may go as long as six months without speaking to each other, but then I feel the need for the stimulation of her intellectual brilliance. She thinks in an esoteric, abstract fashion and can discuss philosophy for hours. She can be fascinating, but after an hour I can get tired of her. The truth is, our relationship is based on favors we do for each other and out of absolute loneliness. There's no closeness or affection between us. She's extremely cold."

Paul spoke with his own air of intellectual superiority. At first he seemed arrogant, but then his very eccentricity made him interesting. He rarely paused for a response from me, and soon I found I hardly needed to ask him any questions because he was bound to answer them on his own.

"John may have told you that we all met at a lecture series at the Metropolitan Museum of Art in 1961. We are all children of the generation of Ayn Rand and *Atlas Shrugged*. We grew up around that movement. Our relationship wouldn't have continued if we hadn't been drawn to the same philosophy. Helen and John have drifted away from it, but it's still meaningful to me. Moral positions were very, very important. One's career or job was an important value to the movement. A person had to find a purpose. But for Helen it was always,

'I have no special passion. I don't like my job. I don't know how to get a purpose.' It bothered her a great deal.

"She doesn't really care about anything in particular. For example, I have a child out of wedlock myself. I wanted to avoid just what is happening to you. Helen has never understood my efforts to care for my daughter and to try to gain custody of her. She says, 'I don't understand those family connections. They are accidental attachments that don't mean anything to me.'"

"But the way I see it," I said, "here is a woman who is alone in San Francisco. She finds that she has a daughter and two grandchildren living only twenty-five minutes away. I would think that would bring some happiness into her life."

"This woman would laugh out loud if she heard you," said Paul with absolute assuredness. "She is so far away from that kind of person, a person who would enjoy being involved in holidays and doting over grandchildren. Helen hates the way society forces you to have obligations toward relatives, neighbors, friends. All those links that people see as normal literally make her arch her back like a cat.

"Once I took her to see Elia Kazan's movie *America, America*. She said, 'Now, I understand a lot better the meaning of family to you.' But she didn't say it in a nice way. It was more like I was driven by long-established rules of patriarchy and tradition. She looks at people like us with contempt, bemused that family ties mean something to us."

"I guess that explains her lack of feelings for me," I said.

"It's almost as if an element in her mind is missing," Paul went on. "You and I take Thanksgiving and family get-togethers for granted. They're meaningless to her. She talks about her brother in a detached, clinical manner. Yet she was deeply in love with John and deeply hurt by the divorce. She loved John almost like an artist loves his work. She saw in him an integration of purpose and character. I don't think she has ever met anyone of that stature since. I'm sure there have been other men in her life, but nothing really serious."

I was surprised by the intensity with which Paul described that part of Helen's life. While I didn't doubt that she loved John, nothing I'd heard until now had made her seem capable of great passion.

"But in the past ten years, she has never asked about him," Paul continued. "When I brought him up once, she said, 'I wasn't very good at saving a relationship. I didn't know what to do to make a marriage work,' in a little wistful voice, as though she was saying 'I forgot to wash my hands today.'"

"Does she have any other friends but you?" I asked.

"No, I don't think so. It's very difficult for her to meet people. She used to drink because she didn't want to feel unhappiness about the world. She felt like a stranger in society."

I asked him whether he thought her childhood had anything to do with her alienation.

"She's ashamed of her origins, but doesn't want to admit the shame," he explained. "For example, she has a distinctive style of speech, a strange way of pronouncing words like treasure and pleasure," he said, imitating her speech with words that sounded more like "traysure" and "playsure."

"I once teased her about it and she was incredibly insulted. She said sarcastically, 'I'm sorry I don't come from the sophisticated world that you do.' You see, Helen was born in rural America where there was absolutely no appreciation for her superior intelligence. So she must have been terribly frustrated as a child and gave up very early on communicating with the human race. *Now* she has an incredible ability for cutting sarcasm. She's a master of it. But there was never any indication of a particular event in her life history that would explain her behavior toward you. She is secretive, open intellectually but not journalistically you might say. She will not tell you the events of her life. You don't even think of asking her those things.

"I accepted her the way she was because she was so superlatively intelligent," he said. "She has always maintained an incredible sense of perfection. She has committed herself to moral rectitude, honesty and truth. That's why the adoption, and lying to you about it, is such a contradiction. It seems she just wants to blot it out of existence. It would make sense she would react this way if she doesn't want to admit it to herself. The only explanation I can think of is that you would literally age her overnight."

"I would age her?" I asked. "What does that mean? She knows how old she is."

"This is a woman who went to Europe to get special medication to rejuvenate her skin fifteen years ago. She's very conscious of what she eats, she drinks health shakes and takes strenuous walks everyday. Her fascination with youth is so strong, it's an obsession. She won't even let me mention how long I've known her in public. I look at her after all these years and it's like *The Picture of Dorian Gray*. She is someone who has fooled time. She looks forty."

"Don't you think it has more to do with her not wanting to have a child?"

"She certainly made statements that she never wanted children, that's true," he conceded. "She considers her cats like her babies. When I show her a picture of my child, she says, 'I can't make the usual comments. I can't do what people usually do, like ogle over baby pictures.'"

"Could giving up a baby have done that to her?" I asked.

"It could easily have not happened to her. It wouldn't have made a difference. She hears me out about my emotional feelings, but won't share hers. I suspect she views having a baby as something society forced her to go through. If she had her druthers, she would have had an abortion."

Finally someone had brought up the one thing I hadn't wanted to think about.

"But she was probably terrified of abortion, legally and medically," Paul continued. "You have no idea how dangerous it was then."

Had she considered and rejected the possibility of abortion? All I knew was that she hadn't taken that road, and what I was really interested in were the other choices she made.

We talked instead about what Helen did after splitting from John.

"She continued to live in New York in this railroad flat on Spring Street," said Paul. "It was a hole in the wall, a tenement. She lived there because she doesn't care. Cockroaches in the kitchen are inconsequential to her. Chores like cleaning she hates with a passion. Simple luxuries are meaningless to her. She could not value a place enough to make any effort to own it. When she grew tired of New York, she lived with me and another person in Los Angeles. After a while, her cat became incontinent and we made comments, so she moved out.

"Her appearance is such a contrast. Her apartment could be an absolute mess but when she went to work she looked like she walked out of *Vogue*. She doesn't go out very much though. She lives frugally and saves so she doesn't have to work. She's very much a homebody. She's a soap opera watcher like you wouldn't believe. She likes the simplicity of their values; the Harlequin romance of it is an attraction to her. Perhaps she enjoys it vicariously."

I nearly laughed out loud. Not because an intellectual like Helen would indulge in such mindless entertainment, but because I secretly loved to do the same thing.

"For a long time, Helen lived without working," he continued. "She had acquired gold—heavy jewelry and ingots— and lived on it for a few years while the price of gold was up. You'd think she would have traveled when she sold all of her gold, but instead she sat home and watched soap operas. When she does have a job, she works hard, but only out of necessity. She hates the routine of work, reporting to authority. It's nothing more to her than a matter of survival, something you have to do to pay the bills."

"Did she ever mention a guy she once knew, Frank Harlett, a con artist she was involved with before John? He lived in Los Angeles during the time you and Helen did."

"She did acknowledge to me early on that there had been a con man in her life who would trick people out of things. I think she told me about it because she knew I was sometimes a trickster. I remember her saying that he and I had similar qualities, so we would have liked each other. But that was shortly after we met, and it was clear that he was no longer part of the new Helen. We were all becoming born again with the philosophy of objectivism. So there was no need to discuss that chapter of her life. It was just whited out, in the past, no longer important."

"Could that be what she is trying to hide by not telling me the truth?" I asked.

"I don't think that is what she is protecting. She gave herself absolution many years ago. She owns no guilt. She couldn't care less what people think of her. Yes, she dresses fashionably, but the values of common courtesy are meaningless, unnecessary. For her, they just open the door to social hypocrisies. She's definitely a feminist at heart, although not militant. Betty Friedan's book *The Feminine Mystique*—she could have written it herself."

For the first time in the conversation, Paul paused. When he spoke again, his tone had changed from that of a social commentator certain of everything he said to someone exploring more sensitive territory.

"There must be some really deep reason in her mind for lying. Admitting to having a child might make her life a lie or would make her have to expose a major flaw. For you, it must be a terrible sense of not being wanted. It's very sad you're not receiving any acknowledgment. All these years she has pretended you never even happened."

Again he hesitated and his voice softened further.

"I think it's rotten of her to deny your identity. She doesn't know how to deal with the problem you're presenting, so she is running in blind terror. If she knew I was contemplating this, or if I confronted her with it, she would probably tell me the same thing—that this is all a horrendous lie."

We were both silent for a moment. Finally he said, "In spite of all I know of her, it's hard to see how she can lie in bed knowing you exist and deny it."

His voice echoed a frustration familiar to me, one that comes from expecting everyone's conscience to speak the same language.

chapter *SEVENTEEN*

I kept the pictures of Helen I was given by my aunt and uncle in a plastic bag from the Art Institute of Chicago. It sat on a bookshelf in the living room, atop piles of photos of my own children that I hadn't yet found the time to organize into neat albums with labels giving them their time and place.

Each time I took out and opened the bag, I hoped to find something I might not have seen before that would connect me in some way to the faces of these strangers. There was my grandmother, Emma Dunne, with her long face and lavender-gray hair, smiling behind her large square glasses. My grandfather, an older version of Uncle Mike, stood proudly in front of a two-toned 1950s-era Dodge. My great-grandmother, Rose McIvers, sat on a chair in front of a towering elm tree looking frail but alert. Dozens of other photos captured the many faces of Helen—from toddler to army private to twenty-something seductress.

I would study the pictures and struggle to fit myself into them, hoping to feel some memory trace, some deeply imprinted familiarity. But no matter how hard I tried, I could have been anyone looking at someone else's family pictures.

A psychologist I heard speak at an adoption seminar said the child's memory of his or her birth mother is always there, stored in different parts of the body. Shortly after the seminar, someone gave me a paper the psychologist had written about her own experiences as an adoptive mother. She described her daughter's separation from her birth mother as a primal wound that took years of therapy to heal. According to her, some adopted children spend much of their lives testing people's love, trying to provoke the very rejection they most fear. In many cases, adoptees refuse to make emotional connections for fear of losing them and they often flee relationships before they can be abandoned themselves.

Reading this, I felt like you do in one of those dreams where you find yourself out in public, naked and exposed. It was as if the author had been spying on me my entire life, seeing my secrets in a way no one else ever had.

One day as I sat looking at the photographs, I remembered something the psychologist had said about the gestures of the birth mother being familiar to an adoptee even forty years later because of the forty weeks spent inside her womb. I opened a pink photo album full of faded pictures of Helen's early years. Inside there were a few snapshots of her at about four, standing in a pasture, tightly embracing a baby doll with both arms close to her chest. She had a pageboy haircut identical to the one I've seen in photos of myself at about the same age.

A very different series of black and white photos showed Helen, probably in her early twenties, in a black sweater and a choker of giant fake white pearls, her face framed by short, dark hair that flipped up around her ears. In some of the pictures she was smoking with a far-off gaze, yet you could tell she was posing for the camera. In others, she was sitting on a couch, staring straight at the photographer with a sultry expression.

Accompanying these pictures of Helen was one of a man holding a camera. The photo was so out of focus that you could tell the man was caught moving or that the person who took it didn't know what she was doing. He appeared older than Helen; his hair was thick and graying and he had ears that were big and stood away from his head like mine do. Otherwise, I couldn't make out anything specific about his features except that he seemed serious, intent upon what he was doing with his camera.

I figured the photo was probably of Frank Harlett, but I couldn't be sure.

During a trip to Chicago for Christmas, I brought the pictures of Helen to show to my adoptive mother. There was one particular photo in the collection that finally triggered my adoptive mother's memory. It showed Helen sitting on the bank of a lake in a red-plaid pants suit. The sun behind her brought out a red sheen in her brunette hair and her porcelain complexion reflected the light. She looked purposefully pensive with her head thrown back and her hazel eyes staring skyward. Though she was consciously posing for the shot, she looked prettier than she did in any other picture I had seen.

"That's her, that's the woman I remember," my mother said when she saw it. "I could never forget that face."

Her words erased any remaining uncertainty that Helen was the same person who handed me through a car window thirty-three years earlier. But just knowing that wasn't enough. There were blank spaces I still needed to fill.

My newest hope lay with the presiding judge of the circuit court of Cook County in Chicago. I had written to him explaining that while I already had identifying information about my birth mother, all the documents about my biological background had been lost in a fire. I requested his permission to have my adoption file opened for medical and personal reasons. In a tersely written letter with no explanation, he refused.

During my visit to Chicago, I found myself outside of the County Office of Supportive Services. Though the story about a fire destroying all of the birth records between 1953 and 1960 had been confirmed by the Adoptees Liberty Movement Association, I wasn't entirely convinced.

I entered the office and asked to talk to a supervisor. After a few minutes, a woman, neatly dressed in a suit, came out and ushered me into her office. I told her I needed to see the records of my biological background, documents that adoptees all over the country were receiving by the truckload.

"Yes, that fire," the woman said, sounding slightly embarrassed. She avoided my gaze for a moment and I knew something was up.

"This may be difficult for you to hear, but I'm afraid that story has been used as a kind of ruse. You see, there was some mismanagement that went on during those years. In some cases, the files were lost while being moved to the warehouse and there may also have been some unfortunate instances of people stealing records."

I rushed back to my parents' apartment building, stormed in the door, and raced from room to room until I found my mother.

"Did you have my birth records taken from the social

service agency like you had my birth certificate taken out of my court file?" I said angrily.

"What are you talking about?" she asked with some exasperation.

I repeated the story the woman had told me.

My mother seemed nervous. She was no longer looking at me as she stuffed some papers back into her address book.

"I really don't remember," she answered. "It's possible, but it was so long ago. I just can't say for sure."

❧

For months, I consumed books about Ayn Rand. I wanted to understand what it was about her ideas that so attracted Helen.

John said Rand was particularly popular with college students who found positive and uplifting answers in her writings. Her books like *The Fountainhead* and *Atlas Shrugged* extolled individualism and capitalism, but that wasn't enough to explain Helen's allegiance to the woman.

Biographies of Rand told me more about her as a person. Rand's intellect, it seemed, was the only side of herself she was willing to show to the world and, with each passing year, she grew more alienated from her emotions. Her life was ruled by cold rationality; ideas were all that mattered. Even the characters in her novels were emotionally remote. Their conversations, like those between Helen and Paul, were philosophical debates that lacked any emotional intimacy.

Rand believed that living for your own self-interest was the highest moral purpose. This was a woman whose most famous essay is titled "The Virtue of Selfishness."

While protective of the professional lives of her inner circle of followers, there was little softness or affection in her relationships. Like Helen, Rand was able to obliterate her need for emotional closeness and her life grew steadily more reclusive.

What struck me the most was how amazingly indifferent Rand was to the idea of family. She had no sympathy whatsoever for ties of blood. "One is simply born into a family, therefore it's of no real significance," she would say. "Accidental attachments" was how Helen described her own family members, parroting Rand. I fit into that category, I thought, along with being "an accident of birth."

I wondered to what extent Helen had adopted Rand's views or whether she was drawn to her because she already shared the same beliefs. What kind of pain would sear a woman's soul so that it stripped her of all maternal instincts?

The two women's backgrounds were very different. Rand grew up in a well-off Jewish family in revolutionary Russia and, as a young woman, fled the onslaught of communism. Sure, Helen had escaped her own kind of tyranny in small-town Pennsylvania, but it didn't seem nearly as dramatic. From what I had learned about Helen's childhood, though, there were similarities. Like her, Rand adored her father who, in turn, admired her intellectual qualities.

Rand worked hard to find success in America and was pathologically aggressive about getting what she wanted. Helen, however, appeared to have no such drive to succeed. While Rand's work obviously replaced any needs she may have had for children or emotional bonds, I couldn't figure out what filled the same void in Helen's life.

Helen may have imitated Rand in escaping the messy emotions of life by dealing only in philosophical abstractions, but she was unlike the kind of characters Rand worshiped in life or wrote about in her novels—men and women who devoted their lives to their work through incredible feats of self-discipline.

In one biography of Rand written by Barbara Brandon, a disillusioned follower whose husband carried on an affair with the novelist, the hero of *Atlas Shrugged* is shown to have serious flaws: "Despite his epic grandeur of intellect and imagination, he is, in the end, a shadowy unknowable abstraction."

Among Helen's pictures was one of her sitting on a beach in a black swimsuit next to a woman with a shy and withdrawn expression. I scanned other pictures to find the woman again. There was one shot of Helen in college with several other girls sitting on the grass in the middle of campus. It was difficult to tell, but none of them appeared to be the same woman. Another photo of Helen at a restaurant with another group of women was more promising but no matter how hard I studied the faces, I couldn't be sure the woman was there. Then I came across a formal portrait of a man and a woman in army uniform. There was no mistaking that this woman was the same as the one in the beach picture. On the back of the portrait in neat cursive handwriting was written: *Sgt. Luke and Private Maureen Foster.*

Knowing that the pictures were probably taken during Helen's stint in the army between 1954 and 1956, only a few years before I was born, I decided to see if I could locate Maureen Foster. I figured there had to be something she could tell me about Helen that would help me piece together what happened to her between then and the time she became pregnant.

Finding someone's phone number was not as easy then as it would be only a few years later with the Internet. I went to the library and scanned telephone directories from all over the country. I started with Chicago, found a few M. Fosters, wrote them down, and went on to New York, Los Angeles and Michigan until my eyes burned and I couldn't look any longer. When I got home, I started making calls. In every case, either the person's name was not Maureen or the number was wrong. I pinned my hopes on one phone number in Chicago, hoping this M. Foster was the one who might have helped Helen through her pregnancy. Helen must have shared her secret with someone, I told myself. I spent weeks repeatedly dialing the number, but no one ever answered.

A short time later, I heard that many adoptees were using a nationwide database of phone listings that could be found on computers in some big libraries. I was told one of the best ones was located at the library in Redwood City, about thirty miles from my home, so I drove there one morning. With help from a librarian, I printed out all of the Fosters whose first names began with an L or M. There, in the middle of the list, were Luke and Maureen Foster in Colorado Springs. I was amazed that, so many years later, they were still together.

I rushed to the library's pay phone and just stared at the receiver for a few minutes, figuring out what I would say. Finally I dialed the number and asked for Maureen Foster.

"Yes, this is Maureen."

"Hello, you don't know me, but my name is Debbie Holtz and I am Helen Dunne's daughter. I was wondering if you remember her? I believe you may have been in the army with her, perhaps at Fort Monmouth in New Jersey?"

"No, I was never at Fort Monmouth," she said carefully.

"Were you ever in the army?" I asked.

"Who did you say you were?" she asked.

I decided to take a chance and tell her I was adopted. Maybe she would have some sympathy if I told her about finding Helen after so many years, and the reaction I had received.

"I have two small children and I am really just looking for important medical history," I said.

"What did she tell you?" Maureen asked.

"She said I had the wrong person, although I know for sure that she is my birth mother. Do you have any idea why she would lie?"

"I don't know any Helen Dunne," she said, sounding nervous. For a moment, I wondered if my mind was playing tricks on me: her voice sounded so much like Helen's, it was hard for me to concentrate. Perhaps, I thought, the similarity was due to their being about the same age. Or maybe it was because they both had a way of evading the truth without being completely dismissive.

I could hear ambivalence in Maureen's voice, not unlike someone who answers a door, sees who it is, and keeps talking through the crack without shutting the door entirely. I told her about the photo I had of her and Luke, reaching for any opening I could find.

"As far as I know, my husband never had a child out of wedlock," she said with some exasperation. "Do you have red hair?"

"No," I said hastily, laughing. "I wasn't implying that your husband is my father. As far as I know, Helen was involved with a second lieutenant while she was at Fort Monmouth."

"Where is Helen now?" she asked. "What is she doing? Is she married?"

"So you do remember her then?"

"No," she said weakly.

"Well, were you in the army in the 1950s?" I asked.

"I'm not going to say," she said, growing more flustered. "So where does Helen live now? Do you have her phone number?"

I didn't know how to respond to her confused lying. It was as if my feet were stuck in sticky syrup and I couldn't move forward. I didn't want to give her Helen's number for fear that she would actually call her, so I switched the subject to my aunt and uncle in Pennsylvania as a way of demonstrating that someone out there believed me.

"Do you have their phone number?" she asked.

I gave her their number because I didn't believe she would ever call them. Also realizing Maureen might have to think about it for a while before she told me the truth about Helen, I gave her my phone number and invited her to call me back.

I hung up feeling disoriented, much the same way I had after talking to Helen for the first time, as if I was standing still but the ground was moving underneath me.

On my way home, I glanced over my shoulder at a sweeping view of San Francisco from the San Mateo Bridge, and I thought of Helen's apartment building near the lush greenery of Golden Gate Park. It was hard to remember when she had been just a name on a piece of paper. Part of me longed for the days when I could still fantasize about a kindhearted woman with extraordinary artistic talent who wished I would find her some day.

When I walked into my house, there was a message on my answering machine from Paul Solia. I immediately called him back.

"I've been doing a lot of thinking since I talked to you last," he said. "I think I need to take a stand with Helen. I'm with you all the way. At first I felt that I didn't want to tackle her. But now I realize the truth of what is going on is much more important to you than anything else. I don't want to lose her as a friend, but I don't want to protect her from reality."

"Has something changed?" I asked.

"Helen stopped here on her way back from a trip to New Mexico. She went there because she was put in contact with an astrologer who told her about a specific street in Taos where she would be happy."

"What happened to the value of rational thinking?"

"Lately, she's gotten more into mystical things like Eastern religion. She believes there have been documented cases of out-of-body experiences, where people are picked up by paramedics, taken to the hospital and pronounced dead only to come back to life and tell the same stories. To me, it's all la-la land.

"When she came back from New Mexico, she said the place the astrologer sent her to wasn't what she wanted. But she liked Santa Fe. She described it as small, but not a hick town, with intellectuals. She still hates small-town America, but she thinks Santa Fe is an arty, upscale place. The galleries and all that gives the town a highbrow quality, a patina of taste, that appeals to her."

I felt panic at the thought of Helen moving away from San Francisco, taking all of her secrets with her.

"That is why I called you. She's been asking my advice about moving there. She has always been at risk of losing her job in San Francisco because she says the company is close to going out of business. But I wouldn't be surprised if it took two months for something to happen."

"So what would you say to her if you confronted her about me?"

"The next time she visits me, I would tell her that she has always valued truth and objectivity," he said. "I would say I can't understand how she can ignore this. The evidence is incontrovertible."

He hesitated.

"But then she would say she doesn't want to talk about it. Practically speaking, we have to realize that she has run away before and she can do it again. If she wants to run, there's nothing I can do to stop her. She'll pick up her bags and leave."

"It sounds like you just talked yourself out of it," I said.

"On the other hand," he continued, as if he didn't hear me, "maybe *you* should try to appeal to her again. If you were to confront her in a public place, she would have to maintain appearances and act with some decorum. At her house, she can pass you off as crazy like she did before. But if you were to go to her in a public place like . . . like her work, she couldn't run away without appearing crazy herself. She can't be in her never-never land at work. There she has to act realistic, not hysterical, or she'll look like a fool."

The idea sounded crazy, but I was running out of options. Suddenly I felt an urgency, as if she could leave any day and I would never have this chance again.

"But if you do it," he warned, "you've got to appear rational and calm. You've got to kill her with kindness. I strongly suggest you rehearse it."

chapter *EIGHTEEN*

Showing up at Helen's office and catching her off guard was not something I could really prepare for. There was no script to memorize, no way I could predict how she would react. I was flying blind and I knew it. It was an encounter fraught with risk. In the past, I had tried to appeal to her conscience, to some deeply buried maternal love. Now I was playing on her fear, pinning her against a wall. It scared me even more to know that this was an all-or-nothing chance. It would either force her to open the door and let me in, if only for a moment, or slam it shut forever.

I persuaded Steve to go with me because I suspected the presence of a man might intimidate her. Helen might be a staunch feminist, "a champion of women's rights before it became fashionable" as John put it, but I figured Ayn Rand's hero worship of men must have somehow rubbed off on her.

It was two weeks before my thirty-fourth birthday the morning Steve and I pulled out of the driveway to drive to San Francisco. Even though it was already May and the sun was shining, my hands and shoulders trembled as Steve and I tried to anticipate the possible scenarios. I must have asked

"What if?" as many times as he said, "Calm down." I kept my mind occupied during the ride by giving Steve changing advice on the best route to take to her company, located in the Marina District.

We parked the car down the street from the building and sat for a few minutes while I brushed my hair and put on some lipstick. I thought about how, except for our brief encounter outside of her apartment, the last time Helen and I had been in each other's presence, she was handing me over to strangers. I tried to imagine what this time would be like, but I came up blank.

By the time we started walking toward the building, I was breathing in such shallow, quick bursts that I wondered if I would be able to speak. More than a few times I stopped and suggested to Steve that we reconsider, but he pushed me on. I clutched a blue folder containing my birth certificate and other documents to my chest.

"Let me do the talking in the beginning," he said.

I was happy to let him.

We walked in to a large outer office with a receptionist sitting at a desk in the middle of the room.

"Hi. We're here to see Helen Dunne," Steve said with exaggerated politeness.

"Is she expecting you?"

"No, she isn't."

"Who shall I say is here?"

"Steve and Debbie Holtz."

The receptionist picked up the phone and I could hear her repeating the information. She hung up more quickly than I expected.

"She's coming downstairs," she said, looking at Steve and then glancing briefly at me.

It couldn't have been more than thirty seconds before Helen appeared in a nearby doorway. She looked at Steve and then at me, with a faint glimmer of recognition. She looked self-consciously at the receptionist and then back at us.

"Why don't you come upstairs to the conference room?" she said in a cordial voice as she turned back up a short stairway.

We followed her up and into a room at the top of the stairs. Inside was a large rectangular table. She stopped at the door and let us pass. We took seats on the far side of the table facing her. The moment I heard the door close, Helen's restraint disappeared.

"What are you doing here?"

"Helen, I'm Debbie's husband, Steve. We just want to talk to you for a few minutes."

"How dare you come here?" she asked, barely containing her rage. I could tell by the way she kept glancing over her shoulder through an office window, she was being careful not to speak too loudly.

"There's no reason to get upset," Steve said with incredible composure. "We don't mean you any harm. We're just looking for some information."

I couldn't speak. I just studied Helen, engraving her image on my memory. She seemed taller than I remembered as she stood with her back against the door and her hands behind her, still touching the doorknob. Her dark brunette hair fell in a stylish curve above her shoulders. Her face looked like she was about forty-five, with no obvious wrinkles, just a little more filled out and mature than the photographs of her from more than three decades ago.

"We understand that you're not interested in a relationship with Debbie . . . ," Steve continued, but was quickly interrupted.

"I've told you everything I know," she insisted.

"But you haven't told me anything," I blurted out. "You haven't even admitted that you are my mother . . . "

"Debbie has spent her entire life wondering who her parents are and she just needs to know," Steve interceded. "If you're not willing to talk to her, then at least tell her who her father is and we promise you'll never hear from us again."

Helen stood silently for a moment, staring not at either one of us but almost between us.

"If you leave right now, I will discuss this with you on the telephone," she said slowly, as though she were striving for control.

"And when will you talk to me?" I asked.

"This weekend," she said. "You may call me on Saturday, as long as you leave right now."

Steve and I looked at each other, and then he turned to Helen. "All right," he said. "Then Debbie can call you this weekend?"

"Yes," she said as she turned and opened the door. As I passed her to leave, I tried to look into her face, but she turned her gaze to the floor.

"So, what do you think?" I asked Steve once we were outside.

"Well, I think we had an effect on her," he said. "At least she agreed to talk to you."

Whatever impression we did make on her, I thought, at least the next time Helen and I talked, we would be able to move beyond the conundrum of our true identities and finally begin to discuss what really happened thirty-four years earlier.

We traveled over the Bay Bridge in silence for awhile. I wondered, as I often did when we drove over the long, double-decked span, how it manages to stay up under the weight of so many cars.

"Do you think I look anything like her?" I asked Steve. I wanted to resemble Helen, not for reasons of beauty, but for the inescapable proof of connection it would provide.

"Not really," he said, thinking for a minute. "But from a purely anatomical point of view, you have a similar facial structure."

❧

Other people's adoption stories have always fascinated me. They may all involve the same intrinsic issues, yet they have different designs and textures. It's like the way every spider's web is a unique creation. Each one may seem to have a similar roundish shape, but if you look closely enough, their intricate patterns all contain some strands that veer off in unexpected directions or just fail to connect with the next one.

So it is with tales of reunions. Some are ultimately successful and others are not, but what is true about almost every one of them is they are complicated and rarely easy. I have heard dozens of stories since I started meeting adoptees and birth parents. Sometimes people are filled with love the minute they are found by their lost children or parents. But as time passes, they find that the road to the reunion was a lot less bumpy than the one they must take to build a relationship after so many lost years. Then, of course, there are the people who don't want to be found. Sometimes it takes months or years, if ever, for them to come around.

The one constant in the whole roller-coaster ride is the enduring hope that lives in the heart of each searcher. One woman once told our group how she believed she was named after a Barbra Streisand song, so she always left a recording of it on her answering machine in anticipation of her mother calling her one day.

Each story holds its own unique moments of poignancy. A woman who found her brother said he stopped stuttering midway through their first conversation. He said, "I lost something in my life and I began to stutter when I was six. Now I know that what I lost was you."

While I have met adoptees whose birth mothers tell them they gave them up once and still want nothing to do with them, it is rare to hear of a mother who repeatedly refuses to admit who she is.

The American Adoption Congress has found that less than 5 percent of birth parents who are contacted by their relinquished children reject them, with about half of those eventually relenting. The number of women who flatly deny their role as a birth parent is considered much smaller.

"When a woman relinquishes her child, the circumstances surrounding the relinquishment or placement of the child and how she is made to feel about herself have a lot to do with how she receives the child calling her," said Kate Burke, who was president of the American Adoption Congress when I interviewed her for an article I was researching.

"I think the pain involved in giving a child up for adoption doesn't go away," she said. "Having a child resurface brings up that pain fresh and raw. Some women have a harder time dealing with that than others."

⁓

It was with these thoughts in mind that I locked myself in my bedroom on the following Saturday morning to call Helen. Steve and the children were having breakfast in the kitchen. Even though I needed a quiet place to make the call,

I asked them not to leave the house because I didn't want to be alone when it was over.

I held a pen in my hand and a pad of paper in front of me as a way to record the conversation and stay focused. I was so nervous I had to dial the number twice after pushing the wrong buttons the first time.

The phone rang four times before she picked it up.

"Hello, Helen. This is Debbie calling."

"What is it you'd like to say to me?" she asked in a formal tone.

"Well," I stammered. "You said I could call you. Like my husband told you, I'm just looking for information about my family background."

"I understand that you haven't believed anything I've said."

"Well, that's because you didn't tell me the truth before," I said, trying not to be harsh.

"You're totally convinced of a relationship between us, so there's no point in my trying to convince you otherwise," she said.

There was a long silence. I didn't know what to say because I realized we were back to square one. I had been wrong to assume that she would give up the old routine.

"Listen," I said. "We both know the truth, so can you please just tell me who my father was?"

Another long silence.

"There is not much I can say to you, obviously, because you believe what you believe," she said.

She was stonewalling me and I knew that arguing the point would get me nowhere.

"I realize you want nothing to do with me. But if you would just tell me my father's name, you won't have to hear from me again."

Again there was dead silence.

"Was it the lieutenant you met in the army or was it Frank Harlett?" The words just slipped out of my mouth.

"You apparently feel you have a right to intrude into my life," she said. "That creates a dangerous situation."

I couldn't believe what I was hearing.

"A dangerous situation for whom? For you or for me?" I asked.

"Well, for me, of course," she said. "When there is an invasion of privacy, that is a precursor to violence."

"Let's not play this game anymore," I responded. Instead of feeling threatened, I found my courage mounting. "Everyone knows you are my mother. If it helps, I know all about the adoption, about all of the money you received. My adoptive parents know I found you and they have no problem with it. And if you felt threatened in any way at the time, by my adoptive father for example, you should know that he's dead and that's all over. You have nothing to worry about."

"Given your fix on this belief that you have, there's nothing I can say," she answered in a robotic sort of way. It was as if she were engaging me in some weird game of circular logic. I kept running and finding myself in the same spot where I began.

"Helen, just tell me who my father is and we can end this."

"Obviously I can't."

"Doesn't it bother you that your name is on all of these documents about my adoption that you say you have nothing to do with? Don't you want to see them?" I asked.

"To what end?" she shot back.

"Helen, are you lying to yourself, or are you just trying to deceive me?"

"I'm giving you an opportunity to get your hatred out," she said patronizingly. "Maybe it will be good for you."

"Listen," I said, trying hard to soften my voice. "You've brought me a lot of pain over the past year, but I don't hate you."

"I just hope you can give this obsession up," she said,

"I'm not obsessed with you. I just want you to tell me who my father was."

"You are creating a dangerous situation," she warned again.

Feeling ensnared, I looked for any way out I could find. Suddenly I remembered John telling me about the fights he had with Helen and her attempts to frighten him—like the time she threatened to drive them off a cliff and into the ocean.

"You know a lot about threats of violence, don't you Helen? You've made similar threats before, haven't you?" I said, without even thinking.

"You have been investigating me, haven't you?"

"Yes, I have."

Her voice had an eerie calm to it as she delivered a line that could easily have come from an Ayn Rand novel: "You've invaded my privacy."

"No, I haven't invaded your privacy. If you had just admitted to me who you really are, none of this would have been necessary."

"Is there anything else you want to say?" She, too, was looking for a way out.

"Is there anything else *you* want to say?" I asked, running out of ideas.

"I think this conversation has come to a close," she said, her hands still firmly on the wheel and in control.

"Right . . . right, Helen. Good-bye." I hung up the phone feeling disgusted. I was mad at myself for expecting this conversation to be different, mad at myself for leaving her office without any answers. She'd had days to prepare for this, plenty of time to polish her performance.

Yet the strangest thing about it was how she never came out and literally denied she was my mother. She never even used the words "I'm not your mother." I kept thinking what a normal person would say, "I'm sorry you have the wrong person, but you're wasting your time on me. Your real mother is out there somewhere."

Was Helen clever or just crazy? Did she think she could fool me?

I picked up the phone and called John.

"She's trying to scare you," he said after hearing the story. "She's trying to warn you off with her veiled threats. She probably won't do anything now—only if you continue. She has so little to live for. That's what makes me nervous."

I told John that I had a feeling Helen was taping the conversation.

"I think that's something she would do," he said. "She's getting ready for whatever you're going to do next. She doesn't know. Maybe she was bluffing. But if she's trying to build up a case against you, the first thing she'd do is contact a lawyer and see if she could fight it. If he said she couldn't, then she'd try to take matters into her own hands. She wouldn't be intimidated by the legal system because she doesn't operate within that system."

John had explanations for her behavior that I never would have thought of. Her mind was an alien place to me.

"She wasn't kidding around," he said. "She has spent her life living in a romantic dream world. What she finds heroic is someone who can stand alone, risk all odds and go ahead. That's why her favorite novel was *The Count of Monte Cristo*.

Debbie, she thinks this is a closed book. She believes you really are invading her privacy and forcing her to take extraordinary measures. If she really feels like a rat with her back against the wall, she will attack."

"I'm sorry I slipped about the threats she made against you, it was just hard for me to think straight," I said.

"It's all right. I'm worried for you, not me. Right now she's on the edge. She knows you're willing to take drastic measures, like going to her work."

John hesitated for a moment and continued in a more deliberate tone.

"Don't take anything she says lightly. You're not protected by a lawyer or the police from something like this. Normal social controls are not principles she lives by. That's why she's a dangerous person. I'll continue to support you as long as you're very, very careful."

chapter NINETEEN

Surreal was the only way to describe my conversations with Helen. Just thinking about them afterward gave me a feeling of vertigo. I was looking for some rationality—a quality that Helen and the other Ayn Rand cohorts extolled—but it was strangely missing from her words.

My ALMA advisor, herself a birth mother, said Helen was turning the tables on me as a way of staying in control of the situation and there was nothing I could say to change her mind.

Paul thought that Helen was running scared and that, given a few days to think about it before my call, she had decided on a strategy of making me believe this was all a figment of my imagination. "She's an extremely literal person," he said. "The words she uses are exactly what she means." That explained, he added, why she never came out and directly denied she was my mother. In her own twisted way, she was telling the truth when she continually repeated, "There's nothing I can say."

Steve, however, was less philosophical.

"She's obviously a very sick person who cut herself off from the experience of having a child and has convinced herself it never happened," he said. "She's extremely unstable and dangerous, and you have to protect yourself and your children by staying as far away from her as possible."

Steve was not the only person who believed that Helen was seriously out of touch with reality. While this was the easiest scenario to accept since it meant that her actions had nothing to do with me, the theory brought me no comfort. To blame Helen's refusal to acknowledge me on some abstract force like madness would mean that no one had any control over this situation, an impossible thought for me to accept. To believe that she was delusional would also mean that I would have to feel sorry for her. Then I could no longer be angry at her and, as ever, I was finding strength in my anger.

So despite everyone else's opinions, the voice of my own instinct was the loudest of all: Helen was a liar. She knew very well who I was. What she was doing by covering up the truth was as deliberate as my attempts to find her had been. She was keeping vigilant guard over the mistakes of her past.

But whether she was crazy or just a liar didn't erase the fact that she could be dangerous, and I had two small children to consider. She knew where I lived from my letters, and though I was not worried for my own safety, Jake and Sarah were more important.

On my thirty-fourth birthday, I finally accepted that Helen was never going to tell me the truth. Though I might never come to terms with having such a person as my mother, time was slipping away and if my father was out there somewhere, I would have to find him myself.

I had just finished reading *The Search for Anna Fisher* by Florence Fisher, an adoptee and the founder of ALMA. She finally found her mother after searching for twenty years. She recounts how the woman first denied the truth, then admitted it but refused to tell her husband and children about the daughter who had come back into her life. Fisher went on to locate her birth father and find some satisfaction in their reunion.

Finding my own father would not be easy. Since I had no idea of the name of Helen's army boyfriend—the lieutenant in the photo—it made the most sense to start with Frank Harlett. And after my last go-around with Helen, my mind was still thinking in terms of swindlers.

My new search began with another scan of the national phone directory listings, this time for everyone with the last name of Harlett. There weren't very many, about thirty, but they all seemed to live in Cleveland or Florida with a smattering in places like New York, Massachusetts and Chicago. Many of the first names sounded Italian: Carmen, Carmela, Angelo and Angela. But there was no Frank.

A picture began to emerge after the first dozen or so calls. Most of the Harletts were related to the Cleveland family, and no one had ever heard of Frank.

I mentioned my adoption search to my neighbors across the street, an elderly couple who were the friendliest people on the block and always eager to help out with my kids or any problem with the house. Their lives revolved around the Mormon Temple, located just a couple of miles away. They told me that the church had its own genealogy research center and suggested I go there.

When I arrived at the Family History Center, I found several retired men and women milling around the reception area of the strikingly modern facility looking for people to help. Having been offered the *Book of Mormon* on several occasions by my neighbors, I briefly wondered if the volunteers would try to convert me to the Church of Jesus Christ of Latter-Day Saints, but they were sincere and gracious.

The first woman to approach me asked what I needed to find and I told her. She gave me a brief tour, first pointing to several rows of files along the wall that contained names of the people who sailed here aboard the Mayflower. I seriously doubted that Frank Harlett's ancestors sailed on the ship with the Pilgrims. Given what I already knew, I figured it was more likely they were either smuggled here or slipped into the country after escaping criminal charges in Italy.

The woman suggested that if the man I was looking for was older than fifty, I should start with the U.S. Social Security Death Index on CD-ROM at a bank of computers in the middle of the room. She showed me how to type in the name and I waited as the machine considered my request. Three names suddenly popped up on the screen. At the bottom of the list was Frank Harlett.

He was dead. The words swirled around in my mind while I waited for some reaction to latch onto, but found none. I wanted to feel sadness but could only feel disappointment. There I was in a religious institution, and I could not summon up the same compassion or grief I normally feel any time I learn of someone's death, even that of a stranger I read about in the newspaper.

Also on the list were a Fred Harlett and a Carmen Harlett. I asked the woman if I could print out the records.

I stared at the sheets she handed me. The one with Frank's name said he was born in 1910. I calculated the numbers in my head. That would mean he would be eighty-three if he were still alive, more than twenty years older than Helen. Yes, he was the one, I thought. My eyes scanned the small type. Frank died in Los Angeles in November of 1985, eight years earlier. He was born in New York, just as Helen had written about my father on my birth certificate, but using a different name.

There was also Fred Harlett, who was born in Massachusetts in 1890 and died in 1965. Carmen Harlett was born in 1882 and died in Cleveland in 1969.

The church volunteer offered to show me the state of California death records and I found another Fred R. Harlett, who died in Los Angeles in 1986, only two months after Frank. The woman told me about other files I could search: census records, city directories from the nineteenth century, immigration logs from the 1700s. But my mind was racing and I could no longer focus.

For the time being, I decided to ignore all the others and focus on Frank. That afternoon, I wrote a letter to the Los Angeles County Recorder and requested his death certificate. Two weeks later, I held it in my hand. Framed by an ornately designed blue border and bearing the round seal of the state of California, the official document was all that was left of Frank Harlett.

I read it over many times. Frank's parents and occupation were listed as unknown. He lived in an apartment on Franklin Street in Los Angeles and died at Hollywood Presbyterian Medical Center. His cause of death was cardiac arrest due to acute myocardial infarction as a consequence of arteriosclerosis.

I asked Steve what that meant.

"He died of a heart attack," he said and returned to reading a medical journal on his lap.

"It lists a doctor's name," I persisted. "Do you think you could call him and get Frank's medical records?"

"They probably wouldn't tell you much," said Steve, without taking his eyes off the article he was reading.

It took several months of repeated calls to the doctor's office claiming I was his daughter before I received a manila envelope containing Frank's hospital records. It turned out that Frank was a two-pack-a-day smoker who had emphysema. He lived in a retirement home. One day in November, he was rushed to the emergency room in shock.

Reading through pages of medical jargon, I imagined doctors in green surgical outfits poking and prodding the cold and clammy skin of this seventy-five-year-old man with guide wires, needles and balloon pumps. They tried instruments of various shapes and thicknesses to expose and bypass arteries, but to no avail. One failure led to another.

In the end, no one could penetrate an obstruction in his heart.

⌒⌒

Frank Harlett's body was never claimed by any next of kin. It was turned over to the Los Angeles Crematory and burned. Because no one picked up his ashes after three years, they were dumped into a mass grave.

Around the time I was learning of Frank's fate, I read a newspaper story about the deaths of cult members at the Branch Davidian compound in Waco, Texas. It said that cremated bodies are reduced to less than 5 percent of their living mass. According to the Cremation Association of North America, "A 150-pound person will become about six pounds of ash and bone chips."

It seemed to me that Frank's life, as wasted and empty as I imagined it to have been, had shrunk further into oblivion at his death, and he was remembered by no one, not even Helen.

⌐∞⌐

I had left messages with various Harletts and one day I received a call back from a woman named Tony in Florida.

"I was intrigued by your call," she said. "About two years ago, I received a similar call from a woman who was looking for the same man. She said her husband believes Frank Harlett was his father."

I told her that I too believed Frank could have been my father.

"What a strange coincidence," she said. "I'm trying to remember what else she told me. This woman—her name was Yvette—was very nice. I think she said her husband, or his father, was born in Chicago. That's all I can really remember. Oh, and her husband's name is Brian Harlett."

An eerie symmetry was taking shape between myself and a total stranger. I felt as if an invisible force was bringing random lives into alignment in the same way an automatic arm swiftly gathers a jumbled pile of bowling pins into neat rows. It would now be far more difficult to cross Frank off of my short list of "sperm donors"—a phrase used by my mother-in-law to denigrate Helen's choices in men and, however unconsciously, my own biological history.

"These people are hard to find," Tony continued. "I think they move around a lot. Just last year, at Christmas, they sent me a card. Let me find that, because they had a new address."

It turned out that Yvette and Brian Harlett lived in Hollywood, Florida. Their phone number was unlisted. I didn't feel as comfortable about contacting Brian as I had others like John or Paul. Brian Harlett was an unknown quantity, related to a man about whom I imagined the worst.

Before attempting to make any contact, I needed to find out more about him.

I started by running his name through the driver's license records at the Florida Department of Vehicles. There was nothing remarkable, just a few citations for improperly equipped cars and driving without lights. He was tall, over six feet, and nine years older than me. His prior driver's license had been issued in California.

Since I didn't have a phone number for him, I decided to write Brian a letter. I wanted it to intrigue—but not intimidate—him.

> *Dear Brian,*
> *My name is Debbie Holtz. Your name was given to me by Tony Harlett. I recently contacted her while looking for relatives of Frank Harlett and she said your wife had also called her for the same information two years ago.*
> *While searching for my own father, I have received some information about Frank Harlett that may be helpful to you. I would like to talk to you but have been unable to locate your phone number. Please call me at . . .*
> *Sincerely,*
> *Debbie Holtz*

About a week later, Steve and I came home from a dinner out and found a list of messages left by the babysitter. One was from Brian Harlett, who had left his number and said I could call back collect. Hearing that, I was certain that he must be anxious to talk to me. I looked at my watch and realized that it was three hours later in Florida and probably too late to call, so I waited apprehensively until the next day.

From the beginning of our conversation, I could tell that I was descending into the eye of a hurricane. After listening to my story and the little I knew of Frank's relationship with Helen, Brian flooded me with a deluge of information that was often bewildering.

"Frank's name is on my birth certificate," he began. "He was married to Dorothy, my mother, until they divorced in 1955. That's when he walked out and we never saw him again."

"Did you know very much about Frank?" I asked.

"Just what it says on my birth certificate, that he was born in New York City and his occupation is listed as a tool and dye company."

As he was talking, I sifted through a file of papers to find my own birth certificate.

"Mine says that my father was a machine salesman and he was also born in New York," I said, barely able to hide my disappointment. "That sounds pretty similar, doesn't it?"

"It sounds like you could be Frank's daughter," he said. "But . . ."

"What about Chicago?" I persisted, "Tony told me you or Frank were from Chicago and that's where I was born."

"I have a photo of me that says 'baby's first flight from New York to Chicago.' Dorothy said we lived in Chicago for a year because Frank had business there. Something to do with his business making tools."

Frank had connections to people in Chicago, I thought. He must have used them later to arrange my adoption.

"But weren't you born in Chicago?" I asked.

"No," he said. "I was born in Jamaica, New York, and we lived in Queens for a while. My aunt was working as a nurse at Jamaica Hospital."

Jamaica. I thought of the anonymous postcard with the Jamaica, New York postmark: *Helen is very nice.*

"My entire childhood was a living hell," Brian was saying. "I have a brother named Frank Harlett, Jr. He was born in 1949, a year before me. Let me warn you about him. He's a real creep. We fought a lot as kids. It's gotten so bad that Dorothy won't even give me his phone number in Miami. She's afraid I would hurt him. They're both into really shady dealings. That's why my number's unlisted. There were some people related to Dorothy bothering me, carrying on like lunatics."

For the short time while I had entertained the idea that Brian could be my brother, I forgot that I was talking to a stranger about whom I really knew nothing. Now, warning signals were going off in my head at a furious pace.

"Dorothy's no better," he said contemptuously. "Her family are a bunch of hillbillies. She's a pretty creepy character herself. She was involved with the Mafia through Frank and others she knew in New York. She bragged about it. She even got busted for organized gambling when I was about eighteen. Somehow she paid the cops off and got bailed out."

The family portrait Brian was painting seemed dark and depraved until my mind flashed to Manny and his own hardboiled history. I was beginning to imagine nefarious connections between the Harletts and the Skars when Brian's voice interrupted my thoughts.

"I went to live in a foster home when I was eleven, after I was arrested on wayward minor charges. Dorothy and her new husband gave me up to the state, and I lived in places like the Berkshire Farm for Boys and Bronx Youth Home. It was the bottom of the fucking barrel."

He sounded full of anger and I couldn't blame him. It seemed strange, though, that he never referred to Dorothy and Frank as his mother or father. It didn't take long for my question to be answered.

"When I was finally sent home, that's when I started having doubts about who my real parents were. I think I was adopted by Dorothy and Frank. Dorothy used to mention adoption a lot when I was a teenager, in a kind of testing sort of way. I've been doing a lot of digging; that's how we got in touch with Tony. I think my father's name was Fred Harlett. I remember that Dorothy had books with his name on them that he gave her. There were times when she talked about my father and referred to him as Fred."

We started comparing names of the different Harletts we had each talked to and building an imaginary family tree. I told Brian everything I had learned about Frank and Fred, about their death records, and how no one named Harlett I had called admitted knowing who Frank was.

"Nobody will own up to him, " said Brian. "It's like they didn't want to know him. I just think they're all trying to cover Frank up. I talked to a guy named Jay Harlett. He was very nice. He told me a lot. He had been a ward of the state, like me. Fred Harlett was his brother, but since he was fifteen years older than him, he was more like a father to him. Their father, who was also named Fred, was born in 1890 or something like that."

I looked at the death records in front of me. The dates checked out.

"Jay said there was a man in the family, an uncle, who was shorter than Fred. He didn't know his name. But I think that was Frank because Frank was five foot eight and I'm over six feet tall. I think Frank may have been Fred's brother or his cousin. Jay said he'd never heard of Frank, but I don't think he was telling the truth. There's a lot of stuff that's still secret in the family."

I told him that I was familiar with family secrets. I asked Brian whether he had ever questioned Dorothy about these things, but he was evasive.

"I'm tired of the twisted distortions of the truth Dorothy gives me," Brian said bitterly. "I don't even talk to her anymore. Once I find out who my parents really were, I won't look like a jerk anymore. I feel like I've been shooting blanks."

I was so confused by the time I hung up, I started wondering whether Frank ever really existed. For a short time I considered the possibility that Frank and Fred were the same person. But the papers in front of me, death records with different Social Security numbers and dates of birth, convinced me otherwise.

Brian seemed desperate to believe Dorothy and Frank were not his parents. Even if he was right, Frank was presumably still the father of Frank, Jr., a shady character living in Miami who could very well be my brother.

As I tried to imagine him, my mind drifted to the white-sand beaches and broad boulevards of Miami Beach, lined with palm trees and saturated with sunshine. My own memories of being there with my mother and Manny were fuzzy, brought to life only by the photos I had of us on their yacht and in restaurants. Then I thought of the other faces in those pictures, men with slicked back hair who looked like they had something to hide and women draped in jewelry and fancy clothes by their sides.

Once, when I asked my mother about Manny long after he died, she told me, "Manny would have done anything for you. He bought you whatever you wanted. He was devoted to you . . . until the end when he went crazy."

I asked her what she meant by that.

"When Manny was at his worst in the months before he died, drinking brandy all the time, he once came after us with two big butcher knifes. You and I were holding on to each other. He was very drunk. He said, 'You'll die in your own blood.'

"In those last days," she continued, "I used to sleep with you and you'd ask me, 'Mommy, will we die in our own blood?'"

My mind does not allow me to remember that, but the fear lingers deep inside of me. I must have been relieved when Manny vanished from our lives, but fear has a way of breeding fascination. I have always been intrigued by organized crime and people who live on the edge.

The part of me that was open to taking risks would not have let Helen get away with lying to me, would have pressured her until she broke down and told the truth. That same side of me—the little girl who survived being threatened with death by the man she was supposed to trust—would also have picked up the phone and called Frank Harlett, Jr., in Miami.

But that persona was now overshadowed by the faces of my two small children. I was determined they would never live as I had. They would never feel imperiled, running from danger yet secretly drawn to it. They would not be forced to build fortresses around themselves that kept out the good as well as the bad.

The road that led to Frank Harlett had become dark and unnavigable, and the small flashlight I was using to find my way had suddenly gone out. I stopped hunting for clues, tucked away my questions and, for a while, tried hard not to look back.

chapter TWENTY

During the summer of 1993, a battle was raging over the fate of a little girl named Jessica. The sweet, reticent face of the two-and-a-half-year-old girl stared out from the covers of *Time* and *People* magazines. Held in her mother's arms, she reminded me of Sarah, who was the same age and radiated the same shy suspicion about the world outside her family.

On August 3, another photo of Jessica ran in newspapers across the country. This time she was being strapped into a car seat and crying desperately. "Mommy!" she screamed as she was whisked away from the only home she had ever known.

"Whose little girl is this?" one headline asked.

Jessica was caught in a tug-of-war between her adoptive parents and the woman who gave her up shortly after she was born. The struggle ended when the Michigan Supreme Court decided that biology was more important than the bonds between Jessica and the two people who had loved her every day of her short life. It became a litmus test for the nature vs. nurture debate with the emotional life of a baby girl hanging in the balance. The legal arguments in Jessica's case meant little to me. I was drawn to her story in a more visceral way.

Like millions of others, I watched the televised play-by-play accounts of the tortuous weeks before the day when Jessica would be returned to her birth parents. Having spent more than a year searching for my own biological mother and father, I expected to support the court's decision. Jessica would grow up without having to wonder who she really was or bear the shame of knowing that her mother didn't want her.

Instead I was surprised to find myself grieving for her adoptive mother. Her despair touched the mother in me when I imagined how I would feel if someone were to take Sarah away from me forever.

When I watched a lawyer awkwardly carrying a terrified Jessica away, surrounded by dispassionate security guards in dark glasses, her cries echoed my own. I couldn't help but think of myself as a baby handed over to strangers through a car window by a woman whose voice and smell were all that I had known. Her tears were also the ones I never let myself shed when my mother uprooted me from all that had become familiar to go and live with grandparents I barely knew.

But loudest of all, I could hear in Jessica's voice the pleas of my own little girl who loves me completely and trusts that I would never leave her.

A photo captured the signs hung on the adoptive parents' house begging her birth parents: "Please don't take our Jessica away." Below was a drawing of a broken heart with red tears on both sides.

As in other highly publicized adoption battles, the courts treated Jessica as property to be returned to its rightful owner. Her case was the very possibility my adoptive mother had sought to avoid when she absconded with my birth records, hoping to prevent my birth mother from ever finding me. Little did she know she had nothing to fear.

❧

I was out the afternoon my aunt's call came. When I pushed the button on my answering machine, I heard Sylvia's voice.

"Debbie, I called you to tell you that I got a letter from Helen, and if you have time, would you call me? Talk to you later, honey."

I felt an instant sense of foreboding, the result of living with half-truths and unresolved secrets. The Dunnes were like my underground family, usually silent but always lingering just below my consciousness.

When I called her back, she told me Helen had moved to Santa Fe, New Mexico.

"She flew the coop," said Sylvia. "She knew you were there and she was too scared to stay. We thought it was strange that she wrote us a letter with her new address. After all, she's moved before and never let us know where she was."

I was not shocked by the news. It was a move I was somewhat prepared for after my conversation with Paul. It was hard not to believe my visit to her office had caused her to leave San Francisco. I expected to feel hurt by her departure, but I didn't. Her lies had been an abandonment more profound than any physical departure.

What I did feel, almost immediately, was a sense of relief. There was a security in knowing she was far away and would be unlikely to carry out any of her veiled threats.

❧

Although I had never been there, New Mexico had always been alluring to me. I was intrigued by a place that attracts artists simply by the way the sunlight dramatizes its natural beauty. While it might have taken me years to visit New Mexico on my own, and I would never have gone there just to see Helen again, I jumped at the chance to accompany Steve to a medical conference in Albuquerque in the fall of 1994.

It had been over a year since Helen's move. With only sixty-five miles separating the two cities, I couldn't resist planning a day trip to Santa Fe. From the start, I knew that I was going there to see more than the art galleries and adobe architecture; I wanted to see where Helen lived but had no plan of what I would do once I got there. Though Steve also wanted to see Santa Fe, he warned against my paying an unexpected call on Helen.

As we drove north from Albuquerque, not far from the path of the Rio Grande, the highway climbed steadily toward the Jemez Mountains on the northwest horizon and the Sangre de Cristo range to the northeast. Along the way, we passed hills dotted with piñon pines and a striking protrusion of red rock known as La Bajada. I could see why artists flock to New Mexico to capture the vivid colors of the landscape. I, too, felt pulled to the place as though by some odd magnetic force and knew long before we arrived in Santa Fe that I would go to see Helen.

We parked near the center of town and took a walk around, peering through the walled patios to catch a glimpse of the old Spanish courtyards inside. The children were running out of patience, so we stopped ourselves from entering the many shops and galleries we passed. When we arrived at the Plaza in the center of town, we browsed through silver jewelry, Navajo weavings and Pueblo pottery spread out on blankets on the sidewalk.

As a keepsake of a place I doubted I would ever visit again, I bought matching earrings and a necklace by a Hopi artist. He explained that the etching on the silver symbolized the line of life and the steps to heaven.

Knowing our time was limited, I grew more nervous and preoccupied. The bright sun seemed to suck the energy right out of my body. I was sweating under the weight of a heavy sweater and no matter how much water I drank, I remained thirsty.

"I just need a half-hour to go see Helen. It's something I've got to do," I told Steve as Jake and Sarah devoured ice cream cones.

"I can't stop you," he said, "but you should be careful."

I took her address out of my purse and looked at a map to find that she lived on a street on the outskirts of town. We drove a few miles and Steve dropped me off on a corner, saying he would be back in thirty minutes. He asked if he should call the police if I didn't show up.

"I'll be here," I said, getting out of the car.

The street was off the beaten track, a far cry from the quaint adobe buildings and brick walkways closer to town. Standing before me was a straight line of rather rundown apartment complexes that could have been found almost anywhere.

I walked up to Helen's building several times and then quickly retreated across the street to hide behind a tree. It was hard enough to figure out what I should say, but with her I also had to plan for the unexpected. Each time I approached the building, I felt my heart pounding against the wall of my chest and wondered what makes it do that. Does fear force too much blood to gather there and the muscle, engorged and in danger of bursting, frantically beats to get rid of it?

At last, I mustered the courage to walk up an outside stairway to the second floor. Taking a few deep breaths, I knocked on the door. I was careful to stay out of view this time, remembering how Helen had refused to open the door when I visited her in San Francisco. I knocked again and again. I put my ear up to the door but heard nothing.

I decided to look inside. Through a narrow opening in the vertical blinds covering the front window I surveyed the room. It was dark, but I could make out a table or a desk near the window with papers and an adding machine on top of it. Farther into the room I saw the back of a computer. There was a framed painting or photograph, I couldn't be sure which, of an older man hanging from a far wall. I wondered if it was Helen's father, but it was impossible for me to tell.

Then something else caught my attention. It was a large picture of a woman above the couch. She looked so much like my adoptive mother I gasped. My mind told me it couldn't be. I could only see it from an angle. I moved my head from side to side, took off my glasses and put them back on, trying to get a better look at it. It appeared to be a framed poster, so I considered that maybe it was Ayn Rand. But the woman was blondish and prettier than Rand. Her head seemed to float against the pale background with no body and I couldn't make out if there was anything else in the picture.

Worried that Helen would walk up and catch me spying, I peered through the window one last time and then walked back down the stairs. The door to one of the apartments stood open, with several people ambling in and out of an impromptu garage sale. In front, a card table was covered with old appliances and knickknacks, and old clothes were stacked around it on the ground. I went over to look, pretending I was interested in what they were selling.

A man with long brown stringy hair hanging down past his shoulders and several greenish tattoos on both arms was sitting on a chair. "Howdy," he said as I examined a Betty Boop cookie jar with a crack running down its back.

"Hi," I said. "I was just upstairs looking for one of your neighbors, Helen Dunne, in apartment 205. She doesn't seem to be home. Do you know her at all?"

"Yeah, I saw her leave earlier this morning. I don't know her name. She kind of keeps to herself. Sometimes she waves."

We talked for a short time about the high cost of living in Santa Fe. He had grown up there and bemoaned the onslaught of celebrities and New Age types who were drawn there.

A few guys who had been sitting in a van walked over and joined the conversation. "We're the visitors from hell," they said, laughing and pulling some beers from a brown paper bag.

"I guess I am too," I said. "At least to the person I've come to visit."

I looked at my watch and realized Steve and the kids would be pulling up in five minutes. I couldn't just go without leaving something behind so Helen would know I had been there. I took a notebook out of my purse and wrote:

> *Helen,*
> *You've escaped to a beautiful place. I was visiting the area and stopped by to say hello.*
> *I want you to know that I haven't forgotten and neither should you.*
> *Sincerely,*
> *Debbie (born Shirley Jane on May 14, 1959)*

It was a message I gave little thought to and, written in haste, it may have sounded more like a threat than the reminder I intended it to be. Without thinking twice, I left the note tucked into the crack in the apartment door and quickly left. Steve was waiting for me on the corner, with both children asleep in the backseat.

"How did it go?" he asked.

I told him she hadn't been home.

"Honestly, I'm relieved that I didn't have to come face to face with her. But I left her a note. Just letting her know that she hasn't gotten away with her lies was enough for me. I just don't want her to forget . . . "

"Debbie, don't you see she has forgotten?" he said. "She forgot a long time ago."

I hardly heard him. I was already trying to imagine Helen's reaction to the note. I pictured her reading it, walking out to the balcony and looking around to make sure I was gone, and then taking the note to the kitchen, tearing it in half and throwing it away. Or did she open a desk drawer and drop the paper into a file of her own? I could not guess what she would be thinking. Despite everything I had been told about Helen, she remained an enigma.

One of the most well-known stories of the Navajo people is one they still tell their children. After the Navajo were defeated by the U.S. Army in 1865, more than nine thousand Navajo were sent as prisoners to Fort Sumner, New Mexico—three hundred miles from their homes. Many died in "The Long Walk" to the fort and many more perished while being held there. Three years later, those who remained were allowed to return to their homeland.

What force, I wondered, impels people who are ripped away from their place of origin to always long to return?

chapter TWENTY-ONE

There's a Yiddish word, *Mensch*, which means "a real human being"—not a superhero, but a decent person with a giving heart who tries his best to do the right thing.

My second adoptive father was a mensch. After he married my mother when I was nine, he went to court and gave me his name. He probably knew when he picked me up in Minnesota to bring me back to Chicago that I was a troubled child, but he persevered.

"I suspected it would be hard to get to know you," he told me years later, "but it went very well between us. It always did."

From the beginning, he treated me as his own, not as an adopted child or a stepdaughter. Even when he had to be away on a business trip, he would always manage to be back in time for father-daughter gym nights or school assemblies. He wrote me funny letters when I was away at camp, often on postcards he collected on his travels, pretending he was off in more exotic places. When I was in college in California, he would write during the dead of winter in

Chicago and joke about the beautiful, sunny weather they were having.

He provided the first stability and unconditional love I had ever known. Though I may not have realized it then, he was a life preserver I hung onto in turbulent seas.

My dad tried to do the same for my brother but, by the age of twenty-one, he had already drifted too far off course. When Howie was arrested in Boston in 1969 for possessing and distributing drugs shortly after my parents were married, my dad flew there with his pockets full of cash to bail him out. He brought Howie back to Chicago and gave him a job. Howie's recovery didn't last long. A couple of months later, he was dead.

⚬∞⚬

Lying in an open casket at his funeral, my dad was not the man I remembered. He was no longer the rosy-faced man with playful blue eyes whose smile radiated like a burst of sunshine. Gone was the giant stomach that made him look pregnant since he did not carry weight anywhere else. Eating was his greatest pleasure, particularly rich desserts topped with dollops of whipped cream.

He had become a pale, emaciated ghost. I cringed at the way death diminishes a person. Yet as I stood over his casket, I found it difficult to say good-bye to this stranger. I hoped that one day I could erase this image of him and remember the way his face erupted in laughter when someone told a good joke or the way he beamed the day he held my son in his arms for the first time.

His metamorphosis did not happen overnight. Shortly after my trip to Santa Fe, he suffered a stroke that left him partially paralyzed and dependent on the help of others.

Though many in his condition would have stopped working, he continued because it was all he had left. He could no longer even enjoy food because his illness stripped him of his appetite.

Going to the office every day was a kind of charade because all he could really do was shuffle papers around his desk. Nobody wanted to buy insurance from an old man in a wheelchair who slurred his words. Money was running out and my mother could barely afford to pay for people to help my dad get dressed or go to the bathroom. Taking physical care of another person did not come naturally to my mother and, by that time, she was losing her eyesight. She moved him into a nursing home, sold their apartment and moved away from Chicago to be closer to her own family.

My mother said she did what she had to for her own survival. Despite her reasons for leaving my dad, I couldn't help feeling that she had abandoned him. It touched off an estrangement between us that only grew worse with time.

In the last few years of his life, I tried to visit my dad as much as I could but with two small children, finding the time to fly two thousand miles away was never easy. When I did visit, he would stare for hours at the television, randomly changing channels by pushing the buttons on the remote control with his good hand, and dozing off while we were talking. He was easily frustrated by his physical limitations and often refused to even try to walk. His illness made him bitter, just as a sweet red wine left untouched for too long turns to vinegar. I could only briefly glimpse his former self behind the shadow of his illness, but he was stubborn and refused to let go.

As long as my dad was alive, I could not bring myself to make any further effort to solve the riddle of who had been my birth father. I felt that I owed him a single-hearted allegiance, particularly while he was sick.

He died only days before his seventy-eighth birthday. By then my mother and I were no longer speaking, and I felt that I had lost both of my parents. Any hope that the funeral would end our alienation vanished when the immediate family gathered in a room off the chapel. My mother kissed Steve on the cheek. As she turned to me, I said, "Hello, Mom." I wanted for us to put aside our grudges and care for each other: a child who had lost another parent and a woman who had lost another husband. But she only briefly glanced at me, anger darting from her eyes, and walked past.

During the service, I watched her listening to the rabbi's words and prayers. I watched as she nervously fingered a crumpled wad of white tissue, occasionally dabbing her eyes with it. As always, she was dressed impeccably. Her navy-blue suit and white silk blouse didn't have a spot or a wrinkle. Tasteful gold earrings fell beneath her two-inch-high helmet of teased blond hair. She was prettier and younger looking than other women her age because she had never given up on herself.

I started to think about both of my mothers. Together we formed a triangle; I the horizontal line connected to both and my mothers the diagonal lines, beginning separately yet gravitating toward one another.

The significant differences between the two women could not be denied. Luxury and material possessions were my mother's lifeblood. They defined her, were the air she needed to breathe. Helen, on the other hand, seemed to care little for material trappings. It didn't matter to her whether she was surrounded by fine furnishings or was ushered into restaurants and buildings by doormen. She lived within the walls of her mind, involved in matters of the cosmos but unable to figure out how to pump gas into her car. While my mother liked to read society columns and an occasional celebrity biography, Helen's tastes veered more toward books like *The Count of Monte Cristo*. I thought about the hero of that story: an unjustly accused man who escapes from prison, seeks to uncover a vast treasure and adopts a new identity, forcing people to wonder who he really is.

The women seemed as far apart as the North and South Poles, yet they occupied similar moral climates. They were both self-centered, secretive about the past and overly concerned with their appearances. They fled small-town childhoods to reinvent themselves in the sophisticated images they yearned for. As young women, they each ventured into the criminal underworld, attracted by easy money and a kind of cheap glamour that set them apart from their dull, ordinary families.

Their lives had only intersected for a brief moment when one handed a baby to the other through a darkened car window. One sold a baby and the other bought one, each motivated by a self-interest that had nothing to do with maternal instincts.

After the rabbi finished his eulogy, I watched as people lined up before my mother to offer their condolences. She thrived on social interaction, deriving her vitality from friends and acquaintances with whom I had never been able to compete for her attention.

Helen, however, had no social life. I had been told she was terrified of people, particularly the mindlessness of crowds, coming to believe in recent years that in a previous life she was some kind of healer who was stoned to death by an angry mob.

Describing her to a psychologist and a psychiatrist I knew resulted in the same conclusion. She was likely a "schizoid personality," they both said, someone who is indifferent to social relationships and whose range of emotions is so restricted that her personality appears flat. Unlike others who long for closeness but avoid it out of fear, people like Helen neither seek nor desire friends or family. They prefer to be loners and appear cold and aloof to the world. Vague about goals and numb to the feelings of others, they tend to be self-absorbed and choose solitary activities.

"Could a person have been born that way, or did some trauma in her life cause it?" I asked.

Schizoid personalities were usually abused kids, my friends told me. They were often the children of alcoholics and didn't know how to react to the fluctuating behavior of their parents. Emotional deprivation, like the lack of love and affection from their parents that my uncle described, can repress a child's efforts to express herself.

I remembered hearing how my grandmother had lost a son before Helen was born. I pictured Helen as a baby, her arms flailing about, groping for affection, but never cuddled or cooed at. I imagined Helen's mother, still depressed by her son's death, cleaning drawers in the kitchen while Helen cried in a basket alone in the other room.

"The mind is a much safer place to retreat to," said my friend Sue, who was also adopted and was familiar with my story. "Philosophy becomes a form of escape."

◦◦◦◦◦

When the funeral was over, I walked outside into the muggy air of the Chicago summer, feeling as if I was choking. I walked around to the other side of the building where no one could see me, leaned against the brick wall and cried so hard my knees buckled and I slid down to the ground.

I thought about how much I missed my dad and how I never really told him how much I appreciated him. And I thought of the two women from whom I wanted what neither could give.

chapter TWENTY-TWO

After the trip to Santa Fe, I had given up trying to learn anything new about Helen or hoping she would change her mind. My aunt and uncle never called me, and I called them only occasionally, usually on Christmas. I focused my energy on taking care of Jake and Sarah, and being as good a mother as I could.

Four years after I first found Helen, I received a call from my cousin Patty, Sylvia and Mike's estranged daughter. The call pierced a silence that had grown around my search. It didn't take long to learn that nothing about Patty was quiet or subtle.

"It's against my better judgment to call you," said Patty in a low, gravelly voice. "I know my dad hasn't always believed you, but my daughter Lisa came to live with me last year and she's told me all about you. I'm calling because she wants me to. Normally I just don't get involved in things."

"Well, I'm glad you did," I said as politely as I could. I was curious about what she had to say.

"I've been trying to get your number from my mother for months, but she kept telling me she had misplaced it. When

Lisa first moved here last summer, she tried to bring your picture to show me, but Sylvia took it away from her. I even tried to call newspapers looking for you because Lisa said you were a reporter, but I was spelling your name wrong. And then last week, my mother called and gave me your number."

I had considered calling Patty myself after my trip to Pennsylvania, but so much of what my aunt had told me about her reminded me of Helen that I had stopped myself.

"Do you look like Helen?" she asked.

"No, I don't see much resemblance."

"Your voice sounds remarkably like Helen's."

"It's funny you should say that," I said. "I've been told that before."

"I'm intrigued by you even though you were never with Helen. I would have given anything when I was a child to be Helen's daughter."

Maybe that was the reason she was calling me, I thought—out of some weird mix of envy and curiosity.

"Helen was always there for me," Patty said suddenly, as if setting some ground rules. "I'm not nearly as cold as Helen, but we're on the same plateau. When my dad was sick, my mother called me. I asked, 'What can *I* do?' Helen said the same thing when her mother died. That's just the way we are."

Wonderful, I thought.

"The only time I ever saw Helen cry was when she came home when Lisa was born," Patty continued. "It baffled everyone because she never came home otherwise. She cried when she left. She said, 'I'll never be back here and I'll probably never see Lisa again.'

"You see, Helen and my dad grew up with an alcoholic father. They were never poor. Helen never struggled for grades and never conformed to society. She would do things that never occurred to her were off the wall. Like wear stovepipe pants and a big sweater with white pom-poms in 1980. She paid for my honeymoon and then invited herself along. She insisted we go to visit Monticello because she's fascinated with history. It was more like a tour-guide honeymoon. We slept in one room with two beds. As intelligent as she is, she has no common sense at all."

It scarcely mattered that I could not think up any immediate response; Patty talked fast and didn't wait for answers.

"She's not very good with people. She doesn't like to admit mistakes. Admitting she is your mother would mean she had a lot of explaining to do. She would say, 'It's too late to fix it so why bother?'

"I've always known about you," Patty said suddenly. "I remember the whole incident. I tried to tell my parents about it, but my dad wouldn't listen. After my grandmother died, there was a fight over the inheritance and I told my dad, 'You know Helen has children.'"

"Children?" I asked, my voice purposely calm but my insides churning madly.

"There was a guy Helen met in the army, I think his name was Scott. Early on, he came with Helen on a train from New York. He came to Lockhart lots of times, for something like seven or ten years, and had long extensive conversations with my grandmother. Helen stopped in Lockhart before she moved from New York to California. The next day, after Helen left, the guy came to my grandma's. Sometimes he would visit my grandmother and bring along a little boy named Robert. He was a couple of years older than me. I remember because from the time I was a toddler, I was always at my grandma's. After I was seven, I lived there permanently."

"Why are you so sure the boy was Helen's son?" I asked.

"My grandma kept papers in a big cedar chest. Once I peeked at them. They had birth dates on them: one child was born in April and one in May. I remember something about Chicago and Connecticut . . . "

"Are you saying Helen had two children—that I have a brother?" I asked incredulously.

"My grandmother made me vow never to say anything to Helen or she wouldn't come home again," Patty went on as if she didn't hear me. "My grandmother spent her whole life in constant awe of Helen. She would never let anyone say derogatory things about her. After she moved away, my grandmother wrote her a letter every Saturday. 'Just so she never forgets I'm here,' she would say. My dad did everything for his mother, but Helen did whatever she wanted. No matter how much dad did for Emma, she always looked at him like he was nothing and Helen was everything. My grandma sent Helen twenty-five dollars every week. It was funny because Helen always had money, but I remember she was in some kind of trouble in New York with a man. An older man. I think I met him once when we went up to Rochester. He was a doughy kind of guy. I thought he was the man who owned the accounting firm she worked for."

That could have been Frank Harlett, I thought.

"My grandma did to me what she did to Helen. She put us both on a pedestal, never thought we could do any wrong. She was very manipulative but never showed any emotion. She ruined my life."

"Do you know where those papers are, where that old chest is now?" I persisted.

"I don't know, it could be in my parents' attic. But my mother tends to throw everything out."

It was hard to think about anything else but the possibility that I could have a brother out there somewhere. Ever since losing Howie, I had felt like an amputee with phantom pains. I barely remembered him yet I felt his absence almost every day. I couldn't understand why my need for an older brother ran so deep, but I found some comfort in knowing my daughter would have one.

It also occurred to me that if Helen had given up another child, then perhaps my heart could finally accept what my mind had come to believe; it wasn't me that Helen rejected, but the idea of a child, any child.

"Why do you think Helen lied when I called her?" I asked Patty.

"She was probably devastated. You don't understand: to admit you had children but didn't raise them, to Helen that meant you were a horrible person. I know because that's how I feel. I guarantee you she does want to have contact with you. She just doesn't know how to deal with the questions in between. If she could pick it up from today and not from yesterday, she would."

It was a view of Helen I had never heard before. Although they were words I wanted to believe, I figured they were about as likely as the lost island of Atlantis popping out of the sea.

"I'm mad at Helen sometimes," Patty said with sudden force. "Because of her, I lost eight years with my kids and lost my life with my father, whom I adored. Maybe if I hadn't listened to her, I wouldn't have."

"Did she tell you to give up your children?" I asked.

"She convinced me the kids would be OK with Sylvia. That it was better for them and for me. I was going to live with Helen in Los Angeles. She said she could get me a job. That's the way it is with Helen; she's like my grandma was. She wants to set everything up for you as long as you live by her rules. You know, she's really the one who made me hate Lockhart."

Patty seemed to have a way of blaming everyone else for her own mistakes.

"Once when I was very young, we took Helen to the airport," she recalled. "I was crying. She came back down the runway and said; 'What are you doing?' I answered, 'I don't want you to go.' 'And crying's going to change that?' she asked me. She was angry. Later she called and said, 'Don't ever do that again.'"

I could envision the scene as clearly as if I was watching a film. Even though I had never spent any real time with Helen, her speech patterns and behavior had grown to seem as familiar as those of a character in an absorbing novel.

"Helen loves the city but likes to take long walks in the woods," Patty continued. "Once, when I went with her on a hike, she made me stay three trees behind her. I wasn't allowed to talk. I know it sounds ridiculous, but I would have liked her to be my mom. She couldn't bathe me or do my hair, but she was good at cool stuff like going on about philosophies of life that were only important when I got older. But as smart as she is, Helen has no patience. I can't imagine what she would have been like raising a child."

"So what about your son, is he living with you too?"

"No," she said.

"How old is he now?"

"He's ten or eleven, I'm not sure which."

I wondered about a woman who couldn't remember her own son's age; what could be missing from her heart? Maybe Patty and Helen shared some strange family trait that left out all maternal feelings.

"When I was younger," Patty said, "I wanted to be just like Helen. And I guess I did turn out like her. I regret a lot of it now. I regret the stuff with my kids."

Patty filled in a few gaps in our family medical history—she and Helen both get tired and moody from eating starchy food; they have nervous facial twitches; and Helen gets severe migraine headaches from being around florescent lamps. We ended the call, promising to talk again. I agreed to send her the picture I had of the second lieutenant so she could see whether it was the same man she remembered.

She called me back about two weeks later.

"That's the man," she said. "The reason I remember him so vividly is because he looks like my uncle on my mother's side."

It was just the news I wanted to hear. Believing my father was a handsome army lieutenant was a lot easier to live with than wondering if I was the daughter of a con man who nobody would admit to knowing.

"You know, Debbie, the last time I talked to you, I turned around to Lisa and said, 'Why didn't I ever look for her before?' I guess it was out of loyalty to Emma and Helen. If it wasn't for Lisa, I wouldn't have called you at all. If I had tried to find you years ago before you found my parents, I wouldn't have known whether you knew you were adopted or not and would have had to explain it all to you."

"I've always known I was adopted," I said.

"If you had appeared ten years ago, you would have shown Helen's age and she couldn't have tolerated that," said Patty, reminding me of what Paul had said.

"It's no different now," I said.

"Helen doesn't have any problem with cutting people off," she said. "I can guarantee you will never get any confirmation of who your father was, even if she does admit she's your mother."

"I don't think that's going to happen any time soon," I said.

"You and I are not all that different," she said, her voice softer. "I feel like I have no one to lean on. I was alone most of my childhood. If you had been there, we would have had each other. How close we could have been."

Her words made me feel more connected to the Dunnes than I ever had since my search began. I imagined what it would have been like growing up in that small Pennsylvania town, throwing snowballs in the cemetery and collecting wild-flowers on the hillsides in the summer. Perhaps Patty would have been like a sister to me. I wondered why my grandmother hadn't taken me in if she knew all along that Helen had given birth to a daughter. She seemed to prefer girls. How different my life would have been. Would I have gone to college? Would I have had children and given them away?

"I've had a lot of problems," Patty continued. "I took my grandmother's death really hard and did a lot of stupid things. I felt alone and like all I had was Helen. I tried to get comfort from her and didn't get anything. It made me hard. I've had very little contact with my parents for the past seven years. You're the last connection I have to my family."

We hung up after making plans for me to visit her in Pittsburgh the following summer.

❧

Weeks went by before I heard from Patty again. She called while I was out one night and the babysitter left me a note: *Your cousin Patty called. She needs to know your exact date of birth. She spoke to your mother. You can call her anytime.*

An alarm went off in my head. I was going to have to prove myself again, I thought—prove I was who I said I was.

"I talked to Helen," Patty said right away. "She brought up a very good point. When exactly is your birthday? Because Helen said she was at my parents' wedding in April of 1959."

"My birthday is in May and she couldn't have been there without people knowing she was pregnant," I said impatiently. "So what else did she say?"

"She was quite receptive," said Patty. "She wanted to know what you said, what questions I asked you."

She recounted their conversation:

"I talked to Debbie Holtz. Do you remember her?" asked Patty.

"No," Helen answered.

"She's your daughter."

"Oh." The phone went silent.

"This girl I talked to has a lot of evidence," Patty continued.

"You're taking this woman's word? I can't believe you contacted this woman! What were you thinking?" Helen asked with exasperation. "She could have been anyone. There was no reason for you to believe she was a part of our family."

"She visited my parents and I remember seeing documents in Grandma's chest about her," said Patty.

"Mother had a tendency to hold onto too many things," said Helen. "So what did you talk to her about?"

"She's extremely curious about our family and her medical history."

"Is there something wrong with her?"

"No, she just wants to know her medical history," said Patty.

"You're a better person to ask than me. Did you satisfy all of her questions?"

"Not all of them."

"Did you fail to mention that I have a history of hypoglycemia?"

"I mentioned it."

"So what do you think?" Helen asked.

"I think she's telling me the truth."

"Anyone can say anything," said Helen. "Have you met her?"

"No, but I want to. There's a good possibility that Debbie will come to Pittsburgh this summer. I want to meet her, she seems very nice."

"If you're thinking you're going to get someone like yourself, you're wrong," said Helen adamantly. "She was raised in a totally different environment. You were raised in the country, in the woods. Maybe you've changed your ways of thinking since you moved to Pittsburgh, but she had a different upbringing. She grew up in the city, raised by people you don't know, from a completely different status socially and now you want to merge with her as family?"

"She seems very nice on the phone."

"Anyone can talk on the telephone."

"You know, she has two children."

"Oh, yes, there're children involved."

"She sent pictures of herself and a man she thinks is her father."

"Oh, she did, did she?" Helen asked. "Where did she get that?"

"From my parents," said Patty. "It reminded me of a man, someone you met in the army, who used to visit us. Who was he?"

"Just an acquaintance. We kept in touch over the years, but there was no real romantic involvement."

"What was his name?"

"That's irrelevant," said Helen. "He has nothing to do with that woman."

"Wasn't there a boy?"

"That was my friend's son," Helen said evasively, then continued, "Could you send me that photograph? I would be interested in having a copy. What other documents does this woman have? Does she have Mom's papers?"

"This woman researched this all on her own. Whatever she has, she got on her own."

"*I'm extremely sorry if that woman has caused you any inconvenience or discomfort,*" *said Helen.*

"*I asked her how you looked these days,*" *said Patty.*

"*Did she tell you I look old?*"

"*No, she said you look good.*"

"*I don't look old,*" *Helen said.* "*How old are you now?*"

"*I'm thirty-six.*"

"*I didn't realize you were that old. So much time has passed.*"

"*I was surprised to hear that this girl doesn't look like you because she sounds just like you on the telephone,*" *said Patty.*

"*Actually, she looks more like I do from the mouth up,*" *said Helen.* "*But she's not built like us.*"

"*I'd like to meet her.*"

"*Maybe you should do what you have to do to satisfy your curiosity,*" *said Helen.*

"*I'm not trying to corner you, I'm only asking you these questions for myself,*" *said Patty.* "*I know how you must feel since I've lost seven years with my own children.*"

"*I don't have anything to say concerning that,*" *replied Helen.*

"*But what about the paperwork I saw?*"

"*Patty, why, if you saw all these things, did you wait all these years to ask me? I would have explained them to you.*"

"*But you're not explaining them now.*"

"*Patty, I would have given you more credit than that. Your parents married on April 22, 1959, and I certainly wasn't pregnant at their wedding. Who else has she contacted in the family?*"

"*Well, my parents, Aunt Millie, and I'm not sure who else,*" *said Patty.*

"*Millie? What does she know about my life?*" *Helen asked indignantly.*

"*I only want you to tell me if this is true,*" *Patty pleaded.*

Suddenly the phone went dead, Patty said. She went down the block to a neighbor's house, but found out phone

Coincidence

service was out on the whole block. She went to a friend's house to call Helen back, but Patty said by then her line was busy. It was a scenario difficult for me to believe; it made more sense that Helen just hung up, but I chalked it up as one in a long line of bizarre coincidences.

Patty's rendition of her conversation with Helen stunned me. It seemed as though Helen's curiosity had gotten the better of her, forcing her to momentarily drop her guard. It also came as a surprise to Patty.

"It was a different response than I anticipated from her," she said. "It threw me off. I thought she would say she had no reason to talk about this. Instead she did exactly the opposite. Helen's questions convinced me more than ever that she is your mother. I never thought curiosity would overwhelm Helen, but it has."

"Did you notice how she never said, 'This is not my child' or 'She's not my daughter'?" I asked Patty. "She could have just said, 'I don't know who this person is' and refused to discuss it anymore."

Lying, especially where Helen was concerned, came in many different shades of gray. It seemed to me that she was doing damage control, trying to get as much information as she could to figure out where she stood.

"But what about the thing with the wedding?" she asked me.

"I think if you call your parents you'll find out that she was never there," I said.

"You're probably right. I'm irritated that she said that. I just want her to tell me the truth," said Patty. "I'm not even you and this bothers me. I can't imagine how you must feel. Well, I'm glad you're around. I hope we can form a friendship."

"I think we already have," I said.

❧

I called my aunt the following day. She confirmed, as I expected, that Helen was not at her wedding. In fact, they couldn't even find her to send her an invitation. Helen did show up shortly after Patty was born, and showed particular interest in the new baby, even helping to care for her briefly. Were some maternal feelings lingering inside Helen then from having given birth so recently?

Flush with newfound confidence and wanting to develop the kind of relationship with Patty that I could not with Helen or even my aunt or uncle, I went ahead and bought airline tickets for Sarah and me to visit Patty and Lisa the following July. It would be a different kind of trip than my last one to Pennsylvania. This time I would be meeting someone who had found *me*, who believed who I was because she had always known my story. With my aunt and uncle, I felt like I was constantly pursuing them and being pushed back, time after time, by an undercurrent of ambivalence.

Sure, I knew Patty had a jaded past. But awareness of my own multitude of mistakes made it easier to accept hers. She was only five months younger than I was and we both grew up lonely. There was symmetry between us. Through her, I had the chance of finally finding a place in my own history.

I gave Patty the benefit of the doubt when she didn't respond to my letters or phone calls in March and April. I convinced myself that she was busy or distracted by her financial problems.

But, in May, she hung up on me when I called. After that, she stopped answering the phone altogether. Her silence spoke of more than doubts. I was sure her reasons for avoiding me began and ended with Helen.

In June, I wrote Patty a letter on a card I bought in Big Sur. On it was a picture of a girl with long blond hair and angel wings, wearing a flowing white gown, sadly looking at a girl next to her who is wearing a skirt patterned with berry vines and solemnly staring at her hands crossed on her lap. A moon and a barren tree sit between them in the background.

In the letter, I said I couldn't see what I had done to deserve her thoughtlessness and that her apparent decision to cast me off was a loss to both of us.

It wasn't until September that she answered the phone.

"I can't talk now," she said, her voice cold and slippery.

"Just don't hang up, OK?" I pleaded. "Why did you blow me off?"

"I don't know why I did it."

"Did Helen threaten you?"

"Sort of," she said. "I can't explain it to you. I'll write or call you again when I can. Bye."

The phone clicked in my ear and I knew I would never hear from Patty again.

I stared at the phone for a few minutes, then picked it up and called my aunt. I quickly told her what happened.

"I think they probably called Helen to tell her you were coming, and she put the red flag out and stopped them," said Sylvia.

I told her what Patty had said: that my grandmother had known about my birth.

"Don't believe it. Patty was just trying to get on your good side. It would have killed Grandma Dunne knowing there was a child out there. She would have gone and hunted you out. Patty dreams but she lies. Mike says the only time Patty doesn't lie is when she has her mouth closed. He says Helen and Patty are made from the same mold, they're exactly alike."

"So, does that mean she lied about the lieutenant visiting Lockhart?" I asked.

"There was a man and I do believe his name was Scott, and I think he's the same man in the picture, dark-haired and nice looking. I know there was a boy. . . . I didn't remember before, my mind isn't so good anymore, but I asked Mike and he said he remembered his mother mowing the lawn one day and she told him a young man and his son were visiting her. She was mad that Helen wasn't more interested in him. Emma arranged so we weren't around when he came. Patty was there. She would remember."

"So you do think she's telling the truth about that?" I asked.

"Maybe she does tell the truth sometimes," said Sylvia.

Looking for any truth I could find, I counted on that.

chapter TWENTY-THREE

I waited for two years after talking to Patty before I picked up my search again. That may have been because I couldn't stand the idea of any further disappointment, or maybe because so many people told me it would be nearly impossible to find a man with only a photograph to go on.

Once I did resume, though, I plunged into tracking down the nameless lieutenant as much for the sheer challenge of it as in any real hope of finding my father. I have never met an adoptee, woman or man, who wanted to find a father first. It is always the mother we have a desperate need to reconnect with; she's the one with whom we share a physical history. No other intimate experience can be compared to the nine months spent inside another's body. It creates not only a biological bond, but also a kind of psychic link understandable only in the most visceral way. A common thread through the dozens of stories I have heard is that, depending on the outcome of an adoptee's search for her mother, the father either becomes the icing on the cake or a meaningful consolation prize.

I hoped that finding my father, who could very well have no idea I exist, would give me a sense of satisfaction, a way to silently prove to Helen that she had not succeeded in rewriting history, that she didn't have total control over my past.

Looking for the lieutenant was the triathlon of needle-in-a-haystack searches. Like the unsigned postcard, a mystery that remained unsolved on my living room mantel, the photo of the nameless soldier was a nagging question waiting to be answered.

They both reminded me of the anonymity of adoption and the role adoptees are expected to play in concealing other people's secrets. I remembered stories I had been told about adoptees sitting across the desk from social workers who hold the truth of their origins at their fingertips yet refuse to divulge them. I thought of the arbitrary laws that allow adoptees in some states to find out crucial knowledge about their backgrounds while the same information is forbidden to those born in states with different rules governing adoption.

I knew Helen would never tell me who my father was, and I knew the chances of my ever learning the identity of the postcard's author were slim. Chasing the phantom lieutenant, while a long shot, held out the greatest promise.

Knowing very little about the military, I first sought out expert advice. I was introduced to a retired army colonel, a neighbor of another adoptee I knew. She told him about my photos and he said he'd be happy to look at them.

Perched high in the East Bay hills, the colonel's house reached dramatically to the sky with diagonal roof lines and looked out on the surrounding hills of golden brown through windows of various geometric shapes.

The colonel greeted me at the front door. He was a thin man, with a youthful vigor that belied his age, which I estimated to be nearing seventy. He was shorter than I expected, perhaps because I envisioned all higher-ups in the military to resemble John Wayne.

Inside, the house was remarkably free of clutter. The varnish on the wood floors and paneling gleamed. No streaks or specks of dust marred the giant glass coffee table in the living room. I imagined that the colonel and his wife must have given careful thought to the placement of each framed photo of the colonel with his army buddies. As he led me to the living room couch, I passed by a prominent wall display of military memorabilia, at the center of which was his West Point diploma.

After we'd gotten acquainted, I took my photographs out of an envelope and laid them on the table. First, I showed him the formal portraits of Helen.

"Enlisted, private first class," he declared. His faded blue eyes, enlarged by the bifocals he wore, kept darting between the pictures. "She was in the WAC, what we called the Women's Army Corps at that time. They trained separately from the men and lived in separate barracks. They could work in jobs with men, even though they primarily did secretarial work back then. Now it's a different story. Women do everything short of fighting."

I showed him Helen's dog tags, still dangling from the same silver chain she must have worn them on.

"These show you her years in the service," said the colonel. "Women normally enlisted for three years. So here you can see that her term started in 1954. She entered as a private and it seems she was promoted to private first class. She could have gone—she was eligible—to the WAC officer candidate school."

Another one of her missed opportunities, I thought.

"Oh, yes," he added. "Her blood type was O."

Blood was the one tangible link that tied us together yet I had never thought to compare ours before. My blood genotype was AO, meaning I must have gotten the "A" from my father.

I showed the colonel a large photo of Helen and a girlfriend, smiling and posing next to a tree on a gravel bluff. Helen wore a conservative skirt and blouse, but her smile was that of a Cheshire cat and her white-checkered sunglasses were a flashy style statement. I was sure the other woman was Maureen Foster. She was wearing a varsity letter sweater with the initial M on the pocket. Behind and below them you could see a huge expanse of buildings that stretched out to the ocean, all white with dark roofs, looking as though they were all part of the same child's play set.

The colonel said that although he couldn't be sure, the women might have been standing in front of Fort Monmouth. I remembered reading that the fort was located near the seashore, in the middle of one of the most beautiful resort areas in the Northeast.

I showed him the most important photo of all, the one that demanded the most answers—the one of the nameless man with the shy smile and dimpled chin. I had studied it so many times that I was convinced his eyes were the same shape as mine and might even be blue.

"You're right," he said, staring at the photo he held only inches from his nose. "He was a lieutenant. He was a lieutenant in the Signal Corps." He pointed to the double-flag pins on his lapels. "This photo was taken upon his being commissioned. It's impossible to tell if he was a first or second lieutenant because I can't see whether his bars are silver or gold. But it doesn't matter because they usually only stay a second lieutenant for six months to a year and then they're promoted."

You could tell by his authoritative tone that the colonel's identity was still firmly intertwined with the military. The sharp edge of his expertise was softened by nostalgia, the kind that comes with having loved a career so much that you can't imagine having done anything else.

"He's wearing the older uniform, the original dark green one that was used from the mid-forties to around '57 or '58."

"Is there any way to tell where he's from?" I asked.

"Look at the insignia on his sleeve," he said, pointing at a four-leaf clover enclosed in a diamond shape. "He was from the Fourth Army, based in San Antonio, Texas. The Fourth covered a lot of the Southwestern U.S., including Texas and New Mexico.

"At that time, officers were sent to Fort Monmouth because it was home to the Signal Corps School. They were the real experts in the high-tech stuff of the time—battlefield communication, radio, you name it."

Still holding the picture, the colonel got up and walked briskly to the other side of the room. He took a magnifying glass out of a drawer and returned to sit beside me on the couch.

"If you go to West Point Academy, you wear a ring on your left ring finger," he said proudly. I quickly spotted the gold insignia band on the colonel's finger.

"I don't see one on this man's finger. So he either got commissioned out of college or through the ROTC and was sent to Fort Monmouth for basic officer training. Or he could have enlisted and then joined officer candidate school. To be an officer you have to have shown leadership ability."

The colonel explained that most men stayed in the army on active duty for only a few years. But those like himself, who perform well enough to get offered a regular commission, are expected to spend their lives in the army.

I had grown up with a decidedly '60s mentality even though I was ten years too late to be a bonafide member of that generation. I had some radical credentials, probably enough to have an FBI file opened: I protested against South African apartheid in college, was arrested protesting nuclear weapons at the Lawrence Livermore Laboratory and had a knee-jerk distrust of anyone in uniform. Yet now I wanted my father to be this symbol of power and mainstream propriety. It seemed a whole lot better than the swarthy alternative personified by Frank Harlett.

The colonel's only suggestion for identifying the lieutenant was to sift through archives of photos at the fort itself. As I was leaving his house, he told me he wished he could have helped me more.

It turned out that no photographic records existed any longer at Fort Monmouth; they had likely been shipped off to another fort in Georgia.

So I started from scratch. The Internet now offered possibilities that hadn't been available to me just a few years earlier. I posted messages on every military site and veterans' chat room I could find asking for help in identifying the picture from people who may have been at Fort Monmouth around the same time. My postings sat alongside hundreds of others from veterans looking for their old buddies and children born overseas in search of their American soldier fathers. The difference was that they knew the names of the men they were trying to find. The surprisingly few people who responded to my Internet posts did not recognize the lieutenant once I sent them his picture.

I contacted the *Army Times* to purchase an ad featuring the photo, but the newspaper refused to run it without a name. The Freedom of Information Act, a tool I had used many times as a journalist, enabled me to get a veteran's rank, dates of service and town he last lived in—but only if I had a name.

Frustrated and discouraged, I finally broke down and sought help—a military locator service.

"Without having a name, the search is going to be very long and very frustrating," Dick, the former army officer who ran the service, said after I first told him of my strange request. "What else can you tell me about this individual? Why do you want to find him?"

I told him the whole story and he was surprisingly sympathetic. He agreed to take on my case, unusual as it seemed, even though he was accustomed to searching for lost friends and relatives with known identities.

It took months of applying to the National Personnel Records Center in St. Louis before Dick was given permission to view the microfilms containing the rosters of officers from Fort Monmouth. When he finally sat down to view the tapes covering 1953 to 1956, they could not be read. They were worthless because the films were so out of focus that it was impossible to make out any of the names on them. To make matters worse, he said, it appeared that Helen's personnel file was lost in a notorious 1973 fire at the army records center.

This was starting to feel strangely reminiscent of all of the other official records I had sought that were either missing or had been destroyed.

Finally, though, Dick was able to send me hundreds of pages of what the army calls "morning reports," records that kept daily track of the comings and goings of officers on an army base. The huge bundle of photocopied lists contained thousands of names and birth dates of men who joined the fort's student officer detachment in 1954.

I had chosen a specific army training unit from numbers I spotted on an envelope sent to Helen from an army photographer. Knowing it was a crapshoot, Dick suggested I look for the name Scott and then, if that failed, for officers who came from the Fourth Army.

It turned out that everyone started out as a second lieutenant. Large groups of them would join the unit from civilian life for a three-month officer-training course. Chances were good, Dick told me, that someone who trained there at the same time might recognize the man in the photo.

My decidedly unscientific method for choosing which men to find was to look for unusual names. It was easier that way to track them through Internet phone directories.

I devised a story: My mother was based at Fort Monmouth and to commemorate the fortieth anniversary of her discharge, I was trying to organize a surprise reunion of her army friends. It would mean so much, I said, since she is recovering from a serious illness. As for the lieutenant's name, her memory was a bit foggy, although she thinks it may have been Scott.

Most of them bought it. One man after another, each name more offbeat than the last, agreed to look at the photo, but later told me the face was not familiar to them. "Forty-three years is a long time," several of them commented. In turn, they gave me other names.

"He's a fine looking young fella, isn't he?" one man commented.

There were a few guys with whom I had long, friendly conversations. One man, who told me his life story in a speeded-up Texas drawl, called me back several times just to check on my progress. I finally broke down and told him the true story and he regaled me with tales of the romantic exploits of his army buddies after they were shipped off to Japan and Germany.

"He may not know he has a daughter," the man said. "But he might be happy to find out. I know I would be real pleased to come across somebody like you."

Just when I was losing hope of ever finding the lieutenant, Steve was invited to another medical conference, this time in Denver, Colorado. While we were there, I talked Steve into making a side trip to Colorado Springs to visit Maureen Foster, the woman in the photos who knew Helen but refused to admit it.

Arriving at her house unannounced, I knocked on the door while Steve and the children waited in the car. Maureen opened the door, obviously unprepared for a visitor. Although it was the afternoon, she looked a bit disheveled, wearing a house robe with her hair unbrushed. I told her who I was and her expression suddenly resembled a deer caught in headlights. Still, she asked me in and I followed her as she flitted around the house, straightening her hair and apologizing for the mess.

"I didn't realize you live nearby," she said.

"I don't. We're staying in Denver and stopped by on our way to visit some friends," I said.

"I have to apologize," she said as we sat down in the living room. "I thought it was some sort of prank when you first called me."

"So you do know Helen?" I asked.

"Yes," she said, reluctantly.

"From the army?"

"No, from before."

"From the Pennsylvania State Teacher's College?"

"Yes."

"When was that?"

"In 1952 and '53," she said. "After we were done, every-one went their separate ways and we never corresponded."

I took out the photos of Helen and her friend posing on the hillside and another of them sitting on a beach and handed them to Maureen.

"That's not me," she said, shaking her head but not tak-ing her eyes off of the picture.

Then I took out the picture of Maureen and her husband in their army uniforms and placed it in front of her.

"Yes, that's me."

"The woman in the other pictures looks remarkably like you," I persisted.

"Where did you say Helen was based?" she asked, ignor-ing my question.

"Fort Monmouth."

"We were never there," she said.

"Then how did Helen get your army picture?"

"I probably sent it to her," she said, sounding more flus-tered than ever. "We were all recruited into the army from the teacher's college. I think the military recruited students there to get the lesbians out of the Women's Army Corps." She laughed nervously.

"Anyway, I sure do remember Helen when we were at the college though. We were all supposed to get up in front of the class as student teachers and Helen was petrified of it. She was too shy to do her student teaching. That's why she dropped out."

She rattled on nervously about some inconsequential events at the school. Occasionally we heard noises from the children who Steve had let out of the car to run around the sidewalk. Maureen looked over her shoulder a few times, staring blankly out the window and then turned back to look at me.

"Helen was such a nice, kindhearted girl," she recalled, making me wonder if we were talking about the same person.

"She was an egghead," Maureen went on. "Very intelligent, but without much common sense. Kind of like Einstein. People had to tie his shoes for him, you know."

Definitely sounding more like Helen, I thought.

I told Maureen how Helen had lied to me when I found her.

"I can't imagine why," she said. "Something must have happened to her. Someone must have hurt her real bad, that's why she's trying to hurt you. Maybe it was some kind of a situation, like a redneck who threatened her or a married guy. Helen wouldn't do something unkind deliberately unless she was threatened in some way. I just remember her as a sweet darling."

She asked me about myself, and I told her about my children and Steve. But I hesitated to tell her I was a newspaper reporter, worried it would make her even more nervous.

"I don't know, the older I get the flakier I get," she said with an uncomfortable laugh. "Maybe Helen really doesn't remember you."

"How could you forget having a child?" I asked with polite exasperation.

"Well, you're such a dear. It's her loss. I would love to have a daughter like you."

Finally, I took out the picture of the lieutenant and handed it to her.

"I don't recognize him," she said, shaking her head.

"Would you mind showing the picture to your husband?" I asked. "Maybe he might remember him."

"No, he wouldn't know," she said abruptly. "He didn't even know Helen."

Maureen wrote my address and phone number down and promised "to keep me in mind."

She walked me outside and I introduced her to Steve. As we walked toward the car, she said in a voice that seemed to float suddenly out of the air and just as quickly vanish back into it: "Your mother was one of the nicest people I ever met."

Later that year, I received a Thanksgiving card from Maureen with pictures of pumpkins and carnations on it. I had never before seen a Thanksgiving greeting card. Inside she wrote: "I will keep trying for you."

I wasn't sure what she meant by that.

⌒∞⌒

When I returned home, I was about to start a new round of calls to former army officers when I received a call one day from a woman named Laura Christopher.

"I'm a friend of Jack and Carol Brudno," she said. "You sent them a photograph of a man who you're trying to identify, and I think I may be able to help you."

"Yes," was all I could say.

"I lived at Fort Monmouth when I was a teenager," she went on. "We lived on officer's row because my father was based there. The bachelor officers' quarters were posted nearby, and my friends and I used to go to their parties. I remember this man because he was such a good-looking guy that all of the girls went a little crazy over him. I can't be 100 percent sure, but I think his name was William Markham."

I knew the minute she said the name that she had identified the right person. I shuddered for a moment and then found myself pacing the floor. The father's name listed on my birth certificate was also William. William Dunne. Helen had used his real first name. He had to be my father, I thought over and over again.

"Do you remember anything else about him?" I asked, trying hard to contain my exhilaration.

"He was from Texas, I think. I remember that he ended up getting married there. A lot of them stayed on and were stationed on the post, but he left."

"Thank you so much, you've helped me more than you can know," I said, making sure to get off the phone before she could ask me any questions about my reasons for looking for him.

From the beginning I knew that searching for the lieutenant was a gamble. If he was my father, and I found him, there was a risk that he would do to me what Helen had: he could reject me. It wasn't so much being turned away by a stranger that I feared, as that it might reopen the old wound that had been healing for several years now. I didn't have complete faith that the stitches would hold.

Yet once I had his name, there was no turning back. It didn't take me long to find out that there were more than a few William Markhams in Texas. Before I started phoning, I wanted to do some research on this man to find out what kind of a person he was.

It's amazing how much you can learn when you have a name. It was only a matter of weeks before the military locator I had hired sent me William's military service record. He was from Galveston and had attended Texas A&M University, receiving a bachelor's degree in industrial engineering.

With some difficulty, I tracked down his yearbook pictures from both high school and college. I was grateful that I had somewhere to put my energies because I wasn't yet ready to call him.

Thanks to some helpful school librarians, I received the photocopies in the mail very quickly. The photos, though incredibly grainy, showed variations of the William Markham I had grown familiar with from his army picture. There was William as cadet captain in his college ROTC program, standing at attention before rows of other would-be soldiers; William, dressed in a formal uniform, a girl in a ball gown on his arm, posing before a line of flags; a somber-looking teenager in his high school yearbook; and then a more mature and handsome version of himself in his college graduation portrait.

Once I was certain that I had the right person, I started making phone calls to William Markhams all over Texas. Eventually I reached a woman named Kathy Markham in Lubbock. I told her I was looking for a William who had been at Fort Monmouth in the mid-fifties. Her husband had been there, she said, but he was out of town right now. She even told me he was a teacher at Texas Tech University. But she didn't once ask why I was looking for him.

I wrote William a letter, enclosing the army photograph, and asked him to call me. I offered no explanation.

A week later, I still hadn't heard from him. I left a message on his answering machine at the university, where I found out he was a senior lecturer in petroleum engineering. I reminded him about the photo I sent and again asked him to call me.

One morning before the sun had risen, the phone rang. Steve picked it up and then turned to me: "I think it's the lieutenant from Texas calling."

I shot out of bed, my mind struggling to keep up with my body as I raced to the kitchen to pick up the portable phone.

At the same time, I was searching for the pad of paper on which I had written a prepared speech.

"Thank you so much for returning my call," I said, stalling while I found the paper in the dining room cabinet.

"Well, I've been traveling," he said. "The picture you sent me was of myself in a Fourth Army uniform taken, I think, at the time when I was commissioned."

His voice was serious, and I knew he must want to know how I got it.

"I know you don't know me," I said cautiously. "But if you have a few minutes, I would like to tell you the story of how I came to call you."

"That's fine," he said.

My mind was like an engine struggling to rev up on a frigid morning without much fuel. I longed for a cup of strong coffee.

"I was put up for adoption when I was born," I started, trying not to sound like I was reading from prepared text. "In my thirties, after I had two children, I had a need for their sake as well as mine to know my biological background. I don't want or need anything else. I am well educated and I live well.

"When I started my search seven years ago, I was lucky to have my original birth certificate, which listed Helen Dunne as my mother. I found her but, unfortunately, she has no interest in talking to me. We have no contact now. At first it hurt very much but later I realized that she is a loner who doesn't even keep in touch with her family. So it was up to me to find out the truth of my origins. Helen's family in Pennsylvania welcomed me and were very forthright. They told me as much as they could.

"As far as finding my father, though, I had to rely on any leads that I was given. One thing I knew was that Helen had told her former husband that she had been in love with an army lieutenant while based at Fort Monmouth. Also, my aunt and uncle gave me a photograph—the one that I sent you.

"I've spent quite a long time trying to find you. It hasn't been easy. I just want you to understand that I'm not looking for anything except the truth about myself. All I really need to know for my own peace of mind is where I come from and that's why I called you. I was hoping you could tell me whatever you remember about that time in the 1950s."

My heart was beating so fast that I was having trouble catching my breath.

"I dated Helen Dunne, I do recall that," he said, without a trace of agitation. "Whether she was in love with me, I can't address that. Under no circumstances did I feel that was mutual. Once I left Fort Monmouth, we never had any additional contact. She was a nice lady, I remember that. I do remember going out with her."

"I was born in 1959. Helen's family said you visited them in Pennsylvania several times through the early 1960s, after Helen was discharged from the army," I said.

"That's not correct," he said patiently and without hesitation. "I got out of the army in June of 1957 and returned to Texas immediately thereafter. On December 2, 1956, I was married to my current wife. So as you can see, my being your father is not biologically possible."

"Not biologically possible." The words echoed in my ears, getting louder each time.

For a few seconds, it occurred to me to try to argue with him, ask him to reconsider, to assure him that he could be honest, that he had nothing to fear from me. But reality had slapped me in the face and I couldn't help believing everything he had said. He had put together a puzzle and all of the pieces seemed to fit into place.

"Thank you again for returning my call," I said. "I appreciate your honesty."

After hanging up, I looked at William's army records again. Suddenly I saw things I must have refused to see before. An annual audit, signed by William two days after I was born in 1959, said he was employed in Texas, married and had one child.

Then I dug out my birth certificate. Perhaps Helen had used his first name on it out of a hopeless wish that he had fathered her child instead of disappearing from her life. Or maybe it was a cruel joke, born out of her disappointment with having loved someone who did not feel the same way about her.

⚬◆⚬

My son has a friend named Ben Murphy. He is smart, more mature than his eleven years, and often wears a pensive expression, as though he is pondering some deep philosophical issues. He is open and friendly, without the posturing that often accompanies preadolescent boys.

He is also adopted.

At my son's twelfth birthday party, amid the commotion of children unleashing all of their pent-up energy, Ben was somber and quiet. He sat away from the others, unable or unwilling to join the revelry. I kept my eye on him as I scurried around, cutting up pizza, pouring soda and putting candles on the cake.

When the children went downstairs to listen to music and dance, Ben came into the kitchen.

"Debbie," he said. "You might have noticed that I'm a little sad today."

"I did notice that, Ben. Would you like to tell me what's bothering you?"

"I don't know if you know this, but I'm adopted. I know my birth mother and we talk sometimes. She couldn't take care of me so she gave me to my parents."

Ben's was an "open adoption"—the newest answer to the quandaries of adoption—where identities are no longer hidden and both sets of parents can decide whether or not to have contact, how much or how little.

"I've been wondering about my father lately," Ben went on. "I asked my birth mother about him. She wrote me a long letter that I got about a week ago. She said she wasn't careful, that she had a one-night stand. She doesn't remember his name."

He delivered the information with such resolve that I admired his courage. "One-night stand" just rolled off his lips as though it were a familiar concept to him, although I knew it wasn't. Yet he seemed to understand the mistakes of adults in a way no child his age should have to. Despite how much pain the secrets of my adoption had caused, I couldn't imagine coping with that kind of bitter truth when I was Ben's age.

Suddenly tears filled Ben's eyes and his lip began to quiver.

"I don't think I'm ever going to know who my dad is," he said.

I walked closer to him and kneeled down so I could look straight into his eyes.

"You know, Ben, I was adopted too and I found out just a short time ago that I'm never going to know for sure who my dad was either. I know how hard that is to accept."

"You were adopted?" he asked, his watery eyes widening.

"Yes."

"I've never met anyone my entire life who was adopted before," he said. His face remained serious, yet I could see a faint smile breaking out around the corners of his mouth.

Like Ben, I was the only person I knew who was adopted when I was his age and for a long time afterward. His reaction showed me that, somehow, this small piece of information made a difference to him. Suddenly he was no longer the only person carrying the heavy load.

"You may never know who your dad was," I said. "But you have something very special. You have two parents who love you very much."

"I read that letter from my birth mother by myself for three days before I showed it to my parents," he said.

"Did it help you to show it to them?" I asked.

"Yes," he said.

I hugged him and said quietly into his ear, "They will always be there to help you with all of this, and I will too if you ever just want to talk about it."

In the hours that followed, I kept imagining Ben sitting alone in his bedroom, reading the story of how he came into existence as if watching some gritty, adult movie. Children, it seemed to me, should be allowed to fantasize their creation being the result of some great love affair or romantic comedy —at least until they have enough of their own experiences to accept that adults often make choices that destroy the magic of fairy tales.

I thought a lot about my conversation with Ben. Perhaps what shocked me the most was my own reaction: I felt angry at his birth mother for being so damn honest.

Not having been part of an open adoption myself, I could not say for sure whether it helps alleviate the grief of an adoptee, whether there can ever be a panacea for abandonment. Ben might understand his own mother's reasons for giving him up more clearly than I will ever understand Helen's, but the truth is that knowledge doesn't have the power of emotion.

For after the discordant voices of our adoptive parents and birth parents diminish and recede into the background, Ben and I will ultimately be left alone to heal our own wounds. We'll have to find out who we are, not in other people, but within ourselves.

chapter TWENTY-FOUR

Remembering can be a gift and a curse. Russian psychologist Aleksandr Luria wrote about a soldier who suffered a severe head wound. The injury knocked out all limits to his memory—he could recall virtually everything that he had ever seen, heard, smelled or tasted. But what seemed to be a phenomenal gift brought him little happiness. His vast memory left no room for anything else. He could not derive any meaning from his vivid recollections nor could he fully experience the present.

Yet the idea of a memory that knows no bounds intrigued me. I had spent years trying to recover memories that were lost to a kind of emotional anesthesia. Couldn't it be possible, though, that forgetting plays a part in remembering what is essential? We all revise and reinterpret the past in an effort to extract the meaning we want or need from it.

Manny Skar may have been a crook and a womanizer, but when she thinks of him thirty-five years later, what my adoptive mother remembers best is his charisma, her passion for him and the exciting life they shared. "As miserable as I was with him," she told me, "that was the happiest time in my life."

It's not so different when I remember David. The way he made me laugh tends to crowd out all the times he didn't call, or was too stoned to pay any attention to me. Yet my brother, whom David was supposed to replace, is a blank to me. My mother tells me he was protective, hovering, adoring of me, and that I always looked forward to his coming home. I want so much to retrieve those memories, but all I am left with is a lingering guilt over having survived what he did not.

Historians and genealogists commandeer the past as if it's the only way to make sense of the present, scrutinizing events that happened hundreds of years ago. Seven years after finding my birth mother, my own family tree was still withered and bare.

That changed one day when I received a letter from an elderly cousin in Maryland. I had called him a few months earlier just because he was the only member of the distant Dunne family whose name was William, like the father listed on my birth certificate.

I opened the large envelope and pulled out a stack of papers. There was a pamphlet about a famous tennis player who had found strength in Christ, a bookmark celebrating "40 years of service to the Lord" on family radio, and a small card with a picture of a church in Baltimore and its schedule of Sunday services. On the back of it, William proudly wrote "Our family church will be one hundred years old in 2004."

Next I found a six-page handwritten letter. *Dear Cousin Debbie, It was a pleasant surprise to hear from someone I never knew existed.* While he had addressed the letter to me, I felt as if it was really meant for Shirley Jane Dunne. After seven years, the Dunne family still seemed like a collection of storybook characters to me.

He went on to talk about his faith in Jesus and how the Dunne family worshiped for generations in the Baptist Church in Lockhart. *Many have died in the faith of our Lord Jesus and I expect to see them in heaven.*

His letter was filled with family stories.

> *From 1925 on we would make about three trips a year to Lockhart. Your grandpa ran a garage and had pumps there right close to Uncle Henry's general store and the post office. . . . Everyone looked up to your great-grandparents Geoff and Rose Dunne. They had a large thirteen-room house, a huge barn, a large icehouse. They kept cows, and sold their milk to the milk company, and also had sheep and hogs and chickens. The best cold spring water was piped down from the hill and there was a pond close to the house. . . . My greatest event of the year was going to Lockhart. . . .You would have liked your grandparents Dunne. They were good hardworking people. They lived just on the edge of town, on what was part of the Dunne estate. The federal government had given Elias Dunne 640 acres as payment from his time in the war of 1812 . . .*

He asked me about my adoptive family and said he hoped it had turned out to be a good thing for me. The last time he remembered seeing Helen was in 1948, at their grandmother's funeral. He signed the letter, *Your long lost cousin William Dunne.*

I turned the page to find a copy of The Mayflower Compact, a declaration of independence signed by those who had made the voyage in 1620 from England to Cape Cod. Of the forty-one men listed as passengers on the ship, William had underlined seven of them, who he claimed were ancestors of his father. On the back of the paper, he talked about the Pilgrims by name as if he had known them. *The Dunnes are descendents of four Mayflower families, who were all interrelated. Eli Tilley fell overboard and that's a story in itself,* he wrote with the confidence of a true insider. He suggested I get a book on the Mayflower and read all about them.

What followed were eleven pages of small cursive handwriting tracing fourteen generations of the Dunne family back to Somerset, England, in 1585. In painstaking detail, William recounted the names and years of birth, marriage and death of dozens of ancestors. Beginning with 1891, he even listed causes of death—diphtheria, typhoid fever, accidents, cancer. On the back of one of the pages, he wrote that all of the family's aunts and uncles have passed away and of the two hundred Dunne cousins still living, he is the oldest—the patriarch.

I continued to scan down the lines of names and dates, marveling at the man's devotion to ancestry, his absolute acceptance of birthright. Then my eyes fixed on number thirty-one of a list of second cousins, the great-grandchildren of Geoff and Rose Dunne:

Shirley Jane Dunne, May 14, 1959 to Helen Rose Dunne

Shirley Jane, my alter ego, was sandwiched between names of people I did not know and would probably never meet. It was as if I had climbed onto someone else's tree, but was so well camouflaged that no one could tell I didn't belong there. At the bottom of the paper, he wrote that my children belong among the list of third cousins.

Wasn't this what I always wanted, I thought, to be a part of something larger than myself, instead of just driftwood, long ago broken apart from the tree from which it grew? But how could I be connected to these ghosts from the past when family members who were still alive wanted nothing to do with me?

The problem with documenting bloodlines on paper, I thought, is that it ignores the fragility of human relationships. For example, who would ever know what really happened between Justus Dunne and his son, Josiah, in the early 1800s? Were they always close, or did they drift apart and never speak again?

As I studied the papers, losing my way as I moved from one branch of the family tree to another, I thought about the ever-growing emphasis on genetics. Scientists, hoping to cure diseases, are focusing on genetically isolated places like Iceland, where nearly everyone on the frigid island descended from a small group of ninth-century Norse and Celtic settlers. Not surprisingly, Icelanders are passionate genealogists and researching family trees is a national pastime.

Genetic material is what ties us to our relatives, but it's also what makes us stand apart. Everybody on earth, with the exception of identical twins, is made up of different DNA. You can change your name, but you can never alter your genetic makeup. Nearly every cell of a person's body contains twenty-three pairs of chromosomes, bundles of DNA that carry the thirty thousand genes that make up the blueprint for a complete person. It is an invisible but distinct fingerprint that can be detected in a drop of saliva or a single strand of hair. Police now use it to identify suspects who might otherwise have gotten away and to exonerate the innocent, solving murders that are sometimes decades old. A newspaper story about one famous DNA expert described him tirelessly sifting through tiny fragments of bone, teeth, paint and clothing, "searching for fibers of truth."

Adoptees have also turned to DNA testing to confirm their links to birth relatives. Early on in my search, a few people suggested that I get Helen to submit to a DNA match—as if some scientist looking through a powerful microscope would be any more convincing to her than the undeniable truth embedded in her past.

But several years after learning about him, I did consider calling Frank Harlett, Jr., in Miami and asking him to take a DNA test so I would know once and for all whether we shared the same father. Beleaguered by unanswered questions, I was no longer scared of how dangerous he might be. One night, alone with a glass of wine, I finally picked up the telephone.

A woman answered and said he wasn't there. She was cagey, refusing at first to admit she was his wife. But the more I told her of my story, the more intrigued she became, and before long she opened up. They were estranged, she said, and she wasn't sure where he was. I told her about my conversations with his brother, Brian, how he said Frank and his mother were dubious characters and that he doubted Frank, Sr., was his real father.

"They're full brothers," she said without hesitation. "They're only a year apart. I've seen photographs of them when they were babies. They look alike. Their father left when they were five and they never saw him again. They had a very hard childhood."

I remembered the bitterness in Brian Harlett's voice. Like me, he had tried hard to reconstruct the past in the hope of finding something better. Neither of us wanted to believe Frank Harlett was our father so we vainly looked for others to fill the role.

Frank's wife said that she would try to track him down and give him my message, but I wasn't surprised when he didn't call back.

⸻

The last time I talked to Paul Solia, he told me he doesn't believe in biological determinism—the idea that we could just as well have lived another person's life and still be who we are. While it may be a basic need of every person to know who their parents are, he said, inevitably, "we all make ourselves."

Sometimes we don't realize the truth of our words until we say them out loud. I had told my son's friend Ben that although he may never know who his birth father was, he now has parents who love him and will help him absorb any pain caused by his adoption.

I, too, was lucky enough to have parents willing to take me down the road to adulthood, rocky as it may have been. As my anger toward Helen slowly alchemized into acquiescence, my relationship with my adoptive mother grew closer. The years have smoothed our edges and taught us to refine our expectations of one another. What I had for so long refused to see behind all of her extravagance and implacability was that she loved me.

While the search for my history only strengthened the bonds with my children, that did not hold true for my relationship with Steve. I am reminded of something Helen once said of her own marriage: "I wasn't very good at saving a relationship." But that, as the saying goes, is another story.

There was a time when it felt like the losses of my childhood magnified the greatest loss of all—being rejected by my birth mother, not once, but twice. Now, though, I believe those early experiences gave me the courage to ask the questions and the strength to withstand the answers.

⌘

Over the years, I would occasionally take out my collection of photographs of Helen hoping that a fresh look at them would provide a clue I had previously missed. When Sylvia first offered the pictures to me, I accepted them because I knew they were all I would ever have of my mother. I felt that I deserved them. They were my consolation prize.

But one day as I sat looking at them, I realized that had changed. One picture showed Helen as a baby, standing up on wobbly legs and holding onto her father's arm with both hands. This was her history, not mine.

I shuffled through all of the other pictures that documented her early life: snapshots of her army friends, of her grandmother, of a high school boyfriend. They were a part of Helen, not of me.

I went up to the attic, where I kept old shipping boxes. I took down the sturdiest one I could find. Digging in a drawer in the kitchen, I found some tissue paper from an old gift. I lined the bottom of the box with it. One by one, I placed each picture inside.

On a piece of plain, white paper, I wrote:

> *Helen,*
> *I am returning these photographs to you because you are the one who should have them. They belong to you.*
> *Debbie*

I placed the paper on top of the pile of pictures, closed the box and taped it shut.

Acknowledgments

It is with deep appreciation that I thank my adoptive mother for encouraging me to write this book despite the pain she knew it would cause her.

The words would never have found their way onto these pages without the unwavering support and insights of Polly Bloomberg Fretter. For her generosity of time and of spirit, I will forever be grateful.

Thanks also to my editor, Kevin Bentley, for his careful eye and sense of humor.

The friendship of Claudia Sternbach, Uli Mueller, Essy Bahri, Lorri Holt, Gail Taback and Barbara Mueller got me through the rough spots and enabled me to glimpse the future.

Delores Thom is deserving of the utmost thanks for her caring and concern about me and the hundreds of other adoptees and birth parents who have walked through her door over the years.

I am also grateful to my fellow travelers on the adoption journey—Ann Green, Bobbie Wheeler and Sue Drese—whose understanding and support prevented me from giving up.

Perhaps the greatest lessons of my experience would not have been learned without Ben Murphy, who shared his own story with honesty and courage.

Like the rainbow created by a storm, my friendship with "John D'Lorio" is one I will always value.

And for all the tears and laughter David has brought to my life, it's the laughter I remember the most.

Most of all, for their patience, love and wisdom, I thank my children Jake and Sarah, who make it all worthwhile.